WAITE HOYT

WAITE HOYT

A Biography of the
Yankees' Schoolboy Wonder

William A. Cook

McFarland & Company, Inc., Publishers
Jefferson, North Carolina, and London

LIBRARY OF CONGRESS CATALOGUING-IN-PUBLICATION DATA

Cook, William A., 1944–
    Waite Hoyt : a biography of the Yankees'
schoolboy wonder / William A. Cook.
        p.   cm.
    Includes bibliographical references and index.

    ISBN 0-7864-1960-1 (softcover : 50# alkaline paper)

    1. Hoyt, Waite, 1899–1984.   2. Baseball players—United
States—   Biography.   3. New York Yankees (Baseball team)
I. Title.
GV865.H69C66   2004
796.357'092 — dc22   2004015881

British Library cataloguing data are available

Manufactured in the United States of America

Cover photograph of Waite Hoyt (courtesy National Baseball Hall of
Fame Library, Cooperstown, N.Y.)

McFarland & Company, Inc., Publishers
    Box 611, Jefferson, North Carolina 28640
        www.mcfarlandpub.com

To three fantastic great-nephews:

Michael Cunningham
Taylor Ehrman
Reed Ehrman

Always play the game with a passion and make big plans.

Contents

Introduction

The story of Waite Hoyt is an atypical biography. It is far more than just the story of another Hall of Fame ballplayer. In the case of Hoyt it is a journey through the history of professional baseball in the twentieth century. For 50 years between 1915 and 1965 Hoyt was employed in the national pastime as a batting practice pitcher, a minor league player, a major league player and a radio broadcaster. Then in 1972 he made a brief encore as a television broadcaster before returning to retirement. His remarkable life was filled with trials and tribulations, triumphs and tragedy. However, for this incredibly talented man the triumphs far outweighed the tragedies. It seems as if Waite Hoyt would have been a success in just about any endeavor.

Born and raised in Brooklyn, New York, at the turn of the twentieth century, as a young boy Waite Hoyt rooted for the Brooklyn Superbas (forerunners to the Dodgers) playing their games in Washington Park. As a youth he saw Ebbets Field built brick by brick. As a teenager he became a pitcher on his high school team at Erasmus Hall High School, where his fast ball overwhelmed his peers. Dubbed the Schoolboy Wonder at age fifteen, he was signed to pitch batting practice for the New York Giants, where he closely studied the pitching methods of the great Christy Mathewson.

After paying his dues in the minor leagues, Hoyt became a major league pitcher and played under three of the most legendary managers in the history of the game: John McGraw, Miller Huggins and Connie Mack. In fact, he played with most of the game's immortals. Hoyt was in uniform for the opening of Yankee Stadium in 1923 and was a teammate of Babe Ruth and Lou Gehrig during the glory days of the New York

1

Yankees' "Murderers' Row" teams in the 1920s. He played with Al Simmons, Jimmie Foxx, Mickey Cochrane and Lefty Grove on the Philadelphia Athletics and later played with Pie Traynor, Arky Vaughn and Paul Waner on the Pittsburgh Pirates.

If the immortals of the game were not his teammates, then they opposed him on the field. Walter Johnson, George Sisler, Ty Cobb, Tris Speaker, Shoeless Joe Jackson, Rogers Hornsby, Ray Schalk, Rabbit Maranville, Eddie Collins, Carl Hubbell, Dizzy Dean, Bill Terry, Ernie Lombardi, Mel Ott and countless others faced Hoyt on the mound. Even the great Joe DiMaggio in his rookie season faced Hoyt in an exhibition game played at Forbes Field.

In all, Hoyt's friendships and associations in baseball spanned nearly a century, from Ty Cobb to Pete Rose. Maybe it was just coincidence, perhaps it was destiny; nonetheless, Waite Hoyt at one time or another crossed paths with all the legends of the game.

And he held his own. In the nine years that Hoyt pitched on the New York Yankees he averaged 17 wins a season. Overall he won 237 games in his 21-year big league career and pitched in seven World Series—six of them with the Yankees, one with the Athletics. Humble in his success, when asked what had made him a great pitcher he attributed it to being a teammate of Babe Ruth.

But there was more to Hoyt's natural abilities than just his extraordinary talent to throw a baseball. In the off season he was a vaudevillian and played the Palace Theatre in New York. He also operated a funeral parlor (hence his later moniker "the Merry Mortician.") He was a painter and a writer, and he even played polo one year in the off season to stay in shape. He was a man preoccupied with appearance, who dressed to the nines and always kept his hair neatly coiffed. Although he was born and raised in Brooklyn there was not a trace of the borough's infamous accent in his speech. Hoyt spoke in very elegant, almost aristocratic tones. He enunciated each word so very precise as to make one wonder if he had an Ivy League education. So complete was the package that *New York Sun* reporter Will Wedge referred to Hoyt as the Aristocrat of Baseball.

Hoyt's playing days in baseball came to an end in 1938 where they had started, in Brooklyn. He had risen from playing pick-up games in the vacant lots of Flatbush shortly after the turn of the century to become a high school phenom. He toiled for a brief while in the minors, and after 21 years in the major leagues he was given his unconditional release by the Dodgers. But when Hoyt received his release the season was still young and the desire to compete was still deep within his soul. Therefore, Hoyt finished up the 1938 season pitching for the Bushwicks, a semi-pro team in Brooklyn.

For Hoyt, getting his walking papers from the Dodgers became the key that opened the door to the next phase of his career. From the pitcher's mound Hoyt moved behind the microphone and began a radio job with WOR in New York, where he gave a wrap-up segment following Red Barber's play-by-play broadcasts of Dodgers games. Then, in 1942, his big break came as he was hired by the Burger Brewing Company to broadcast the Cincinnati Reds games on radio station WKRC in Cincinnati. As natural a broadcaster as he had been a pitcher, Hoyt went on to become a broadcasting legend in Cincinnati, providing the familiar play-by-play of the Reds games on radio for 24 years until his retirement following the 1965 season.

During rain delays in Reds games Hoyt's monologues became enormously popular with his listening audience. His ruminations on his experiences as a player and tales of Babe Ruth became so popular that they even attracted listeners who did not follow the Reds. Hoyt was a pioneering former ball player in radio broadcasting. Had he failed, his failure might have prevented others of the legion of professional athletes who fill the air waves today from becoming broadcasters. Instead, his success probably inspired those who followed.

When Hoyt received a telephone call in 1969 that the Old Timers committee had elected him to the National Baseball Hall of Fame, he broke down and cried. He was successful, it seemed, in almost anything he did; yet Hoyt's life was not without personal failures and crises. Although he was a devoted family man, his first marriage ended in divorce. When he arrived in Cincinnati in late 1941, he brought not only his extraordinary talent but also a chronic problem with alcohol abuse. The demons of alcoholism eventually caught up with him in 1945 and forced him to confront his personal weakness. But Hoyt—a big league pitcher who was known as one who performed at his best under tight situations—rose to the challenge, grappled with the monkey on his back and with sheer will power, a strong determination to succeed and the assistance of Alcoholics Anonymous (AA) licked his addiction. After entering the AA program and admitting to himself that he was powerless over alcohol, Hoyt never allowed another drop of John Barleycorn to pass over his lips for the remaining 39 years of his life. His sobriety was remarkable for many reasons, not the least of which was the fact that in addition to being a baseball broadcaster, he was also a beer pitchman for the team's radio broadcast sponsor Burger Beer.

One of the most important aspects of Hoyt's life was his friendship with Babe Ruth. According to Branch Rickey, no one knew the Babe better than Waite Hoyt. Hoyt was a teammate of the Babe's on the Boston

Red Sox when Babe broke the major league record of 27 home runs in 1919. They were teammates on the New York Yankees when Babe hit a record-breaking 60 home runs in 1927. Later Hoyt was a member of the opposing Pittsburgh Pirates when Babe, playing for the Boston Braves in 1935, hit the last home run of his career, number 714. Hoyt told people, "Believe everything that you hear about Babe Ruth regardless of how outlandish the story may be. That's the way he was."

On the day that Babe Ruth died — August 16, 1948 — Hoyt was about to begin broadcasting a Cincinnati Reds game when he was handed the message off the news wire. He told his audience to remain with him following the game for some words of remembrance about the Bambino. Hoyt's eulogy of Ruth that evening lasted for over an hour and was a stunning moment in broadcasting history. Hoyt then left for New York, where he served as an honorary pallbearer at Ruth's funeral.

Following his official retirement in 1965 Hoyt lived on for 19 years, but never really found contentment. Without broadcasting, there seemed to be a void in his life. Although still very much in demand as a speaker and enormously popular in the Greater Cincinnati community, in retirement Hoyt was not able to find a proper outlet for his still blossoming creative streak and love of the game. After a series of heart attacks Hoyt died on August 25, 1984, just a few weeks from his 85th birthday, and was laid to rest in Spring Grove Cemetery in Cincinnati. Coincidentally, Miller Huggins — his favorite manager on those glorious Yankees teams of the Roaring Twenties — had been buried there in 1929.

This work represents one of the first published comprehensive accounts of the life of Waite Hoyt. There have only been a few other attempts to tell his life story in print, apparently because of Hoyt's personality. Several authors made efforts to collaborate with him on a biography, but one by one the projects crashed and burned as Hoyt demanded a standard of storytelling that made the work extremely arduous and complicated. A manuscript by Bob Smith of Boston was ready to be published when Hoyt requested that it be withdrawn because it did not meet his expectations. A later attempt by Sherly Bills of Cincinnati also failed to reach the printing press. Still, Waite Hoyt remains a very important figure in baseball history and excerpts making references to his experiences in the game occur in no fewer than 342 published works currently on the market.

Here, then, is one humble attempt to tell the extraordinary story of this remarkable man. May it represent, at least, a chance to remember the many hours of joy that he brought to fans on the ballfield and over the airwaves — and perhaps to hear the familiar laughter once again.

1

The Schoolboy Wonder

In the 1890s, just prior to its incorporation in the City of New York, *Harper's* Magazine said of Brooklyn, "The City has no promenade for the display of fashion, and its people are fond of boasting that whatever electrical force it is that makes us metropolitan, that keeps all New-Yorkers under a strain, and that charges even the night air like a magnificent essence of strong coffee is lacking in beautiful Brooklyn. Rest, comfort, and cozy homes, that bring independence even to the poor, are the richest offerings of this lovely sister of the metropolis."[1]

In 1899, as the new millennium loomed ever closer to the now incorporated Brooklyn, the borough had grown to a population of over 900,000. One of those newly arrived Brooklyn souls—born on September 9, 1899, at 96 Second Place in Flatbush — was Waite Charles Hoyt. (During his life Hoyt would take great delight in writing out his birth date as "9-9-99.") He was the son of ElLuise, 28 years old, and Addison "Ad" Hoyt, 27 years old. Ad earned his living as a vaudevillian. He was a minstrel comedian with a fine baritone voice.

In 1905 Waite Hoyt began his schooling at P.S. 92 at Parkside and Rogers Avenue. He often stated that he was dismissed from the school for what he called "conduct unbecoming an American boy. I was ejected on fourteen counts. None of which I can remember," said Hoyt.[2] As the Hoyt family traversed around the borough, Waite then attended P.S. 90 through the sixth grade before moving on to P.S. 89. It was about the time that he arrived at P.S. 89 that he also began to play organized baseball. According to Hoyt, "When I had my marks I played second base. When I didn't I pitched. While at P.S. 89 we played a game with P.S. 90. So I treated it like a joke and showed up in an Eaton collar and packet and spiked shoes, played second base, made four errors, lost the ball game and was graduated with high honors."[3]

Hoyt had actually learned to play ball in alleys alongside theatres with vaudeville troups and with neighborhood friends on the many vacant lots in Flatbush as Brooklyn continued to develop early in the twentieth century. At first Waite's hand was too small to fit around a regular baseball, so Ad Hoyt bought him a tennis ball and a five-cent bat. Hoyt delighted in slugging the ball across the vacant lot. When he was about eight years old his grandmother bought him his first wood bat — a black and white one — at a drug store. "I was proud of that bat, but I never got a chance to use it, because when the weather grew warmer, the first kid that used it broke it the first time he swung. There were kids' teams all over Flatbush. A new one sprang up every week. One team would get sore, break up and there'd be two new teams. Nobody can say that I can't pitch down an alley, because that's where I learned to pitch — in the alleys of theatres, playing ball with the actors."[4]

And pitch Hoyt did, with incredible skill. He entered Erasmus Hall High School in Brooklyn, a secondary school with an alumni roll that reads like a who's who list. Hoyt himself did not graduate from Erasmus, leaving school early to pursue his baseball career. However, among the illustrious Erasmus Hall alumni are professional football Hall of Fame quarterback Sid Luckman (1935), actors Eli Wallach (1932) and Jeff Chandler (1935), writer Bernard Malamud (1932) of *The Natural,* cartoon mogul Joseph Barbera (1928) of Hanna-Barbera, major league pitcher Don McMahon (1948), Chicago Bulls and White Sox owner Jerry Reinsdorf (1953), songbird Barbra Streisand (1959), basketball great Bill Cunningham (1960), and even *Happy Days* actor Donny Most (1970), just to name a few.

In his first year at Erasmus Hall High School Hoyt did not make the baseball team because he did not make the required grades: "I flunked my first-year Latin, because I couldn't get 'E Pluribus Unum' straight and because I asked my instructor what effect Latin had on a curve ball."[5] By 1915 Hoyt was 15 years old, weighed 165 pounds and was considered big for his age. He had also become the starting pitcher for Erasmus Hall, and according to Ad Hoyt, who followed his son's progress on the diamond with more than just a casual interest, Waite was selected to pitch all the important games. Pitching for Erasmus Hall, Hoyt was overpowering with his fastball, curve and control. His high school coach, Dick Allen, rounded out his pitching repertoire by teaching him to throw a palm ball that would become an insurance policy for Hoyt in the late stages of his major league career.

Ever so quickly, Hoyt's reputation as a superior hurler began to leak out of Flatbush. In fact, so promising had he become that professional teams began to scout him. While still 15 years old, in June 1915 Hoyt was offered and declined a contract with New Haven in the Colonial League. Then the renegade Federal League, which had been a minor league, suddenly burst onto the national scene to challenge the established American and National leagues. With a large bank roll, the Federals began to sign established major league stars such as Edd Roush, Eddie Plank, Hal Chase, Chief Bender and Three Fingers Brown. The Federals also offered a contract to young Waite Hoyt, which he declined. Furthermore, with the insistence of his father, Waite even declined an opportunity for a tryout with the St. Louis Browns. Ad Hoyt's reasoning in the matter was two-fold: one, he wasn't sure young Waite was ready for major league competition yet. Two, at that point in time there were three big league teams playing in New York, and Ad felt that if Waite was going to blossom at an early age as a big league pitcher, then he needed support and guidance; playing close to home was therefore in his best interest.

With Ad clearly in control of Waite's destiny in baseball, Waite began working out with the Brooklyn Robins, pitching batting practice through an invitation from Nap Rucker and Jack Coombs. Ad Hoyt was an ardent baseball fan and he easily recognized the natural ability in his son. Also, through his show business experience, Ad knew the value of marketing and was working as an early version of an agent for his son. Ad had made the acquaintance of Charles "Red" Dooin of the New York Giants and subsequently Dooin started to show up at Ebbets Field to scout Waite. Soon thereafter Dooin began to report back to Giants manager John McGraw on Hoyt's abilities and Little Napoleon, as McGraw was often called, took an instant interest in the youngster. According to Ad Hoyt, "During a Brooklyn–New York series at Ebbets Field, Charles Dooin called McGraw's attention to Hoyt's style and form while he was pitching batting practice. After McGraw watched Hoyt for several days he finally made the decision to give the kid a tryout at the Polo Grounds."[6]

At the direction of McGraw, Dooin stopped to talk with Hoyt along the sidelines and asked, "Do you belong to the Brooklyn club?"[7]

"No," replied Hoyt. "Nobody's even spoken to me."[8]

Dooin then asked, "Would you like to workout with the Giants?"

"When?"

"As soon as we get back to the Polo Grounds."

"Sure," Waite said. "I'll be there."[9]

So for several weeks Hoyt was kept busy shuttling back and forth between Brooklyn and Manhattan on the subway, reporting to the Polo

Grounds and working out with the Giants. However, John McGraw was tight lipped on his opinion of the kid. Finally Hoyt, a high-strung youngster who was growing tired of the tedious subway commute each day from Brooklyn to the Polo Grounds in upper Manhattan, could no longer stand the perceived run-around that he was getting from McGraw. Without warning Hoyt burst into McGraw's office and startled him with a verbal outburst. "I'm tired of working this way. To hell with it," proclaimed Hoyt.[10]

Now, confronting McGraw in this manner might not have been the wisest course of action. After all, at that time McGraw was the unchallenged Mr. Baseball in New York. He had been in the game for well over 25 years as a player and a manager, and had won four pennants with the Giants since taking over as manager in 1902. Furthermore, McGraw ran the Giants ball club with a dictatorial management style and was agitated by Hoyt's aggression. Yet, lucky for Hoyt, at the same time McGraw admired the kid's sense of spirit. As a result Waite Hoyt was immediately signed to

Waite Hoyt

an optional contract for $90 per month and a $5 bonus. A newspaper account of his signing by the Giants stated, "Hoyt put on a uniform Saturday and surprised the New York players with his speed, curves and control. Dooin says that he will keep an eye on the Brooklyn prodigy until he is old enough to play professional ball."[11]

Hoyt's style also got the attention of the legendary Giants pitcher Christy Mathewson. Mathewson liked the kid's spunk and immediately befriended the young hurler and attempted to encourage him to consider attending his Alma Mater, Bucknell University, where he had been president of his class and a standout football player. Hoyt admired Mathewson and used the opportunity of being close to him to seriously study his style on the mound, but for now college was out of the question.

When John McGraw signed Waite Hoyt to play for the Giants in August 1915, it made him the youngest player ever signed by a major league team at that time. As Waite was not yet 16 years old, Ad Hoyt signed for his son. As for the bonus payment of $5, Hoyt stated, "The Giants gave me $5 for signing and my father took it away from me immediately. He felt it was much too much money for a kid to have on his person at one time."[12]

Following his signing by the Giants, Hoyt continued to pitch in amateur, semi-pro and

John McGraw (National Baseball Hall of Fame Library, Cooperstown, N.Y.).

exhibition games during the summer of 1915, playing with the Wyandotte A. C. team that won the championship of the *Brooklyn Eagle* and *Brooklyn Times* leagues. In fact, the Wyandotte A. C. team of 1915 was a talented bunch and had several players on the team that eventually played on major league teams. Among the Wyandotte squad was Clint Blume, a pitcher for the New York Giants in 1922 and 1923, as well as Gene "Red" Sheridan, an infielder who played a few games for Brooklyn in 1918 and 1920, and Ed Goebel, who played 37 games in the outfield for the Washington Nationals in 1922. But Waite Hoyt was without question the superstar on the Wyandotte team. During the 1915 season, including his high school competition, Hoyt played on teams that won championships in three different amateur leagues. He pitched in 36 games, winning 33 games while losing only three. Along the way that year he pitched four no-hitters. Then came September; the glorious summer was over and Hoyt returned to high school at Erasmus Hall. That October during the 1915 World Series in Philadelphia, John McGraw told a reporter from The *Public Ledger* that Waite Hoyt was good enough to pitch in the majors right now.

However, 1915 was not just about baseball with Hoyt, but also the year that he met the lady he would eventually marry — Dorothy Pyle, a lovely young lady with black hair and green eyes. The first meeting of the two happened at a dance around Memorial Day that year at the St. George Hotel in Brooklyn. Recalling his first meeting with the lovely Miss Pyle, Hoyt stated, "It was one of those formal spring dances, and the men were supposed to wear white flannel pants. It was raining buckets and I remember I brought my white pants in a suitcase and when I put them on in the men's room they were too short. I looked like Henry Hjelvorsen just landed. But the others looked as funny as I did. So I met my wife."[13] However, their meeting was not instant matrimony, as Waite's baseball career would bring a separation to their relationship until the early 1920s when they would once again begin to see each other.

When the spring of 1916 arrived Hoyt returned to the mound for Erasmus Hall High School and was absolutely sensational. In one of his first starts he pitched a no-hitter against New Utrecht at the West End Oval in which he fanned 10 batters while walking only one.

	1	2	3	4	5	6	7	8	9	R	H	E
Erasumus	0	0	0	0	2	0	1	0	2	5	11	1
New Utrecht	0	0	0	0	0	0	0	0	0	0	0	2

Batteries: Hoyt and McPhey (Erasmus)
        Carlson and Smith (New Utrecht)

On April 28 at the Parade Grounds in Brooklyn, facing Morris High from the Bronx, Hoyt locked up in a thrilling pitching duel with a youngster by the name of Meaney. Meaney had held the opposition hitless and taken a 2–0 lead into the top of the ninth when Erasmus Hall High scored three runs to win the game. Ed Goebel, Hoyt's Wyandotte A. C. teammate, started the rally off Meaney with a one-out single and then stole second. McPhee, the Erasmus catcher, then followed with a hit, sending Goebel to third. Waite Hoyt was next up and smashed a hit to right field, scoring both Goebel and McPhee. The next batter was fanned by Meaney, but Barasch then singled to left, scoring Hoyt with the winning run. According to Ad Hoyt, 16-year-old Waite pitched three games for Erasmus Hall in the month of April 1916, winning them all, with two of them being no-hitters within four days of each other.

In May 1916, Hoyt left high school to join the Mt. Carmel team in the Pennsylvania State League, where he pitched in six games with a won-lost record of 5–1. In the only game Hoyt lost at Mr. Carmel (by a score of 3–2), the game went 19 innings and he pitched the entire game, giving up nine hits and one base on balls. However, within a month the league disbanded and Hoyt was given $25 — a week's pay — and returned to New York to pitch for the semi-pro Degon-Grays.

In June Hoyt was signed to a regular playing contract by the New York Giants and seemed to be right on track for a spot on the Giants' major league roster within a year or two at most. But suddenly the fast track that Hoyt had been on slowed to a crawl. Upon signing with the Giants, John McGraw loaned Hoyt to Hartford of the Eastern League. Hoyt never started a game in Hartford. When John McGraw became informed that young Hoyt was being persuaded to sign an agreement with the Hartford club, he quickly recalled him and immediately ordered that he be sent back to New York. Then in July Hoyt somehow contracted blood poisoning in both hands. To recuperate he was sent out of the city to the countryside. Then, while still battling the disease he was ordered to report to Lynn of the Eastern League, where that club had suddenly come up short on starting pitchers. Forced into action at once and still weakened, he lost four straight games at Lynn. Finally, in August, as the infection subsided, he won four out of five games, including a two-hitter against Portland to win the Eastern League Championship. Hoyt finished the season at Lynn with a 4–5 record. In September he was returned to the New York Giants contractually, but was not placed on the roster. Hoyt pitched in a few local games in Brooklyn and then returned to school. Overall, his record for the 1916 season with Erasmus Hall High School, Mt. Carmel, Hartford, Lynn and the local teams in Brooklyn had been 22–8 with two no-hitters.

In January 1917 the Hoyt family was living at 52 Clarkson Street in Brooklyn. Watie was now 17 years old and found himself in the middle of a contract dispute between Hartford and the New York Giants, who were both laying claim to owning his services. Subsequently, the National Commission met on the matter and awarded Hoyt to the Giants. McGraw now having Hoyt officially in the fold, invited him to spring training with the Giants in Marlin, Texas. However, when the regular season began Hoyt found himself in Memphis with the Chicks rather than Manhattan with the Giants.

Hoyt's introduction to Southern League hospitality was rough going. On April 12 he was beaten by Little Rock 3–2 and on April 16 was roughed up by New Orleans 6–1. On April 21, as the Chicks hitters seemed to all be in a slump at the same time, he lost to Nashville 1–0. Then suddenly it all started to come together again for Hoyt. On April 28 he beat Nashville 2–1 in one of those tight games that would become Hoyt's forte throughout his big league career. (A few years later, when Hoyt became one of the aces of the New York Yankees pitching staff, he discovered that owners of major league ball clubs were a strange breed. Jacob Ruppert, co-owner of the club, asked Hoyt why he couldn't win games 10–1 like Bob Shawkey or Carl Mays— why did he always have to win games 1–0 and 2–1, which made Ruppert so very nauseous.

On May 10, *New York American* writer O. B. Keeler went to Memphis to check on Hoyt's progress and witnessed the Atlanta Crackers serving up a 3–2 loss to the kid. Subsequently, on May 20 Keeler made the following remarks in his column: "Waite Hoyt is about ripe and he is seventeen and never been kissed by a safety razor or any other kind. He looks like a great big kid — a high school boy. And that's what he is. Also, he is a pitcher. Oh, man — Waite Hoyt is a pitcher! I went out to see Waite Hoyt pitch for Memphis last Thursday against Atlanta and the Crackers gave him a nice little beating and they took him out in the shank of the game and that doesn't cut the skimpiest figure in my estimate of Mr. Hoyt's ability as a pitcher. The Crackers just naturally were hitting and the Chicks were not fielding and Mr. Hoyt's stuff fine as it was simply wouldn't get by. But they had an awful time making as many as three runs off this amazing infant at that."[14]

Mike Donlin, manager of the Memphis Chicks, was impressed with Hoyt too. "He looks like Christy Mathewson at the same age," said Donlin.[15] However, Donlin said that Hoyt brought one fault from high school to Memphis with him: "He still is trying to pitch it past 'em. I keep telling him there are several other players on his side and to give them a chance to earn their board and lodging. Make 'em hit bad ones, I tell him. And he's learning it. When he gets it — good night!"[16]

Hoyt wound up pitching in 17 games for Memphis in 1917 with a record of 3–9 before being sent to finish up the season with Montreal in the International League. With the Royals Hoyt pitched in 28 games and finished with a record of 7–17, but his ERA was only 2.51. More important for Hoyt, though, was that his manager at Montreal was Dan Howley, who would later manage the St. Louis Browns (1927–1929) and the Cincinnati Reds (1930–1932). It was under Howley's mentorship that Hoyt really learned how to pitch rather than just throw. Ten years later in 1927, when Hoyt was an established major league star, he stated in an interview with Frederick G. Lieb, "Howley taught me more about pitching than all the other minor league managers I worked for combined. I wasn't the easiest kid to handle, but Howley was one of the most patient men I ever knew. He kept working with me day after day, trying to encourage me and showing me why it would pay me to follow his advice. He not only told you a thing but also why it was done that way and why it was better than other ways· I still feel indebted to Dan for much of the success that I acquired as a big league pitcher."[17]

Indebted as Hoyt might have been to Dan Howley on the field, he also couldn't forget that he had taken advantage of him off the field by exploiting his youthful naiveté. The Montreal Royals had on the team a pitcher nicknamed Bugs who was well known as a practical joker. Knowing this, Howley decided to have some fun and assigned Bugs and Hoyt as roommates. Subsequently, the Royals players, being in on the plot, began characterizing Bugs as certifiably insane to the unsuspecting 17-year-old Hoyt. The other players, told Hoyt that Bugs would walk in his sleep and could become extremely dangerous when he was intoxicated. Thoroughly indoctrinated by the other players Hoyt took their word as the gospel truth and planned to keep an eye on Bugs.

According to a retrospective story about this incident printed in *The Sporting News* on April 2, 1942, the web of deception was completely woven and ready to draw Hoyt in as the Royals rolled into Baltimore and stopped at a small but dignified family hotel most often utilized by elderly ladies: "One night as the clock struck 12, Waite was in bed reading, when his roomie staggered in. He stood at the foot of Hoyt's bed, with his eyes closed and muttered: 'If ya don't like a guy, I shay jush cut hish throat. See! Slice 'em up. I always shay.'[18]

Bugs then began to do all sort of strange things, like taking an imaginary drink from an empty pitcher, and eventually flung his clothing off and laid down on the bed muttering something and then began to snore. A startled Hoyt watched Bugs' every move. Then all at once Bugs sprang up in bed, got a razor strop, hooked it on the bed post and began honing. "Cut their throats—'ats what I always shay."[19]

As the mortified Hoyt lay in bed totally frozen in fear, Bugs began to make wild passes at the air with the razor, then suddenly went back to bed. Hoyt then waited until he thought Bugs had fallen asleep and decide to bolt out of the room fast as possible. He quickly pulled his pants on over his pajamas and started to quietly move towards the door. Just as he turned the knob, Bugs jumped out of bed, eyes blazing wildly! "No ya don't. Ya won't leave!"[20] From somewhere Bugs pulled out a small pearl-handled gun and with his eyes closed pointed it directly at Hoyt. That was enough for Hoyt. He threw the door open and dashed down the hallway at a full gallop, down one flight of stairs, then another, until he saw a room with the door open. In he ran and closed the door behind him. Soon he heard footsteps coming down the stairs. Quickly he noticed that the room was filled with feminine articles— powder puffs, filly clothes lying over chairs, etc. He decided that it was in his best interest to evacuate the room, but when he opened the door he found himself face-to-face with two elderly women. Startled, they screamed and Hoyt screamed too! Waite then spent the remainder of the night in another room. In the morning everyone checked out — the two elderly ladies, Hoyt, Bugs and the ball club. The Royals paid for an extra room. A week later Hoyt was informed that the whole episode was a big joke. On April 6, 1917, the United States declared war on Germany and entered into World War I. When the war came along the Ad Hoyt Minstrels broke up as four members of the quintet were drafted into military service. Consequently, Addison Hoyt walked away from show business and never entertained again. In the spring of 1918 Waite Hoyt was again at the spring training camp of the New York Giants in Marlin, Texas. But when the team started to move north he was dropped off in Nashville. Pitching again in the Southern Association, Hoyt saw action in 19 games and had a record of 5–10, but once again had a terrific ERA of 2.73. However, due to the ever increasing demands on teams by the country's involvement in World War I, the Nashville club lost many of it's players to military service and ceased operations.

In fact, by July it was not known if there would be any major league baseball or not for the balance of the 1918 season. A "work or fight" edict had been issued by Provost Marshall General Enoch Crowder in May and as a result baseball was declared a nonessential endeavor in support of the war effort. Suddenly major league rosters were being depleted by players marching off to war. Labor Day — Monday, September 2, 1918 — was designated as the end of the season. With the war raging in France, the push was on now to recruit major league ballplayers. The U.S. Navy was openly attempting to sign major leaguers. In fact the Navy was hopeful that they could sign all the players on every major league roster at once and even drafted a special letter. "We are asking them to join the Navy because we want the best men we can get,"[21] declared Captain William A. Moffett at the Great Lakes Naval Training Center, located in Great Lakes, Illinois. Baseball officials were asking General Crowder to rescind his "work or fight" order in regard to baseball; they felt that if it was enforced less than 60 players would remain on major league rosters, and with no time to recruit new players the season — and millions of dollars in revenue — would be lost.

On the morning of July 18, 1918, as fans around the country anxiously awaited the arrival of the morning papers to see if the major league season would be scuttled, Waite Hoyt finally got his first taste of big league life when John McGraw brought him up to the New York Giants. Hoyt made his debut in the major leagues on July 24, 1918, when McGraw sent him in to pitch in a game against the St. Louis Cardinals in the ninth inning. With the legendary Jim Thorpe playing behind him in left field, Hoyt struck out two of the three batters he faced as the Giants won the game 3–2, sweeping a doubleheader from the last-place Cardinals to climb within three games of the front-running Chicago Cubs.

Hoyt had been the fourth Giants pitcher to enter the game, following Slim Sallee, Ferdie Schupp and Jack Ogden. The following day the *New York Times* remarked, "The game was a cavalcade of Giant pitchers. Sallee led the procession for an inning, and then Ferdie Schupp took a hand. In the fifth inning Jack Ogden showed his wares, which were below standard, and in the ninth the Brooklyn schoolboy, Waite Hoyt, made his first appearance in a game under Coogan's Bluff. Of the whole lot, young Hoyt did the best flinging. He fanned two of the three batsmen who faced him."[22] At that point Hoyt thought he had made it. But John McGraw really didn't have any plans for Hoyt and instead used him to carry out silly agendas such as stationing him in a hidden cubicle at the end of the dugout to heckle umpire Bill Klem. McGraw felt that Hoyt, not yet 19 years old, still lacked experience and eventually shipped him over to Newark of the International League.

In today's terms, regarding his management style, John McGraw would be considered a control freak. When irritated, he often loudly admonished a player with a stream of profanity right in front of the whole team. Often he kept players around for hours after a game to brow beat them. Hall of Fame member Edd Roush of the Reds had previously played 39 games for McGraw in 1916. In 1928 he was traded back to the Giants and at first refused to go as he utterly despised McGraw. Even Hall of Fame second baseman Frankie Frisch had trouble playing for McGraw. Hoyt says that "Frisch couldn't play for McGraw—he did for a while and had several big years under Mac's fire and brimstone—but after a while it wore Frankie down so much that Mac had to get rid of him. Frisch and McGraw had many an argument—and serious ones."[23]

In 1918 McGraw was both frustrated and angry. His 1917 National League champion team was not playing up to their potential and he had his hands full chasing the Chicago Cubs as the war consumed his players. Outfielder Benny Kauff was hitting .315 when he was drafted, and pitcher Rube Benton had enlisted, while pitcher Jeff Tesreau and first baseman Walter Holke left the club to work in war industries. Third baseman Eddie Grant had left the team to join the Army during 1917 and was killed in action on October 5, 1918, in the Argonne Forest. With a shortened season the Giants finished second, 10½ games behind the Cubs. So when the young, hot-tempered Waite Hoyt explosively protested his demotion to Newark, it sealed his fate with McGraw and the New York Giants. Little Napoleon had had enough of Hoyt's challenging him. So Hoyt finished the 1918 season at Newark pitching in five games with a record of 2–3 and

ERA of 2.09. Then that club also folded up for the season due to the war effort.

Discouraged, Hoyt quit professional baseball, accepted a job and joined the Baltimore Dry Docks, an independent team in a shipyard league. (Ironically, Babe Ruth had actually jumped to the Baltimore Dry Docks for one game during the 1918 season after a dispute with Boston Red Sox, but quickly found himself back in Beantown and on the mound for the 1918 World Series against the Chicago Cubs.)

By the end of World War I 247 major league players would serve in the United States armed services, including 25 future members of the Hall of Fame. At the end of the 1918 season, Waite Hoyt found himself deciding what he could do for the war effort too. A friend of Hoyt's, Ed Moran was attending Middlebury College in Vermont where a considerable group of young men were attending through the Students Army Training Corps (SATC). The Army paid the men's room and board while they were on the campus. Moran asked Hoyt to join him at Middlebury. However, for Hoyt there was an outstanding credentialing problem. He had not graduated from Erasmus Hall High School and therefore did not have the 15 credits (or 12 credits and 3 conditions) necessary to take the required Regent's exam in the New York State school system. Moran convinced Hoyt that with the war going on that they might relax the standards and admit him to Middlebury.

According to an interview with Hoyt for the *Purple & Gold* by James D. Bunting and Alan C. Johnson, when Hoyt arrived on the campus of Middlebury College in the fall of 1918 he went directly to the dean's office, where he was questioned on how many credits he had from high school. In reality, Hoyt had only 10 credits, as he had quit high school in his junior year to play ball. However, he told the dean that he had 12 credits and 3 conditionals. The dean said, "We have to have your Regent's Card."[24] Hoyt stated that he did not possess a Regent's Card and the dean suggested that he write to the state capital in Albany and request one. When Hoyt did obtain his Regent's Card from Albany, sure enough, it listed him as having but 10 credits. So, feeling that the whole affair was impossible, Hoyt tore the card up and threw it away. Now the college semester was about to begin and he had no credentialing material. Hoyt did what all good pitchers would do in such a tight spot — he bore down and decided he was going to pitch his way out of the jam.

His strategy involved an act of subterfuge by developing a scheme in which he would make it to the dean's office the very last minute before the close of registration. Therefore, he developed a plan of action to arrange a happenstance meeting with the dean at the point where two paths crossed on the campus. On the day of deployment Hoyt watched from a vantage point far enough away to see the dean approaching the point where he planned to intercept him. As the dean slowly moved down the path Hoyt took off running hard from his station so as to exhaust himself in an attempt to reach the dean's office. Feigning exhaustion, Hoyt's timing was exact as he encountered the dean at the cross point of the two paths. "I was just on my way to your office. My card came this morning," exclaimed a panting Hoyt.[25] Then, as the dean curiously watched him, Hoyt began to nervously shuffle through his pant's pockets and shirt. "That card came this morning. Just like I told you, there were 12 credits. Where is that card?"[26] After about five minutes of speaking and searching through his clothing, Hoyt exclaimed, "Jeez, don't tell me I lost that card!"[27] Apparently all that thespian exposure he had in his developing years around the Ad Hoyt Minstrels paid off as the dean for some reason believed his story and he was admitted to Middlebury College.

But Hoyt's college experience was to be short lived. On November 11, 1918, at 11:00 A.M. — or as the more popular recitation of the date goes, at the eleventh hour of the eleventh day of the eleventh month — "the war to end all wars" ended with the signing of the Armistice on the western front. When Hoyt went home for the Christmas holidays he did not return to Middlebury College. As for his future in baseball, at that point Hoyt was tired of playing in the minor leagues and did not really know what he would do.

However, others did have plans for his future. With the war over in the spring of 1919 and still under contract to the Giants, John McGraw decided to send Hoyt to Rochester. Once again Hoyt got into an explosive argument with McGraw over his salary and refused to report to Rochester. Also, Hoyt did not like the fact that he would have the same manager at Rochester that he had at Newark. When Hoyt turned down the Rochester assignment he received an offer to pitch for the Fisk Tire Company team at Chicopee Falls. Fisk wanted young men not only to play baseball, but to learn to become salesmen for the growing company.

After thinking it all over and consulting with his father, Waite turned down the Fisk offer and instead returned to pitch for the Baltimore Dry Docks. In June, the front office at Rochester came to the realization that they would not be able to sign Hoyt. So they traded his contract to New Orleans for $2,500 and a player by the name of Al Nixon an infielder who had played for Brooklyn in 1915 and again from 1917 to 1918. But again Hoyt refused to cooperate Nixon had refused to report to New Orleans and now Hoyt was sticking to his guns too, and had absolutely no desire to report to the Crescent City club. Hoyt had previously played at Memphis and Nashville and did not like the hot, humid conditions that one had to play under in the Southern Association. Therefore, turning his back on New Orleans, he continued to pitch for the Baltimore Dry Docks.

In 1919 Blue Laws regarding major league baseball on Sundays were still much in effect. So the Baltimore Dry Docks, although an independent team, often played major league clubs on Sundays. Subsequently, in one of the Sunday games that Hoyt pitched for the Dry Docks he beat the Cincinnati Reds 1–0, allowing only four hits. Now, the 1919 Cincinnati Reds were on their way to winning to the National League pennant that year; they would soon outdistance John McGraw and his second-place New York Giants by nine games while racking up a .686 winning percentage. It was an understatement to say it was quite remarkable that a 19-year-old kid with one inning of major league experience had shut out the Reds. In fact, it was an amazing feat.

The catcher on the Dry Docks was Norm McNeil, who contractually belonged to the Boston Red Sox. Seeing the potential in Hoyt, McNeil contacted Ed Barrow, manager of the Red Sox. Subsequently, Barrow sent a scout to Baltimore to monitor Hoyt, and based on the favorable report that was sent back to Boston, Hoyt was invited to come to Washington and pitch batting practice when the Red Sox made their next road trip there. At that point in the season Hoyt had not yet signed a contract with either Rochester or New Orleans. The prevailing protocol of the time was that if a player had signed a contract with a minor league club then the major leagues would consider that player signed. However, if a player had not signed a contract then the big leagues considered him a free agent. Such was the case with Waite Hoyt in 1919.

Apparently Ed Barrow liked what he saw and in late July offered Hoyt a contract with the Red Sox calling for $600 a month. However, the contract had a condition. Hoyt was sensitized by what he felt had been a pointless protracted tour of duty in the minor leagues at the hands of John McGraw and the New York Giants. Therefore he wanted Barrow to agree to start him in a game within four days of signing his contract. Reflecting on his contract demand from the Red Sox, Hoyt later remarked, "Barrow got sore at this, but he admired my stand."[28] Subsequently, Barrow put the clause in Hoyt's contract and kept his promise. Waite Hoyt was headed for the big leagues and never looked back.

2

Boston

In late July 1919 Waite Hoyt's grueling tour of the minors and industrial leagues came to an end when he reported to the Boston Red Sox. Finally he was a big leaguer. Upon arriving in Boston and entering Fenway Park, Red Sox manager Ed Barrow began to show Hoyt around. He introduced him to the office staff, the ground crew and other behind-the-scenes personnel that kept the team's operations going. Then they entered the Red Sox clubhouse, where the players were all sitting in front of the wide red wire cages that served as lockers at the time. Barrow began to slowly move down the line and introduce Hoyt to his teammates: Harry Hooper, Stuffy McInnis, Red Shannon, Sad Sam Jones, Bullet Joe Bush, Allen Russell, Wally Schange, etc. As Hoyt passed by shaking their hands, they all gazed upon him with a sort of curious wonderment. Hoyt stated later that while the team was aware of his signing, the arrival of a 19-year-old kid in the major leagues was still something of novelty.

Upon reaching one player's locker Hoyt encountered a guy pulling on his baseball socks. His description of the player was that "His huge head bent toward the floor, his black, shaggy, curly hair dripping downward like a bottle of spilled ink."[1] It was Babe Ruth. Ed Barrow said, "Babe, look here a minute."[2] Ruth sat up, turned around and looked Hoyt over from head to toe, then said, "Pretty young to be in the big league aren't you kid."[3] Hoyt replied, "Yep — same age you were when you came up, Babe."[4] However, before another word could be spoken Barrow stated that the kid would take care of himself.

For Hoyt, that day became the beginning of a 29-year, sometimes on and sometimes off, friendship with Ruth. In 1948, writing in his eulogy to Ruth, *Babe Ruth As I Knew Him,* Hoyt recalled their first meeting: "For a second I was startled. I sensed that this man was something different than the others that I had met. It might have been his wide, flaring nostrils, his great bulbous nose, his generally unique appearance — the early physical formation which later became so familiar to the American public. But now I prefer to believe it was merely a sixth sense which told me I was meeting someone beyond the usual type of ball player."[5] "In 1919, Babe was a kind of a big good natured goof — who never realized what glory and fame lay ahead."[6]

Actually Babe Ruth was glad to see the 19-year-old Waite Hoyt suddenly appear in the Boston clubhouse. A set of circumstances involving the trade of pitcher Carl Mays to the New York Yankees had forced Ruth, who was in pursuit of the American League home run record, back into the Red Sox starting pitching rotation. By 1919 Babe Ruth was of course an established big league pitcher who had won 80 games and held a record for pitching 29 consecutive scoreless innings in World Series play (a record that stood until 1961 when it was eclipsed by Whitey Ford pitching in the World Series against the Cincinnati Reds). However, suddenly Ruth's power hitting had become the rage of all baseball. By July 29, Ruth had hit 16 home runs, thus tying the American League record set by Socks Seybold in 1902 playing for the Philadelphia Athletics. With Hoyt on the team he would be relegated to only infrequent mound appearances and could participate as a regular in the Red Sox lineup playing in the outfield.

On July 31, four days after Hout joined the Red Sox, Ed Barrow stood by his agreement and Hoyt made his first start against Ty Cobb and the Detroit Tigers, beating them 2–1 in 12 innings. Babe Ruth helped Hoyt in pursuit of his first victory by contributing four hits in six at bats, but failed to hit the record-breaking home run. Hoyt stated years later that he had a terrible headache while warming up for the game. Nonetheless, not only did he go the distance for his first major league victory, but also got the first of his eventual 255 major league hits in the game The game itself was a wild affair and culminated with a brawl under the grandstand as Ty Cobb and Harry Heilmann took on umpire George Moriarity. While it is not known who won that fight, according to Hoyt there was no need to feel sympathetic for Moriarity having to take on two Tigers, as he had a reputation as the toughest umpire with his fists that ever lived.

According to Hoyt, "The feature of that game — as I view it now was the aftermath, as I did not have enough money to wire my father and mother in Brooklyn, much less phone — and my father called the *New York Journal* that night to get the news. Naturally I was on cloud nine, but had no one to tell, or celebrate with. So, I sat in Fenway Park on a bench — in my self-imposed glory — suddenly realizing I had it to do all over again four days later."[7]

Meanwhile, down in New Orleans Julius Heinemann took notice that Hoyt had beaten Detroit and demanded payment for him from the Red Sox. Ed Barrow disagreed with Heinemann and considered Hoyt a free agent. Then Hoyt beat the Cleveland Indians 7–5 in his second start and Heinemann persisted that the Red Sox pay him for Hoyt. Ed Barrow then felt it was in the best interest of the Red Sox to negotiate for Hoyt's release, so he offered Heinemann $2,500. But Heinemann wasn't satisfied with the offer and demanded $5,000. As Barrow and Heinemann were waiting for each to blink in the matter, several days passed and Hoyt started again, this time against the St. Louis Browns. He beat them too, for his third consecutive win since joining the Red Sox. Then simultaneously, both Heinemann and Barrow decided to accept each other's offer. Heinemann wired: "Accept your offer of $2,500.00 for Hoyt's release."[8] At the same time Barrow telegraphed: "Your demand for $5,000.00 for Hoyt's release accepted."[9]

A few minutes after Julius Heinemann's telegraph was sent out to Barrow, a terrific hurricane occurred in Louisiana, blowing down all the telegraph wires and poles around New Orleans. Consequently, it was several days before Ed Barrow's telegram of acceptance of the $5,000.00 terms reached Heinemann in New Orleans. Unfortunately, it was too late for Heinemann to do anything about it, as his message had already reached Barrow in Boston and had been filed with the president of the American League and the National Commission. So the Red Sox now had the contractual rights to Hoyt for $2,500.

A few years later when Hoyt was with the New York Yankees and they made a spring training stop in New

Waite Hoyt (National Baseball Hall of Fame Museum Library, Cooperstown, N.Y.).

Orleans, he caught up with Julius Heinemann and told him that he owed him 10 percent. According to Hoyt, Heinemann never paid a cent for him and Al Nixon never reported to New Orleans either, so in reality Heinemann made $2,500 off him. However, Hoyt said that all Heinemann did was "sing the blues about how he had lost $2,500" in the deal.[10]

As the summer continued, Hoyt enjoyed playing with Babe Ruth, even though Hoyt was now in the Red Sox starting pitching rotation, Babe Ruth was still seeing infrequent mound duty and was scheduled to start a game against Detroit. Ed Barrow called a meeting in the clubhouse prior to the game to go over the Tigers' batting order with Ruth. As Ruth went over the score card, supposedly analyzing the batting order — Bush, Veach, Cobb, Heilmann, etc.— Barrow waited patiently for Ruth's response. Hoyt stated that every hitter got the same comment from Ruth: "I'll pitch high inside and low outside. High inside and low outside. High inside and low outside."[11] Finally Barrow could take it no longer and cut Ruth off, saying, "Aw, forget it, Babe. Just go out and beat 'em."[12] Ruth did just that. In all, Ruth would pitch in 17 games for Boston in 1919.

As Babe Ruth continued his quest for the American League home run record that season, Waite saw his first home run from Ruth — in Fenway Park off of Claude "Lefty" Williams of the Chicago White Sox. Ruth hit the ball on top of the roof of the right field grandstand and his homer won the first game of a doubleheader. Hoyt later said, "Between games, Joe Jackson, Happy Felsch, Buck Weaver, Eddie Cicotte and Eddie Collins sat around talking about Ruth's epic homer, as though it was the forerunner of the atomic bomb. They had never seen anything like it. Neither had the fans— neither had I."[13]

Actually, Hoyt had known Jack Warhop, the first pitcher to give up a home run to Babe Ruth in the major leagues in 1915, Warhop was a resident of Brooklyn and Hoyt knew him well. At the time in 1915 Warhop was pitching for the New York Yankees when on May 6 he got the assignment to pitch against the Boston Red Sox. The Red Sox had just brought up a rookie pitcher (Ruth had pitched in four games for Boston in 1914) from Baltimore by the name of Babe Ruth to pitch against him. In the third inning Ruth led off against Warhop and drove the ball into the upper deck of the Polo Grounds for a home run. Warhop was disgusted with himself giving up a home run, and to a rookie nonetheless. However, Warhop did win out in the long run that day he as he eventually beat Ruth 4–3 in a 13-inning game. What Warhop could not possibly have known that day in 1915, his last year in the majors, was that he was to be first of a long line of major league pitchers against whom Ruth would hit dramatic home runs— 714 of them by the time he retired in 1935.

Ruth's quest for the American League home run record continued in the summer of 1919 when he tied Socks Seybold's record on July 29. Then it was two more weeks before he would hit another home run on August 14 to break the record with 17. Now the modern major league record of 24 home runs, which was set by the Philadelphia Phillies Gavvy Cravath in 1915, was within Ruth's reach. (The all-time record at that point in time was 27 home runs that had been hit by Ed Williamson of the Chicago Colts in 1884). By early September Ruth had hit 20 home runs and was aiming higher. On Saturday, September 20, at Fenway Park the Red Sox were scheduled to play a doubleheader with the Chicago White Sox. The Red Sox had arranged a Babe Ruth Day to honor his achievements during the season and in the ninth inning of the first game Ruth did not let the fans down. He hit a tremendous home run to the opposite field off the White Sox Lefty Williams to tie Williamson's record with his 27th home run of the season. On September 23, 1919, with Ruth needing one more home run to set the all-time home run record, the game between the Yankees and Red Sox at the Polo Grounds was cancelled due to rain. However, a doubleheader was scheduled for the following day. With 5,000 fans on hand the Red Sox beat the Yankees 4–0 in the first game as Ruth went 0-for-3 with Sad Sam Jones pitching a five-hitter.

In the second game Waite Hoyt was scheduled to pitch for Boston against the Yankees Bob Shawkey. In the first inning both teams failed to score. But in the home half of the second inning the Yankees drew first blood, scoring against Hoyt to take a 1–0 lead. Wally Pipp, the Yankees first baseman, beat out an infield tap between first and second and then raced to third on a single to left by Del Pratt. Duff Lewis then followed with a single, scoring Pipp and giving the Yankees the lead off Hoyt.

In the fifth inning Boston mounted a threat. Mike McNally led off by grounding out Peck to Pipp. Then Norm McNeil singled off Shawkey. (This was the same McNeil who had contacted Ed Barrow about Waite Hoyt when he was the catcher for the Baltimore Dry Docks.) Everett Scott was next at bat and followed with a single off Shawkey, McNeil stopping at second. Waite Hoyt banged a single to center, filling the bases. Frank Gilhooley then smashed a hot grounder to Pipp, who threw home to force McNeil. Then the rally died when Oscar Vitt flew out to Sammy Vick in right field.

The game progressed into the ninth inning with the Yankees still leading 1–0. Then, in the top of the ninth, Babe Ruth hit his record-breaking 28th home run over the right-field roof in the Polo Grounds to tie the score 1–1. (A few seasons before, Joe Jackson had hit a home run over the top of the right-field stands, but the ball landed on the roof. Ruth's blast was the first to clear it.) The next day the *New York Times* said in its account of Ruth's record-breaking clout, "Ruth stood firmly on his sturdy legs like the Colossus of Rhodes, and taking a mighty swing at the second ball pitched to him, catapulted the pill for a near altitude and distance record."[14]

When Waite Hoyt went out to the mound to pitch the bottom of the ninth he had not given up a run since the second inning and not allowed a hit to the Yankees or a base runner since the third inning. Hoyt continued to pitch brilliantly through the 9th, 10th, 11th and 12th innings, pitching nine perfect innings from the fourth through the twelfth. Then, in the bottom of the 13th with one out, Wally Pipp tripled off Hoyt, the ball hitting the wall in front of the bleachers in right field. Then Del Pratt hit a sacrifice fly to Ruth in left to score Pipp with the winning run, beating Hoyt 2–1.

Despite being the losing pitcher, the rookie Hoyt had pitched a masterful game and couldn't wait for the newspapers to arrive in the morning so that he could see what the sportswriters would say about his nine perfect innings. In 1948, looking back on the game, Hoyt stated, "I had my first lesson in the cost of playing with the world's greatest ball player. Quite properly, the headlines screamed the news of Babe's cracking the home run record. Vivid descriptions of his 28th homer clearing the grandstand roof. But no mention of me. Down at the end of the piece one line was given to the Boston pitcher. It said 'Hoyt pitched for Boston.'"[15]

However, the fact of the matter is that while the New York press did give the lion's share of the credit to Ruth and his record-breaking home run, nonetheless Hoyt's heroics were mentioned too. In its account of the game the *Boston Herald* stated, "Waite Hoyt, the Brooklyn schoolboy, pitched for the Red Sox in the second and Bob Shawkey officiated for the Yanks. Hoyt gave a remarkable performance of his pitching skill and from the fourth inning to the 13th he did not allow a hit and not a Yankee runner reached first base. In these nine innings the youngster was at the top of his form and pitched with the coolness and skill of a veteran."[16]

September 24, 1919, at New York
Second Game
Box Score

Score by Innings

	1	2	3	4	5	6	7	8	9	10	11	12	13	Totals
Boston	0	0	0	0	0	0	0	0	1	0	0	0	0	1
New York	0	1	0	0	0	0	0	0	0	0	0	0	1	2

Errors: New York, 1 (Fewster)
Boston, 0

September 24, 1919 (*cont.*)

New York	ab	r	h	o	Boston	ab	r	h	o
Vick, rf	5	0	0	3	Gilhooley, rf	6	0	2	3
Peckinpaugh, ss	5	0	1	2	Vitt, 3b	6	0	1	2
Baker, 3b	5	0	0	2	Lamar, cf	6	0	2	1
Pipp, 1b	4	2	2	14	Ruth, lf	4	1	2	2
Pratt, 2b	5	0	1	4	McInnis, 1b	5	0	0	19
Lewis, rf	4	0	1	2	McNally, 2b	5	0	1	1
Fewster, cf	4	0	0	5	McNeil, c	4	0	2	5
Duel	4	0	0	6	Scott, ss	5	0	1	2
Shawkey, p	4	0	0	1	Hoyt, p	5	0	1	1
					Schant, c*	3	0	1	1
Totals	40	2	5	39		49	1	13	37

*Batted for McNeil in eleventh.
†Winning run scored with one out.

On September 27 Babe Ruth hit his 29th home run of the season at Griffith Stadium in Washington as the Red Sox lost a doubleheader to the Nationals. This was the Babe's first home run of the year in Washington and it made him the first player in major league history to hit a home run in every park in the league in the same season. Overall for the 1919 season Ruth led the American League in six batting categories: slugging average, home runs, total bases, runs batted in, home run percentage and runs scored. Also Ruth had pitched in 17 games, finishing with a record of 9–5 and a ERA of 2.97. Regardless of the heroics of Babe Ruth, the Boston Red Sox finished the 1919 season in sixth place in the American League, 20½ games behind the pennant-winning Chicago White Sox. The White Sox then went on to play against the Cincinnati Reds in the most controversial World Series ever held — "the Black Sox scandal."

Waite Hoyt, having turned 20 years old by the end of the season, could no longer be considered a schoolboy. For in 1919 Hoyt had established himself as a big league pitcher, appearing in 13 games while finishing with a record of 4–6 and a 3.26 ERA From this point forward his march to the Hall of Fame had begun.

On January 3, 1920, the Boston Red Sox sold Babe Ruth to the New York Yankees in what all baseball historians seem to agree by acclamation as being "the bad deal of all bad deals." Harry Frazee, the Red Sox owner, was also a Broadway producer and constantly strapped for cash to finance his lavish productions. In early 1920 Frazee found himself again in a bind for cash. First of all, his current Broadway productions were all bombs and he was scrambling to pay off the actors, stage hands, musicians, etc. And Babe Ruth was demanding a new contract. The Babe was currently under a three-year contract calling for $10,000 a year. Now Ruth wanted $20,000. Lastly, Joe Lannin —from whom Frazee had bought the Red Sox in 1916 — was calling for payment on Frazee's notes.

As luck would have it, Harry Frazee's New York City office on Broadway was only a block away from Col. Jacob Ruppert's, the majority owner of the New York Yankees. This made it easy for Frazee to sell off piecemeal parts of the Red Sox to keep his head above water. In fact, during the 1919 season Frazee had sold pitcher Carl Mays to Ruppert for $40,000 and two players. In early 1920 Frazee approached Ruppert with a proposition for the Yankees to obtain Ruth. Ruppert was to give Frazee $125,000 cash for Ruth and also loan him $325,000, with Fenway Park being put up as collateral in the deal. According to Waite Hoyt, Babe Ruth first balked at the thought of going to New York: "He felt secure in Boston. New York was a huge, forbidding place. Ruth always said New York cost him so much dough he couldn't afford to live there. A $20,000 season's contract changed his mind."[17]

In the 1920 season Hoyt pitched against the Yankees twice. On July 25, when Hoyt faced them at the Polo Grounds, Babe Ruth added his name to the growing list of pitchers who could no longer figure out how to pitch to the Babe. According to Hoyt, "I had reasoned that the only way to stop him was to make him supply his own power. I threw him a high looping slow ball. Ruth booped my scientific pitch high into the upper deck of the right field grandstand."[18] In 1920 Ruth would raise the bar on his major league record for the most home runs in a season, hitting 54. (The next highest total in the major leagues for that year was the distant 19 home runs hit by George Sisler of the St. Louis Browns.) Subsequently the sports writers began referring to Ruth as The Sultan of Swat.

Harry Frazer (National Baseball Hall of Fame Museum Library, Cooperstown, N.Y.).

The Cleveland Indians, Chicago White Sox and New York Yankees went down to the wire in the 1920 American Pennant, race with the Indians pulling it out by two games after the news broke on September 29 of a scandal in the 1919 World Series. White Sox owner Charles Comiskey had immediately suspended all eight alleged White Sox players implicated in accepting bribes in the scandal, including Shoeless Joe Jackson. Consequently, with the pennant hanging in the balance and the White Sox now playing with a makeshift lineup, they faded behind the Indians.

Another infamous incident occurred during the 1920 season when on August 16 at the Polo Grounds Ray Chapman, the Cleveland Indians shortstop, was hit in the left temple with a pitch thrown by Carl Mays of the Yankees. Chapman died the next day from complications of a fractured skull. (For the record the death of Ray Chapman is still the only such incident of a player having died as a result of being injured in a game in the history of major league baseball.) Following the Chapman incident it seemed as if all of baseball came down on Carl Mays. According to author Robert Creamer, Mays was particularly in disfavor in Boston, where the Red Sox players felt that he had abandoned them the year before by jumping to the Yankees. Subsequently, the Red Sox players talked about going on strike if Mays was permitted to pitch against them. Ty Cobb of the Detroit Tigers called for Mays' banishment from baseball.

A few years later Carl Mays and Waite Hoyt would become teammates on the New York Yankees. Recalling the Chapman incident, Mays told Hoyt, "Hell, I threw him a curve ball. You don't throw a curve when you're trying to hit somebody."[19] Summing things up, author/statistician Bill James wrote in his book *Whatever Happened to the Hall Fame* that the dislike for Carl Mays generated over the Chapman incident has been key in keeping him out of the Hall of Fame despite having been a better pitcher than contemporaries such as Jim Bagby, Stan Coveleski, Herb Pennock and Waite Hoyt.

With the heart and soul of the Red Sox lineup ripped out by Frazee's dealing of Ruth to New York, Waite Hoyt and the others attempted to fill the void in the 1920 season. However, it was not to be as the Red Sox finished a distant fifth place, 25½ games behind the Cleveland Indians. In fact, Hoyt wasn't much help to the cause as he finished with a season record of 6–6 and 4.38 ERA

Hoyt's mediocre season in 1920 was partly the result of an injury sustained in horseplay. The incident took place in the Red Sox clubhouse at the Polo Grounds during a road trip to New York. There was a light bulb suspended from the ceiling by a cable that was about seven feet from the floor. Several of the Red Sox players, including Hoyt, decided to wager on who could hitch-kick and touch the bulb with one foot. Reminiscing about the incident in 1977, Hoyt stated, "I cannot recall whether I won a bet or not — but I do remember with great clarity, the next day doubling over in pain — and remaining in misery until we reached Boston where I was hustled off to the Phillips House of Massachusetts General Hospital to be operated on for a double hernia. I spent eleven lonely weeks in that place."[20]

In August, after Hoyt had rejoined the Red Sox, he attempted to work himself into shape again without much success. Then misery struck again as his lips became infected. Consequently, he spent three more weeks in Chicago's Mercy Hospital while the team moved on. The infection had a devastating effect on Hoyt's strength and when he once again rejoined the Red Sox in September the only service he could offer was to attempt to throw batting practice. In fact, his arm was so weak he could barely reach the plate when he threw the ball.

When Hoyt came home to Brooklyn following the 1920 season he seriously wondered if his major league career was over. However, Addison Hoyt was full of optimism about his son's future and demanded that he rehabilitate himself by throwing with him three times a week. Waite followed Ad's advice and attempted to strengthen his arm throwing in an empty lot. Often the two would throw in the early morning when the late fall temperatures in Brooklyn were near zero. According to Hoyt, passersby thought they were nuts. But Ad's rehabilitation program for Waite seemed to work, and slowly his arm came around and his pitches suddenly had more smoke on them.

Around Thanksgiving that year, Hoyt later said, his father suddenly began to act mysterious. "He spoke in tantalizing terms about the great Christmas gift you may get, if everything goes right. Of course this only aroused my curiosity. Secretly I began to question his sanity and examine my own. He was certainly going overboard with the mystery bit. The only worthwhile gift I could possibly receive would be a good strong pitching arm."[21] Then, on the morning of December 15 Hoyt was suddenly awakened with a startling revelation! Ad Hoyt was standing over him as he lay in bed, waving the *New York Tribune* and yelling, "Get up — get up, it's here, it's here. Your Christmas present is here."[22] Ad quickly unfurled the newspaper to the sports page and pointed to the headline, "Yanks In Big Trade."[23]

What had happened was that Harry Frazee did it again. This time he had made an eight-player deal with the Yankees, exchanging four of his players for four of the Yankees, including Waite Hoyt. In the deal the Red Sox sent Harry Harper, Wally Schang, Mike McNally and Hoyt to the Yankees in exchange for Muddy Ruel, Del Pratt, Sammy Vick and Hank Thormahlen. Hoyt was coming home to New York.

While Hoyt was the question mark in the trade, some dynamics had been taking place since the end of the season that were in his favor. Ed Barrow had been unhappy managing the Red Sox and seeing his star players shipped out to finance Frazee's theatrical interests. Therefore, when the New York Yankees general manager Harry Sparrow died in May 1920, opportunity knocked for Barrow. According to author Robert W. Creamer, Harry Frazee — who was a drinking buddy of Col. Jacob Ruppert's partner in the Yankees ownership, Col. Tillinghast Huston — recommended Ed Barrow over a few cocktails to replace Sparrow. Subsequently, in October 1920 Ed Barrow left Boston to become the general manager of the New York Yankees. What Hoyt did not know at the time was that Ed Barrow still had the same great confidence in him that he had when he first saw him pitch in 1919 at Washington and that also his father had been making regular trips all through the fall to the Yankees offices in order to report to Barrow on the progress and condition of his arm.

Fifty-seven years later in 1977, looking back on that joyous Christmas season of 1920, Hoyt stated, "When the overpowering spiritual glow of the actual Christmas finally arrived, all about me seemed bathed in an added glow. The candles burned brighter, the tinsel a heightened glistening, the bulbs and ornaments added luster — and the tree itself more stately in its Christmas majesty. The love of family and friends was never more intense."[24] Waite Hoyt was about to experience the most successful years of his major league career and define his place in baseball history.

Prior to 1921 the New York Yankees had never won an American League pennant and had done no better than finishing Second in 1904, 1906 and 1910. Now, thanks to the generosity of Harry Frazee, the New York Yankees would win six American League pennants in the next eight years. Harry Frazee, through his trades with the New York Yankees, had assisted in building one of the most successful and legendary franchises in the history of the game. Not only had Frazee sent the Yankees the biggest superstar in baseball history in Babe Ruth and one of the best catchers in the game in Wally Schang, but in just a few short years had also dealt them an entire starting pitching rotation comprised of future 20-game winners Joe Bush, Sad Sam Jones, Carl Mays, and Waite Hoyt.

Harry Frazee would eventually sell the Boston Red Sox after the 1922 season and finally strike it rich on Broadway in 1925 with the hit show *No No Nannette*. All at once Frazee had a monster hit on his hands with five road companies touring around America and one of the most recognizable tunes of the century in "Tiptoe Through the Tulips." But the legacy of Harry Frazee will throughout eternity be bringing down "the curse of the Bambino" upon Beantown.

Even with Frazee out of the picture the Red Sox would still continue to send quality players to New York. In 1923 Boston would send the Yankees additional help in pitchers Herb Pennock and George Pipgras, both eventual 20-game winners. But the damage had already been done by Harry Frazee and the World Championship team of 1918 would be the last such victory for a Boston Red Sox team in the twentieth century. The Boston Red Sox would finish in fifth place in 1921 and then the franchise would not finish any higher in the standings until 1931, becoming perennial cellar dwellers in the American League and finishing last in 1922, 1923, 1925, 1926, 1927, 1928 ,1929 and 1930.

3

The Polo Grounds Years

Following the 1912 season the New York Highlanders had vacated Hilltop Park, changed their team name to Yankees and begun playing home games at the Polo Grounds. However, the Polo Grounds just happened to be owned by the New York Giants. Nonetheless, for the first eight years the Yankees were a good tenant in the Polo Grounds; they paid the Giants $100,000 a year in rent and were not much trouble. The Giants were at the time considered the premier baseball team in New York, having won six National League pennants since 1904. Manager John McGraw was so popular that he was even invited to cocktail parties in Fifth Avenue mansions. The Yankees, on the other hand, had been a struggling franchise. With the exception of a fourth-place finish in 1916, they had perpetually floundered in the second division of the American League.

After a failed attempt to buy the Giants, Jacob Ruppert and Tillinghast Huston purchased the Yankees for $460,000 on January 1, 1915. By the 1920 season the Yankees had acquired Babe Ruth from Boston and suddenly become very competitive finishing in third place just three games behind the World Champion Cleveland Indians. In 1920 Babe Ruth hit 54 home runs and batted .376. He hit 54 home runs despite the fact that he did not hit his first home run until May. In fact, Ruth's home run total that season actually exceeded that of any team's total in the American League, with the St. Louis Browns coming closest to him with 50.

The Yankees had great pitching too, with Carl Mays winning 26 games and Bob Shawkey 20. With Ruth becoming a huge draw, the Yankees' season attendance in 1920 swelled to an unprecedented 1,289,422. The Yankees actually exceeded the attendance of their landlord by a total of 359,813 and suddenly they were considered a threat to the prestige of John McGraw and the New York Giants in the city.

In May 1920 the Giants (under the new management of Charles A. Stoneham, who had headed the group of investors that purchased the team from the estate of John T. Brush) in 1919 for $1 million dollars issued an eviction order to the Yankees. Although the eviction order was rapidly rescinded, it soured Yankees owners Jacob Ruppert and Tillinghast Huston. Therefore, they began to search for a suitable site on which to build their own stadium and relocate the team. In February 1921 Ruppert and Huston purchased from the estate of William Waldorf Astor for $600,000 a 10-acre site, located across the Harlem River from the Polo Grounds in The Bronx at 161st Street and River Avenue and began to plan their new ballpark.

When Waite Hoyt joined the New York Yankees for the 1921 season, he roomed with teammates Bob Shawkey and Bob Hoffman in an apartment close to the Polo Grounds. He was about to become a major league star and the Roaring Twenties were about to explode on the national scene with an exaggerated excess of glitter that featured flappers, bathtub gin, jazz and a sense of preoccupation with the realization of the American dream. One of the first things Hoyt noticed upon arriving back in New York was the change in Babe Ruth. According to Hoyt, "In Boston he had been a surprised young man — hardly able to assimilate the extravagance of success. Now he was sure of himself. He at last realized he was a man apart and above the ordinary ball player."[1]

Ruth lived in a suite at the Ansonia Hotel with his wife and adopted daughter. Taking advantage of his new status in the Yankees clubhouse, he was demanding special amenities, such as having a pay telephone installed and a waste paper basket by his locker. While baseball in the previous decade had celebrated Ty Cobb as its number one star, the new decade of the twenties reserved that distinction for Babe Ruth. By the end of the 1921 season Ruth would become the biggest gate attraction ever in major league baseball. Waite Hoyt later stated that regardless of his success, the Babe "had no business sense whatever. Salary meant nothing. Money was just metal and paper to be exchanged for whatever he wanted. His mail was some thirty thousand letters a week. He had no secretary — and wouldn't have known what to do with one if he had one. Naturally Babe couldn't read — or answer all those letters— so he just opened and read the pink and the blue and the green ones, and those which smelled of perfume — and tore the rest up. The Yankee ball players, yours truly included, would sort out some of the others. Honestly — we found that Ruth would tear up letters containing checks for as much as one, two and three thousand dollars—sent to him for royalties for the use of his name. Goodness knows how much money Babe threw away by tearing up his mail."[2]

The Cleveland Indians, having beaten the Brooklyn Robins five games to two in the 1920 World Series, were determined to defend their World Championship in 1921 and fought tooth and nail with the Yankees all season long into late September, when they were eventually crippled with injuries to catcher Steve O'Neill and player-manager Tris Speaker (who would finish the season with a .362 batting average). On September 23, with the Indians trailing the Yankees by two games in the standings, they arrived at the Polo Grounds for a four-game head-to-head series. The series would draw 147,000 fans through the turnstiles. The huge crowds at the Polo Grounds were a result of several factors. First of all, many fans were there to see the Yankees in the quest for their first pennant. Then there was Babe Ruth, who

Babe Ruth (National Baseball Hall of Fame Library, Cooperstown, N.Y.).

had already eclipsed his previous record of 54 home runs in a season. Also, as the New York Giants were about to clinch the National League pennant, it looked like a possible all–New York World Series was in the making.

Waite Hoyt started the first game and beat the Indians 4–2 as Babe Ruth stroked three doubles and scored three runs. In game two the Indians pounded the Yankees 9–0. The third game was played on a Sunday and saw the Yankees get out to a 15–0 lead behind the pitching and hitting of starting pitcher Carl Mays, who had three hits. The Yankees eventually won that game 21–7 and Babe Ruth played a very minor role in the victory.

Game four of the series was a wild one; according to Waite Hoyt, two spectators even died in the stands from the stress. So much interest was being generated in Ruth's home run hitting that on New York's East Side carrier pigeons were being sent into the Polo Grounds to bring back returns of Ruth's trips to the plate. Prior to the game manager Miller Huggins had polled the players on who they would like to have as their starting pitcher. The Yankee players selected veteran Jack Quinn. However, after Quinn gave up three runs in the first inning to allow Cleveland a 3–0 lead, Waite Hoyt came in to relieve him. In the bottom of the first Babe Ruth hit his 57th home run. In the third Ruth added an RBI double. Then, in the fifth Ruth hit a two-run homer to give the Yankees a 5–4 lead. It was his 58th of the year. With the Yankees leading in the ninth 8–7, Carl Mays— who had taken over from Hoyt on the mound in the fifth — struck out Steve O'Neill with two base runners on to end it. The Yankees were now in front of the Indians by 4½ games and the pennant looked certain.

On October 1, 1921, the Yankees clinched their first American League pennant when they beat the Philadelphia Athletics at Shibe Park 5–3 in the first game of a doubleheader. In the second game Waite Hoyt started for the Yankees and was going for win number 20. The Yankees quickly built up a 6–0 lead and Hoyt was cruising along having pitched seven terrific innings. However, the fans at Shibe Park were calling for Babe Ruth to pitch. Ruth had previously started one game in the 1921 season and gotten credit for the win against the Detroit Tigers, striking out Ty Cobb twice. Well, with the pennant already wrapped up, Miller Huggins acquiesced to the call of the fans and sent Ruth out to the mound in the top of the eighth. With Hoyt out of the game, suddenly the Athletics bats came alive against the Bambino as they scored six runs to tie the game at 6–6. Amazingly, Miller Huggins let Ruth stay in the game and he shut down the Athletics in the ninth and continued to pitch scoreless ball through the 10th as the game went into extra innings. In the top the 11th inning Ruth hit his 59th home run of the season to give the lead back to the Yankees 7–6 and then concluded his efforts by getting the Athletics out in the bottom of the inning to preserve the victory. However, while Ruth got credit for the win, it cost Waite Hoyt his first chance to become a 20-game winner. Consequently, Waite Hoyt finished the 1921 season with a record of 19–13 and an ERA of 3.10.

Ruth finished the season with a 2–0 record as a pitcher, with a 9.00 ERA His batting statistics for the season were phenomenal: 59 home runs, 171 RBIs and a batting average of .378. However, as good as Ruth's statistics were, he did not win a triple crown, finishing third in the American League batting chase behind Detroit's Harry Heilmann (.394) and Ty Cobb (.389). Following this experience on the mound, Ruth did not pitch another inning in an American League game until 1930.

Suddenly the New York Giants and New York Yankees were about to square off in the first intra-city World Series in 15 years. The first intra-city World Series had taken place between the Chicago White Sox (also known as "the hitless wonders") and the Chicago Cubs in 1906. The White Sox defeated the Chicago Cubs 4–2 in the series. The 1921 World Series would be the first where all the games would be played in the same ballpark. The sportswriters of the time dubbed it a "subway series," as both fans of the Giants and Yankees alike could ride the subway to the Polo Grounds for all the games. In addition, the 1921 World Series would feature opposing brothers, with Bob Meusel playing right field for the Yankees and Emil "Irish" Meusel playing in left field for the Giants. (This, however, was not a first, as brothers Doc Johnston of Cleveland and Jimmie Johnston of Brooklyn had faced each other in the 1920 World Series.)

While the Yankees had tremendous hitting, the odds favored the Giants in the series because of their speed and aggressiveness. With Babe Ruth hitting 59 home runs, Bob Meusel 24, Wally Pipp 8 and Frank "Home Run" Baker 9, the Yankees had set a new major league record of 134 home runs, topping the old record set by the Chicago Nationals in 1894. However, the Giants had power too, and had hit 83 home runs and featured the National League home run king in their lineup — George "Highpockets" Kelly, who had blasted 23 round-trippers. But more apparent was the fact that the Giants had speed. As a team the Giants had hit 91 triples and stolen 144 bases. Frank Frisch, known as The Fordham Flash, had stolen 50 bases which was more than the Yankees' first three leaders in swipes combined — Bob Meusel at 15 and Babe Ruth and Wally Pipp at 14 each. In 1921 the home run had not yet been calculated as an effective way to win games, so the odds-makers were favoring the speedy Giants. However, one unknown entity almost tilted the balance of power in favor of the Yankees: the pitching of Waite Hoyt.

Since 1919 the World Series had been played in a nine-game format. In 1919 the major league club owners had misjudged the post–World War I economy and established a 140-game schedule. When fans flocked through the turnstiles in droves in 1919, the owners developed a scheme to recoup some of the lost revenue by extending the World Series from seven to nine games. Therefore, the 1921 World Series, like the 1919 and 1920 series before it, was to be played out to the best five out of nine games.

Prior to game one, outside the Polo Grounds jobless men who had waited all night to gain an advantage in the ticket lines were selling their places for $5 to eager buyers. Inside the Polo Grounds the governor of New York and mayor of New York City were escorted across the field. The band played "The Star Spangled Banner" as members of both the Giants and Yankees placed a wreath on a stone in deep center field that was erected to honor the memory of former Giants infielder Eddie Grant, who had been killed in World War I. Then game one of the 1921 World Series began and Carl Mays baffled the Giants, pitching a 3–0 shutout and allowing just five hits—four of them to the switch-hitting Frank Frisch.

Prior to the series Giants manager John McGraw had counseled his pitching staff on containing the power of Ruth. "Don't throw that big baboon anything but low curves," ordered McGraw.[3] But Babe Ruth drove in the first run of the series when he singled home Elmer Miller in the first inning off of spitball artist Phil Douglas.

The rivalry between the Giants and Yankees was intense and in many ways petty. Waite Hoyt later stated that just before the 1921 World Series began the Yankees signed a testimonial advertisement for a popular soap. Therefore, each time a Yankee player had to pass the Giants bench returning from first base they were showered with soap cakes. Finally, one of the Yankees picked up one of the cakes and threw it hard into the Giants dugout, just missing McGraw's head. While the soap ballistic attack angered McGraw, he only retaliated with a stream of profanity. However, some years later at a banquet, Hoyt stated, McGraw told him that he was sorry that he ever let the Yankees get away with that.

The following day in game two, with the ball clubs rotating as the home team, Waite Hoyt took over, facing the Giants ace Art Nehf and handing the Giants their second straight shutout at 3–0. Hoyt allowed only two hits in the game. Hoyt always considered this game as the finest game he ever pitched. For Hoyt it was sweet revenge against the Giants and John McGraw, the team that had first signed him and then sent him to languish in the minor leagues. However, it was to be a bitter-sweet victory for the Yankees, as it would ultimately cost them the services of Babe Ruth. In the fifth inning Ruth had stolen second and then proceeded to steal third base. In sliding into the third-base bag Ruth scraped his upper left arm badly, aggravating an unhealed wound he had received sliding into second base during the crucial series with Cleveland in late September. It had become infected.

In the first two games of the series Carl Mays and Waite Hoyt had held the Giants scoreless and only allowed a total of seven hits—five of them to Frank Frisch, who was despite his team's dismal play hitting .625. John McGraw, not in the least daunted by the play of his team in the first two games, sent Fred Toney against Bob Shawkey of the Yankees in game three. With Commissioner Kenesaw Mountain Landis on hand, dressed nattily in an old tan sweater jacket and topcoat and holding a cane, the Yankees scored three runs in the third when Babe Ruth singled, driving in two runs. It looked like they were going to rout the Giants and send them into a three-game-to-none hole in the series. Prior to the game it had been reported in the press that Ruth would not play in the game; he was in fact carrying his arm around in a sling and it was causing him a lot of pain. But throughout the series the Giants had been riding Ruth unmercifully from the bench and he wanted to show them something, so he played despite his ailing arm, finally leaving the game in the eighth.

However, after 20 scoreless innings the Giants finally began to hit and scored four runs in the bottom of the fourth to tie the game. The Giants scored eight more runs in the seventh and ultimately won game three by a score of 13–5, pounding out 20 hits against four Yankees pitchers. Following the game, Yankees' skipper Miller Huggins was surrounded by the press and simply told them, "We can't win 'em all. It was one of those things that will happen to any ball club. Shawkey didn't show the stuff that we expected him to show and his control was bad. In addition to that he faced the Giants at a time when they were due to come back."[4]

In game four Carl Mays pitched a shutout into the eighth inning, when he gave up three runs to the Giants, who went on to win the game 4–2 and even up the best-of-nine series at two games each. Phil Douglas, who had been the losing pitcher in the first game, was the winner this time around as George Burns provided the winning margin for the Giants with a two-run double off Mays. In the ninth inning an ailing Babe Ruth hit the first home run in the series.

In game five Waite Hoyt was back on the mound facing Art Nehf again. The Giants scored an unearned run off Hoyt in the first inning to take a 1–0 lead. George Burns led off for the Giants and grounded the ball to McNally at third, who bobbled it, allowing Burns to reach first base. Dave Bancroft, the Giants shortstop, then forced Burns, Peckinpaugh to Ward. Frank Frisch followed by bouncing a single off Hoyt's glove, with Bancroft going to second. Hoyt then walked the next batter to load the bases. George Kelly then hit a Texas Leaguer, scoring Bancroft.

In the third inning the Yankees evened up the score 1–1. Mike McNally led off with a walk from Nehf, and Schang doubled, sending McNally to third. Following an out by Hoyt, Bancroft to Kelly, with the runners holding their bases, Miller flied to Irish Meusel, scoring McNally. In the fourth inning the Yankees went out ahead in the game by a score of 3–1. Babe Ruth, with his arm hurting him badly, led off the inning by laying down a surprise bunt that caught the entire Giants infield sleeping. Bob Meusel followed with a double to left, scoring Ruth all the way from first base to take them to 2–1 Yankees. As Wally Pipp grounded out Rawlings to Kelly, Meusel took third on the play. Aaron Ward then hit a sacrifice fly to Burns in center field, scoring Meusel for 3–1 Yankees. From the bottom of the fourth through the ninth Hoyt and Nehf both pitched scoreless ball. However, in the eighth the Giants threatened when with one out Ross Youngs got an infield hit and then George Kelly hit the ball to right and Youngs raced into third. But Bob Meusel threw Kelly out at second trying to stretch his single into a double. Hoyt then got Emil Meusel to foul out to Pipp.

　　Waite Hoyt had now won two games in the World Series while not yet yielding an earned run in 18 innings. In the account of the game in the newspapers the next day, remarking about Hoyt's pitching performance, it was stated, "When in that electrical eighth inning the fans were calling for his blood, Waite Hoyt never batted an eyelid. There were two interesting persons watching him closely, but he never gave either of them a thought. One was John J. McGraw and the other was Harry Frazee, owner of the Red Sox. Both have had Hoyt in their employ and both discarded him as hopeless material. Both have lived to feel the burning swish of his Yankee-owned delivery."[5]

　　John McGraw was a practitioner of intimidation and abuse and permitted his players to use it freely against the opposition. At one point during the 1921 World Series the Giants bench began to make fun of Babe Ruth's physical appearance, riding him about the size of his nose and size of his posterior. Also, they began using various racial epithets toward him, thus refueling the old rumor that the Babe was part Negro in his genetic makeup. The razing and questioning of his racial status so inflamed Babe that

Waite Hoyt (National Baseball Hall of Fame Library Cooperstown, N.Y.).

following the game he made a mad dash for the Giants clubhouse, with Bob Meusel close at hand as an ally to settle the score. Bursting into the Giants clubhouse Babe went directly for Johnny Rawlings, who stood a mere 5'8" and weighed all of about 155 pounds. Ruth's boisterous intrusion immediately caused a group of Giants, led by Frank "Pancho" Synder, to intercede on Rawlings behalf. However, the fracas soon became a stand-off as Ruth let the Giants know in no uncertain terms that it was all right to verbally abuse his play on the field, even cuss at him, but going after his physical appearance or accusing him of not being a white man was out of bounds.

The Giants attempted to use the same tactics of verbal intimidation on young Waite Hoyt too. Throughout the early innings of game five the Giants belittled Hoyt from the bench, attempting to rattle him. However, Hoyt retained his composure and answered the Giants by flinging a stone into the dugout and causing a few players to scatter. the *Philadelphia Inquirer* said of Hoyt's performance on the mound, "His attitude towards his foes was an asset. The Giants, tutored by the genial McGraw, had decided that they would talk and ride young Mister Hoyt out of a battle if they could not hit him out of a victory. So they started to use language in one inning that may be imagined and is better not depicted, and Hoyt calmly picked up a stone and threw it into the group of those who were trying to accomplish that fell purpose known as 'getting one's goat.' With that display of personal nerve young Hoyt found no further vocal disturbance from the Giants, and after having demonstrated that he could throw a stone with accuracy and effect, Waite struck out a couple men an inning to prove that he was still master of the art of handling a baseball."[6]

While the 3–1 win gave the Yankees the upper hand in taking a 3–2 lead in the best-of-nine series, they would now have to play the rest of the way without Babe Ruth. Despite being in intense pain Ruth had played in game five with his swollen arm heavily bandaged and a tube draining pus from the wound. So serious had the infection in Ruth's left arm become that he was advised by his physician that to take further chances would risk the possible loss of the arm. Furthermore, the battered Babe was suffering from other injuries sustained during the season. He was still hurting from a sprained left knee that occurred in mid-summer and a pulled tendon in his right leg torn loose when he scored from first base on Bob Meusel's two-base hit in game five. In addition, Ruth also had an open sore on his hip caused by sliding into bases and constantly reopening it. Nonetheless, if Ruth had not been threatened with the permanent loss of his left arm he would have without a shadow of doubt been in the Yankees lineup for game six.

In game six, with Ruth out of the lineup, the Yankees blew an early 5–2 lead to lose the game 8–5. The Yankees had knocked Giants starter Fred Toney out of the game in the first inning, scoring three runs as umpire Moriarity ordered Babe Ruth — dressed in street clothes — out of the Yankees dugout. However, the Giants came back to tie the score at 3–3 in the second inning on home runs by Emil "Irish" Meusel, a two-run blast and Frank Snyder — both off Yankees starter Harry Harper. In the bottom of the second Chick Fewster, who had replaced Ruth in the lineup, hit a two-run homer to give the lead back to the Yankees 5–3. With three home runs in one inning — two by the Giants and one by the Yankees — a new record for home runs in the same inning in a World Series game had been set. The Giants put the game away in the fourth, scoring four runs and then one in the fifth to take an 8–5 lead. Jesse Barnes, using a sharp-breaking curve and hopping fast ball, picked up his second win in relief in the series for the Giants, striking out 10 batters to allow the Giants to once again tie up the series at three games each.

With the largest crowd yet on hand for any of the series games, Carl Mays started game seven for the Yankees against Phil Douglas of the Giants. It was Mays' third start in eight days and Yankees manager Miller Huggins had already announced that if the series went nine games, then Mays would make a fourth start. The game turned out to be another pitchers duel as the Giants edged the Yankees 2–1. The deciding run was scored by the Giants in the bottom of the seventh when with two out Johnny Rawlings got on base as a result of an error by Yankees second baseman Aaron Ward. Frank Snyder then followed with a double to left, scoring Rawlings and giving the Giants a 4–3 advantage in the series.

With Waite Hoyt, who had already won two games, on the mound the Yankees took the field for game eight of the series. The Giants' Art Nehf would face off against Hoyt for the third time in the series. In the first inning George Burns led off against Hoyt and grounded out Baker to Pipp. Dave Bancroft drew a walk off Hoyt and Frank Frisch fouled out to Pipp. Hoyt then walked Ross Youngs as he kicked the mound in disgust when the fourth ball was called. The next batter up was George Kelly, who hit a grounder to Yankees shortstop Roger Peckinpaugh — who let the ball go through his legs, allowing Bancroft to score. It was to be the only run the Giants would need. For the rest of the game Hoyt and Nehf then dueled, throwing up zeros on the scoreboard. In the end Art Nehf and the Giants prevailed, winning the game 1–0, with the World Championship and the championship of New York City to boot. It is less than anti-climatic that following the series on December 20, Roger Peckinpaugh — who made the error in this pivotal game — would be traded by the Yankees to the Boston

Red Sox, who would then deal him to the Washington Nationals for the 1922 season.

In the 1921 World Series Waite Hoyt had pitched three complete games, winning two and losing one while going 27 innings without giving up an earned run. His brilliant performance in the series was the finest since Christy Mathewson had pitched three shutouts against the Philadelphia Athletics in the 1905 fall classic. Later Hoyt would say that he considered the toughest game he ever pitched to be the last game of the 1921 World Series in which he lost to the Giants 1–0. While Babe Ruth and Carl Mays had shown their true courageous colors for the Yankees and Art Nehf, Phil Douglas and Jesse Barnes had pitched extremely well for the Giants, the true hero of the 1921 World Series was hands down the blond-haired kid from Brooklyn, Waite Hoyt.

The 22-year-old Hoyt was now a star in New York City, but like the over-whelming majority of ballplayers of his time, he had to find employment in the off-season to sustain himself. So Hoyt did what came naturally—he went out on the vaudeville circuit. While Addison Hoyt had retired from vaudeville, Hoyt kept the family tradition alive. On October 17, 1921, Hoyt made his debut at Loew's Metropolitan Theatre in Brooklyn. A review of his performance at the time from an unknown newspaper stated, "He warbled a baseball parody 'How Many Times' in a voice that had a fair amount of control, though not as much as his fast ball, but when it came down to telling stories he was a rough diamond." It is of course too bad that the reviewer did not get the opportunity to hear Hoyt become a very polished accomplished storyteller on the radio during his tenure as a baseball broadcaster some twenty years in the future.)

Hoyt moved on with his bookings and appeared at Reisenweber's with Sally Field. In late November, while Hoyt was appearing on the Keith's circuit doing a song and dance routine with Tommy Gordon in Hartford, Connecticut, he announced his engagement to Dorothy Pyle. This was the same Dorothy Pyle who Hoyt had met in 1915 at the high school dance at the St. George Hotel. The two had gone together for a while, but Hoyt's baseball career brought a separation to the relationship. In fact, Miss Pyle had dropped Waite because she felt that he wasn't really interested in anything else other than baseball. That was until they met again during the summer of 1921 at a subway station in Brooklyn and found that the flame between them had never really gone out. Furthermore, at the time Hoyt was widely considered the most handsome pitcher in the major leagues. As one writer of the time put it, the Yankee fans adopted him, and so did Dot.

On November 29, 1921, the *Brooklyn Daily Eagle* formally announced their engagement: "Waite Hoyt, star pitcher of the Yankees in the late World's Series, is to be married in February. Dorothy Pyle, daughter of Harry S. Pyle of Fiske Terrace, is to be the bride. The couple announced their engagement privately a few weeks ago, and set the month for the marriage. Only their closest friends were aware of the coming event until today. Pyle, a graduate of P.S. 139 at Cortelyou Rd. and E. 13th St. and the Packer Institute, is a daughter of Harry T. Pyle, the Flatbush undertaker. She is as well known to the feminine set in Brooklyn as Hoyt is to the baseball fans."[7]

Hoyt had set the date for his marriage to his high school sweetheart as February 1, 1922. The date gave him plenty of time to finish up his nuptials, complete his vaudeville contract with Keith's and then report for the Yankees spring training camp. Following the marriage ceremony Waite and Dorothy honeymooned down on the Jersey shore in Atlantic City. While the two hardly looked any different from the hundreds of other tourists and newlyweds combing the Boardwalk, Hoyt's recent celebrity status could not escape the media and so on February 7, 1922, a picture appeared in *The New York World* of the happy couple smiling brightly from the seat of an Atlantic City push cart.

Back home, the road for the New York Yankees to the 1922 American League pennant was to be a bumpy one. First of all the Yankees had to play the first 34 games of the season without Babe Ruth, and Bob Meusel. It had previously been the custom of many a major league player to supplement his season's salary with money earned from participating in barnstorming tours at the end of the regular season. Such was the case with Babe Ruth who following the regular season liked to scamper about the country barnstorming for cash. The general feeling among the club owners at the time was that such exhibitions cheapened the World Series, as often players from both teams, supplemented by various amateurs, billed the events as a "re-enactment" of the World Series. To that end the owners had passed a rule in 1911 banning any player who had participated in the World Series from playing in any exhibition games following the series.

Regardless of the rule in place, Ruth, along with fellow Yankees Bob Meusel, Carl Mays, Wally Schang and Bill Piercy, decided to ignore the edict and went out on the road. Consequently, newly installed baseball commissioner Judge Kenesaw Mountain Landis enforced the ban and fined all five their World Series shares (which were later returned) and suspended them for the first 34 games of the 1922 season, which kept them out of the lineup until May 20. The one saving grace in this otherwise bad situation for the Yankees was that on December 20, 1921, Billy Piercy was traded to Boston in yet another six-player blunder set up by Harry Frazee; that trade brought the Yankees two more fine pitchers in Joe Bush and Sad Sam Jones. Bush would go on to win 26 games for the Yankees in 1922.

In addition to the loss of Ruth and Meusel to begin the season, Waite Hoyt said that, "The Yankees of 1922 were a collection of ball players operating as a team, but much divided in spirit. There were frequent fights and arguments. It was one hectic period."[8] Babe Ruth was constantly arguing with manager Miller Huggins and at one point the two arrived at a standoff. With the hard-hitting St. Louis Browns constantly nipping at the heels of the Yankees in the standings, Huggins became upset with Ruth's carousing at night on the road. According to Hoyt, Ruth would say, "If you don't like it, why don't you send me home?"[9] To which Huggins would reply, "If you don't want to play for this ball club, why don't you go home?"[10] At that point Ruth would issue an ultimatum to Huggins: "You won't be here next year. It will be either you or me, wait and see."[11] In fact, Waite Hoyt, writing in an article published in *The Sporting News* in October 1952, stated that the question of Huggins' managerial style went all the way up to the Yankees front office. Co-owners Col. Jacob Ruppert and Col. Tillinghast Huston were at loggerheads over Huggins—Ruppert liked him, Huston wanted to fire him.

Despite the loss of Ruth, Meusel and Mays in the lineup, the failure of Sad Sam Jones to pitch consistently and the loss of Joe Bush (who was out the first month of the season due to a cut on his hand,) the Yankees, buoyed by the superior pitching of Hoyt and Bob Shawkey, were out in front in the American League throughout April and into May. Nonetheless, the frustration was showing on the Yankees. Then in May the hotheaded Hoyt got into an argument with Miller Huggins over how to pitch to a batter. Now the press was beginning to question Huggins' lack of discipline on the club.

On May 20 Ruth returned to the lineup and immediately went into a slump. Huggins had thought that perhaps by naming Ruth team captain he would rise to the challenge and assume the leadership role. The experiment lasted for just five days until Ruth got into huge brouhaha with second base umpire George Hildebrand after being called out sliding into second base; he wound up throwing dirt all over the umpire. Following the fracas Ruth then tried to go into the stands after a fan who began heckling him.

As the summer heat rolled in, the American League pennant race at the top of the standings began to seesaw, with the Yankees losing some close ones. On June 19 the Yankees lost to Cleveland 3–2; it was their eighth straight loss. On June 28, Waite Hoyt lost a tough one to the Washington Nationals 1–0. Pitching against Walter Johnson, Hoyt had allowed just two hits going into the ninth when Earl Smith doubled, driving home the winning run for the Nationals. For The Big Train, it was his third straight shutout and 97th of his career. Throughout his career Walter Johnson seemed to have had a jinx on the Yankees, having beaten them all most every time he faced them. However, on July 23 Harry Frazee gave the Yankees yet another shot in the arm when in a six-player deal he sent them third baseman Joe Dugan. Dugan would hit .286 in 60 games and his play at the hot corner would solidify the Yankees infield and prove a major asset down the stretch in September.

It seemed like everyone on the Yankees team had been in a fight with a teammate throughout the summer of 1922. Waite Hoyt later stated, "Hoffman and Devormer had a melee in Detroit. Aaron Ward and Bobby Roth swapped punches. Carl Mays and Devornmer threatened each other. It was a real hectic season."[12] On July 26 in St. Louis the prevailing utter frustration among the Yankees players was never more apparent. First of all, Wally Schang and Bob Meusel got into a fracas on the bench. Then the main event of the afternoon took place when Babe Ruth and Wally Pipp squared off against each other. Pipp had been having trouble with his fielding of late and Ruth, the duly appointed captain of the Yankees, felt it was his responsibility to set Pipp straight. At the end of an inning where Pipp had committed one particularly clumsy play, he entered the New York dugout and proclaimed, "If that big monkey says anything to me, I'll punch him right on that big nose."[13] When Ruth reached the dugout from his position in left field he immediately began to criticize Pipp. According to Hoyt, "Ruth never finished the sentence. Pipp reached out and clouted the Babe right on the promised spot and Babe's already large beak swelled like a blowfish."[14] Then all hell broke loose as Pipp and Ruth started swinging wildly at each other and Home Run Baker

Miller Huggins (National Baseball Hall of Fame Library Cooperstown, N.Y.).

got clouted attempting to break up the melee. The game was held up due to the fact that Ruth was the first batter up in the Yankees' half of the inning and Pipp was scheduled to hit second. Ironically, when peace was restored Ruth and Pipp hit back-to-back home runs. In the ninth Ruth hit another home run and the Yankees beat the Browns by a score of 11–6.

As the dog days of August rolled in the Yankees were hanging tough. But on August 22 at the Polo Grounds the Cleveland Indians defeated the Yankees 6–2 to cut the New York league lead over St. Louis to one half game as the Browns defeated the decimated cellar-dwelling Red Sox 9–4. The following day the Indians once again defeated the Yankees 4–1, while the Browns beat the Red Sox 6–3 as the league seesawed yet again, giving St. Louis a half-game lead over New York. Now the St. Louis Browns were coming to New York featuring Ken Williams, who was leading the league with 32 home runs and also carrying a 28-game hitting streak. George Sisler, who was hitting .416, was on a 22-game hitting streak.

On August 25 at the Polo Grounds, the Yankees and Browns met in a doubleheader before a standing-room-only crowd of 40,000. In the first game Waite Hoyt put an end to the 28-game hitting streak of Williams as he went 0–4, while George Sisler kept his alive with two hits in three at bats. However, Hoyt lost the game 3–1 to Browns hurler Urban Shocker. *The St. Louis Post-Dispatch* described Shocker's performance as "one of the most brilliant games of his career" as he limited the Yankees to seven hits and shut down a ninth-inning rally.

In the nightcap George Sisler kept his hitting streak alive at 24 games, but the Yankees rebounded and beat the Browns 6–5 as they took advantage of some wildness on the part of Browns pitcher Dixie Davis. Nonetheless, the game was a close one and the morale problem on the Yankees team — and its possible impact on the outcome of the 1922 pennant race — was well known throughout baseball. This prompted *New York Baseball* writer Davis J. Walsh to write, "Judged purely by surface appearances the St. Louis Browns are a more plausible pennant winner than the New York Yankees. Team for team they may lack some of the impressive paper scratch of the Yanks, but when it comes down to a question of morale versus morale the affair ceases to be a contest. So close was the decision in fact that the Browns had the tying and winning runs on bases in the ninth when Marty McManus filed to Witt for the final out. An extra base hit at this juncture would have won the pennant. That is the conviction of this writer."[15]

On August 30 at the Polo Grounds, Babe Ruth hit a home run at his first at bat and was called out on strikes the second time. The Babe protested loudly and was exiled by umpire Tom Connolly. On September

1 Ruth was suspended by American League president Ban Johnson for three days for abusing an umpire. It was the fifth suspension in the season for the Ruth and a major league record.

On September 10 the Yankees played their last home games in the Polo Grounds against the Philadelphia Athletics in a doubleheader. At this point there were plans to expand the Polo Grounds to a seating capacity of 56,000, but the Yankees were already looking across the Harlem River at their new ballpark rising out of the dust in a barren section of the Bronx. An overflow crowd of 40,000 fans turned out for the occasion of the Yankees' last home game in Manhattan and another 25,000 were turned away. In the first game Joe Bush beat the Athletics 10–3. Then, in the nightcap Waite Hoyt defeated the Athletics 3–1 as the Yankees set out to play their final 18 games of the 1922 season on the road.

On September 16 the Yankees played the Browns in St. Louis and won 2–1 as Bob Shawkey out-dueled Urban Shocker. In the bottom of the ninth Yankee center fielder Whitey Witt was hit in the head and knocked unconscious by a soda bottle thrown out of the stands. The Browns came back to win the second game of the series. In the third game, with Witt playing with a bandaged head, he knocked in two runs in the ninth to give the Yankees a 3–2 win. Finally, on September 30, after a nip-and-tuck battle throughout the season with the Browns, the Yankees clinched the pennant in Boston, defeating the Red Sox 3–1 as Waite Hoyt and Joe Bush combined efforts for the victory.

The Yankees had won the American League pennant by one game over the St. Louis Browns. Waite Hoyt had once again won 19 games for the Yankees, finishing the 1922 season with a record of 19–12 and an ERA of 3.43. In the stretch drive Hoyt had won five games in four weeks. If the Yankees had hit for him, he would have won well over 20 games. Still, the press was critical of Hoyt — it charged that he had not been true to form and did not have all of his old-time stuff.

Nonetheless, a lot of the rightful credit for the Yankees pennant drive had to be given to Joe Bush. Down the stretch Bush won four games too, and finished the season with a record of 26–7, while Bob Shawkey finished with a record of 20–12. For Babe Ruth it was an off year with all the suspensions. Still, the Babe hit .315 with 35 home runs in 110 games, but finished a distant third in the American home run title chase to Ken Williams of the St. Louis Browns (with 39) and Tilly Walker of the Philadelphia Athletics (with 37).

While the Yankees had just gotten by the Browns by one game in the American League, the New York Giants had outdistanced the Cincinnati Reds by seven games in the National League — despite having a reputation as a club that liked to party hard and despite losing one of their best pitchers in a scandal. Phil Douglas, known as Shufflin Phil, had won two games in the 1921 World Series after losing to Carl Mays 3–0 in the opening game. By mid–August in the 1922 season Douglas had posted a record of 11–4 with an ERA of 2.63. However, he was kicked out of baseball after it was revealed that he had written a letter to a St. Louis Cardinals player stating that for a fee he would sit out the rest of the season, thereby giving the Cardinals a shot at the pennant. Phil Douglas was an incurable alcoholic who would go on week-long benders. Before coming to the Giants he had worn out his welcome with several major league teams, including the Chicago White Sox, Cincinnati Reds, Brooklyn Robins and Chicago Cubs.

With the Giants in the thick of a pennant race with the Reds and Cardinals during the summer of 1922, Douglas suddenly went on one of his infamous week-long benders, which he called "vacations." John McGraw eventually sent out private investigators to locate his missing pitcher. When it was revealed that Douglas had been found passed out in the hallway of his apartment building, he was hauled off to a local police station, where he passed out again, and then against his will was placed in a sanitarium to dry out. After five days he returned to the Giants and John McGraw docked him a week's salary and billed him for the $224.30 sanitarium fee. Annoyed by the perceived arrogance of McGraw in the matter, Douglas wrote to St. Louis Cardinals outfielder Les Mann and offered to "go on a vacation" for the balance of the season for a fee. Mann, knowing that such circumstantial evidence in the 1919 World Series scandal had been cause for the lifetime banishment of Chicago White Sox players Buck Weaver and Shoeless Joe Jackson, immediately approached Cardinals general manager Branch Rickey with the letter. Rickey in turn placed the matter in the hands of baseball commissioner Kenesaw Landis, who immediately banned Douglas from major league baseball for life.

Regardless of the plight of Phil Douglas, a rematch of Huggins' Yankees and McGraw's Giants was about to commence in the 1922 World Series. The experts were predicting a different outcome for the 1922 series based on the fact that the Yankees had five starting pitchers of some considerable class in Waite Hoyt, Carl Mays, Bob Shawkey, Sam Jones and Joe Bush. Interestingly enough, four of the five — Hoyt, Mays, Jones and Bush — had come to the Yankees from the Red Sox courtesy of Harry Frazee. On the other hand, the 1922 Giants were built on speed — with Frankie Frisch again leading the way, supported by newly acquired Heinie Groh and Dave Bancrot, Irish Meusel, Casey Stengel and George Kelly. The 1922 Giants were a great hitting team too. Their team batting average for the season was .305, with seven of the starting eight regulars hitting over .300.

Branch Rickey, general manager of the St. Louis Cardinals, gave the edge to the Yankees in the series: "The fact that the Giants have stolen about twice as many bases as the Yankees does not in itself prove superior speed. That may be due to different methods of attack and managerial tactics. Huggins has five pitchers of unusual ability where McGraw has only two. That's a real advantage. It seems almost impossible for McGraw to offset this pitching advantage of the Yankees."[16]

In the 1922 World Series, major league baseball, after a three-year experiment with a nine-game series, returned to a best-of-seven format. However, the series turned out to be a humiliating one for Hoyt and the Yankees. The Giants out-hit the Yankees, out-scored them, out-pitched them and simply played better baseball. The result was that the Giants won the series 4–0 with one tie. The tie came in the second game, which was called at 4:45 P.M. after 10 innings with the score at 3–3. While the sun was still high in the sky, for some reason umpires George Hildebrand and Bill Klem called the game on account of darkness. When the announcement was made the 37,000 fans in the Polo Grounds went wild. The field was littered with anything a fan could get their hands on and those close to the box of commissioner Landis cursed him in the most vile terms. Landis looking for a way out of this public relations nightmare donated all the gate receipts to local military hospitals for disabled veterans.

Waite Hoyt pitched in two games in the 1922 World Series, relieving Joe Bush in the eighth inning of the 3–2 loss to the Giants in game one and going the first seven innings in game three in a 3–0 loss to the Giants. Hoyt's won-lost record for the series was 0–1, although he finished with a 1.13 ERA Babe Ruth had a terrible series, hitting a paltry .118, did not hit a home run and went hitless in the final three games. In the Yankees clubhouse following the Giants 5–3 win in game five and sweep of the series, Miller Huggins looked glum and spoke in a glum way: "Well, we were licked, but I must hand it to McGraw's team — smart fighting all the time, with far greater pitching than I ever dreamed they could get."[17]

For the second straight year John McGraw had beaten the Yankees in the World Series and this time done it convincingly. Jubilant in his victory and perspiring heavily, McGraw told the press, "No doubt we disappointed many critics, but this club of ours is one of the greatest baseball ever saw. They hit hard, they were smart in the field and on the bases— they rose to every emergency. They did themselves proud. We were supposed to have nothing more than a few wrecks in the box — but Nehf, Ryan, Barnes, Scott and McQuillan came through just as I thought they would. They out-pitched their rivals and they certainly must have surprised the other club. We showed the Yankees more stuff in the box than the Yankees showed us by a big margin."[18]

In 1938, looking back on John McGraw and the 1922 World Series, Waite Hoyt remarked "The '22 series was no contest. The Giants had the better pitching, hitting and — in a word — team in the five games played. McGraw gave me my start in organized baseball; he alone saw major league possibilities in me when I was a fifteen-year-old high school kid. For a quarter of a century he was the most vivid figure in the game and, as such, was a prime mover in making baseball a better spectacle for the fans and a better business for the players. McGraw dominated baseball by the power of his personality and prestige. People paid for the privilege of watching McGraw manage his team, an interest no other man has ever inspired."[19]

Now, with the 1922 season in the record books, Col. Huston sold his interest in the Yankees to Jacob Ruppert, making him now the sole owner of the club. Therefore, even though Miller Huggins had failed for the second straight year to win the World Series and rumors still persisted that he was not capable of providing the needed discipline among the free-spirited Yankees players, his job was secure with Ruppert.

Also, major league baseball had decided to relax its stringent rules on barnstorming. This year barnstorming would be permitted over the off-season if not more than three players from any one club were on a team. A lot of players were rapidly lining up their exhibitions. However, Waite Hoyt was planning to join a group of ballplayers that would make a good-will tour of the Orient, playing ball in Japan, Korea, China, Hawaii and the Philippines with Herbert Hunter. The tour was organized by Herb Hunter, who had played in the major leagues sporadically for four years between 1916–1921 with the Giants, Cubs, Red Sox and Cardinals. Hunter, in addition to being the tour director, would also play second base. However, in order to show the people in the Orient the best possible quality of American baseball, the players selected to go on the tour had to be of all-star quality. Besides Waite Hoyt and his wife, Dorothy, others making the sojourn included Joe Bush and his wife; Herb Pennock of the Boston Red Sox along with wife and daughter; from the Chicago White Sox, Bib Falk, Amos Strunk and his wife; Bert Griffith of the Brooklyn Robbins, Fred Hoffman of the Yankees; from the Giants, George Kelly, Casey Stengel, Emil Meusel and his wife; and Luke Sewell and Riggs Stephenson of the Cleveland Indians. The Cardinals team physician, Dr. John Lavin, and his wife would also join the party. Lastly, Frank "Buck" O'Neil, a correspondent for the *New York Sun*, and his wife would also join the group. O'Neil's mission was to write stories about the trip and to keep score.

Commissioner Landis who had approved the tour, told the players to make sure and behave. To make sure that they did he sent along rough and ready but pious George Moriarity to umpire the games and send reports back to him on the group's activities. The owners, fearing injuries, decided to withhold contract negotiations with the players on the tour until spring training of 1923. The tour group was scheduled to leave Vancouver on October 19, 1922, aboard the *R.M.S. Empress of Canada* and was due to reach Yokohama on October 30 in route to Tokyo. They would arrive back in San Francisco on January 30, 1923.

In the ensuing years Waite Hoyt would point out that there has been an historical misconception that the first baseball tour of Japan was made in 1932 by Babe Ruth, Lefty O'Doul and others. Writing about the trip in the periodical *Greater Cincinnati Sports* in 1977, Hoyt remarked, "The entire conception as presented is not only fallacy but a downright distortion of fact. Despite the presence of Ruth, and other big leaguers, that 1932 jaunt was bush league compared to the extended tour of Japan, Korea, China, Manila and Honolulu a big league All-Star team enjoyed in 1922 — ten years sooner."[20]

The team won all of its games on the tour but one and Hoyt was the losing pitcher. However, earlier in the trip Hoyt had pitched a no-hitter. In one of the exhibition games played in Seoul, Korea, to entertain the students at the University of Seoul, Hoyt pitched part of the game in temperatures of two below zero. But on Thanksgiving Day, November 27, the party was enjoying an off day in Osaka, Japan. It was also the 30th birthday of Joe Bush. Hoyt later said the hotel acquired a turkey from an American ship and that a few of the tour party then decided to throw a surprise party for Bush and combine Thanksgiving with his birthday. The party was arranged to begin in Hoyt's room at 4:00 P.M. and everything was kept very quiet so as to not alert Bush, but to also keep George Moriarity from knowing about it. Drinks were going to be served and the righteous Moriarity was a confirmed prohibitionist. (This was the same Moriarity who had taken on Ty Cobb and Harry Heilmann under the grandstand following Hoyt's debut with the Red Sox in 1919. Furthermore, Moriarity had whipped Cobb in fisticuffs on at least three or four other occasions.)

As the gaiety commenced there was suddenly a thunderous rap on the door of Hoyt's room and a booming voice proclaimed, "Let me in, — stop that — stop that, I say."[21] The door was opened and there stood George Moriarity with his hands on his hips. According to Hoyt a bitter exchange with pushing and shoving ensued and several persons, including himself and Bush, challenged the very capable Moriarity to a fight. After a few moments they succeeded in shoving Moriarity back out into the hall and closed the door. Suddenly the party noticed that during the commotion, newspaper correspondent Frank "Buck" O'Neil had been hiding behind a door so Moriarity could not see him. This so inflamed Joe Bush that he broke a cane over O'Neil's head. O'Neil promptly left the gathering and the party resumed with the homesick group singing "The Star-Spangled Banner."

4

Yankee Stadium

For the second consecutive year the New York Yankees had lost the World Series to the New York Giants. At least in the 1923 season, unlike the previous years, they would not have to face the humiliation of playing their home games in the Polo Grounds, where high above in the stadium rafters the Giants' World Championship pennant blew freely in the breeze and in their psyche. Yankee Stadium, the team's brand-new ball park at 161st Street and River Avenue in the Bronx, was set to open. Jacob Ruppert and Tillinghast Houston had created a masterpiece in stadium architecture.

The plans for the stadium were created by the Cleveland architectural firm of Osborne Engineering and called for a seating capacity of 70,000. The architects did not draw the plans for the stadium until they had studied the layout of every major league ballpark in the country. Consequently, the best features from all these stadiums were incorporated into the plans for Yankee Stadium. The stadium was built with 2,200 tons of concrete and steel by the White Construction Company of New York, which by using a crew of 500 men finished construction in just 284 working days at a cost of $2.5 million.

The stadium was tripled-decked with roofing down the foul lines. However, the stadium's most lasting and recognizable characteristic was its 15-foot façade, which ran along the top of the roof of the triple-deck stands and presented a sort of quiet dignity to the ballpark. A special type of grass was selected for the outfield and 116,000 square feet of sod was transported from Long Island. A drainage system was designed around the outfield with a network of 11 large pipes, while a similar system was constructed under the infield using 24 pipes. The original playing-field dimen-

Opening Day Yankee Stadium —1923: (left to right) Col. Jacob Ruppert, Judge Kenesaw Mountain Landis and Col. Tillinghast L'Hommedieu Huston (National Baseball Hall of Fame Library, Cooperstown, N.Y.).

sions of 281 feet down the left-field line, 460 feet to left center field, 490 feet to deep center, 429 feet to right center field and 295 feet down the right field foul line seemed to favor left-handed hitters like Babe Ruth and would be cause to fuel a historical debate over the ensuing decades. In fact in 1964 Kansas City Athletics owner Charles O. Finley began referring to the short right-field foul line in the stadium as the Yankees pennant porch. Nonetheless, the ballpark was outfitted with fan amenities unheard of at the time, such as eight restrooms each for both men and women located strategically throughout the grandstands and bleachers. Jacob Ruppert even moved the Yankees executive offices from midtown Manhattan to the stadium, occupying offices between the main and mezzanine decks that were accessible by an electric elevator.

On Wednesday, April 18, 1923, Yankees Stadium was all decked out for its first opening day, with the Boston Red Sox providing the opposition. The *New York Times* called Yankee Stadium a "monument to baseball' and stated in its edition on that day, "Down on the Potomac, close by the National Capital, they are thinking about erecting an impressive monument to the national game of baseball. But to the busy borough of the Bronx, close by the shore of Manhattan Island, the real monument to baseball will be unveiled this afternoon — the new Yankee Stadium, erected at a cost of $2,500,000, seating around 70,000 people and comprising in its broad reaches of concrete and steel, the last word in baseball arenas."[1]

For the big event 18,000 tickets had been sold in advance and the remaining 52,000, including 11,000 for the bleachers, were to go on sale the day of the game at 12:30 P.M. when the gates were opened. To accommodate the anticipated record crowd, Yankees business manager Ed Barrow arranged to have 36 ticket windows and 40 turnstiles going full blast. However, when the game began 74,200 fans had squeezed their way into the stadium with another 25,000 being turned away. The game was scheduled to start at 3:00 P.M. The Yankees' American League pennant was raised and then, at the foot of the flagpole in center field, John Philip Sousa — dressed in the full regalia of his bandmaster's uniform — led the Seventh Regiment Band in playing "The Star-Spangled Banner" as the America flag was hoisted to the top. New York governor Alfred E. Smith threw out the first pitch to Yankees catcher Wally Schang, while other assembled dignitaries, such as baseball commissioner Judge Kenesaw Mountain Landis, attired in a long gray overcoat and wide-brim hat, and New York mayor John F. Hylan looked on.

Waite Hoyt was not selected by Miller Huggins as the Yankees starting pitcher; that distinction went to Bob Shawkey, the Yankee with the longest tenure on the team. Shawkey pitched a fine game, defeating the Red Sox 4–1 and yielding just three hits in the process. It was a special day for Yankees shortstop Everett Scott, who played in his 987th consecutive game despite suffering an injury to his ankle from an exhibition game in Springfield, MO. Of course Babe Ruth stole the show, hitting the inaugural home run in the stadium when he drove the ball deep into the right-field bleachers in the third inning with two men on base. As Ruth circled the bases the record crowd rose to its feet and let out a tremendous roar of approval, causing the Babe to tip his cap at arms length as he disappeared into the dugout. (Although Ruth had hit the first home run in the new stadium, the distinction for getting the first hit went to Boston's George Burns, who singled in the second inning with no one on base and one out. The first extra base hit went to Bob Meusel, who doubled.) The press now began to refer to Yankee Stadium as "the house that Ruth built." Of course the press had also been calling Ruth "The Sultan of Swat, but Waite Hoyt always maintained that none of his teammates routinely called him "Babe": "He was known as either the Big Bam, George, or more commonly, 'Jidge.' 'Jidge' was really 'Gigge'— a contraction of his first name, George."[2]

One afternoon in the early summer of 1923 both Hoyt and Ruth were standing by the batting cage at Yankee Stadium when Miller Huggins came up to the cage with a tall, good-looking kid in tow and said, "Let this youngster hit a few."[3] According to Hoyt, "The kid looked shy and awkward."[4] They stepped aside and the kid picked up Ruth's 46-ounce bat. Ruth immediately started to discourage the kid from using it, then suddenly changed his mind. "Go ahead, you can't hurt it. I got others,"[5] said Ruth. The youngster started out hitting a few slow rollers to the infield. Then suddenly all heads went up as they heard that certain crack of the bat that announces that a ball is on its way into the stratosphere. The kid's blast had sailed into the upper reaches of the right-field grandstand. Suddenly he did it again and again. Hoyt and Ruth looked at each other speechless. No one in the American League did this but Babe Ruth. Who was this kid anyway? His name was Lou Gehrig. Gehrig wound up playing in 13 games for the Yankees that year, hitting .423. However, Wally Pipp remained the Yankees regular first baseman through the early part of 1925 season.

Miller Huggins had a lot of respect for Waite Hoyt and often used him as a role model for other players on the team. However, Hoyt had Huggins fooled and the reality was that on many occasions while the Yankees were on the road he was out carousing with Babe Ruth until the street lights went out in the morning. According to one report, "Years later, Hoyt confessed that he could be out with Ruth until 6 A.M., yet get back to the Yankees hotel for a quick shower and change to a coat and tie in time to greet Huggins for breakfast looking as if he'd slept like a baby."[6]

As the 1923 season rolled along and the Yankees were out in front of the pack in the American League, Hoyt and Ruth were getting along pretty well together. However, that was about to change. The Yankees were playing in Washington and Hoyt pitched the third game of a four-game series with the Nationals. Following the game Miller Huggins gave Hoyt permission to return to New York ahead of the team. Now, what Hoyt didn't

realize at the time is that Babe Ruth had been overdosing on his own pub-
licity and considered Hoyt's early departure to New York a personal affront
to his stature as the team's leader. A couple of days later when the team
reunited with Hoyt at Yankee Stadium, Carl Mays came over to Hoyt's
locker and told him that the Babe didn't want to have anything to do with
him anymore. A surprised Hoyt ambled over to Ruth's locker to discuss
the matter. But Ruth stopped Hoyt dead in his tracks before he reached
his locker and said, "Skip it, you and I are through."[7] Hoyt's reply was
short and to the point: "That's okay with me. It's mutual."[8]

However, the feud between Hoyt and Ruth was far from resolved and
all it needed was a spark to re-ignite it. That came later in the season with
Hoyt on the mound and a ball hit into right field that got past Ruth and
went for a double. Hoyt felt that the Babe had dogged it on in the play and
stood on the mound looking in the direction of right field with his arms
thrust out on his hips and a disgusted look upon his face. When Ruth
noticed Hoyt's posture he blew up and came running towards the mound.
Quickly the Yankees infield jumped in, separated the two and play was
resumed. When the inning was finally over Ruth came into the dugout and
jabbed Hoyt with some choice uncomplimentary words. The next inning
Hoyt was knocked out of the box and was off to the showers.

When the game ended Ruth came charging into the Yankees clubhouse and went right for Hoyt, screaming at the top of his lungs, "You
lousy bum, you're not going to show me up!"[9] Hoyt was still steaming mad
himself and responded by stating, "What do you figure to do about it?"[10]
Ruth shouted back, "I'll punch you in your [expletive] nose."[11] To which
Hoyt shouted back, "You're not tied, you fathead."[12] At that point the fur
began to fly as the two began to pummel each other with their fists. Little
Miller Huggins, who weighed 140 pounds soaking wet, quickly jumped into
the middle of the fracas and attempted to separate the two, but all he got
for his peacemaking efforts was a sock in the jaw. Finally, half the team
jumped in and pulled the two apart.

Following their clubhouse fisticuffs Hoyt and Ruth did not speak to
each other again for the remainder of the 1923 season. They didn't make
peace until a year later when the Yankees were traveling on a night train
out of St. Louis. Hoyt and a group of his Yankee teammates were sitting
in the men's wash room on the train when the Babe entered with a few
bottles of beer for the guys. He offered one to Hoyt, who quickly stated,
"No thanks, Babe."[13] However, Ruth was really trying to patch things up
and said to Hoyt, "Aw, go, ahead. It's all over — that argument — a lot of
damn fool nonsense, anyway. Forget it."[14] The reality of the situation was
that Hoyt really liked the big fellow. Eager to put their differences behind

him, Hoyt grabbed a bottle of beer and so ended the feud. Years later Hoyt was to say in regard to Ruth, "If you have a young son who is in the first stages of discovery, a youngster whose days are filled with romping pleasure and glory ... then you have a small edition of Babe Ruth. The guy just never grew up."[15]

There was no feuding, however, in the American League in 1923 as the New York Yankees won 98 games and ran away with the pennant, outdistancing the second-place Detroit Tigers by 16 games. For the Yankees it was their third straight American League pennant. The 1923 Yankees had an excellent pitching staff. Sad Sam Jones won 21 games, while both Joe Bush and Herb Pennock won 19. Waite Hoyt won 17 games, finishing with a season record of 17–9 and ERA of 3.02.

The Yankees were a powerful ball club too. Babe Ruth had a spectacular year, hitting .393 while leading the American League in home runs with 41 and RBIs with 131. Ruth was denied a triple crown as Harry Heilmann of the Detroit Tigers won the batting title with an average of .403. Supporting Ruth were Wally Pipp, who hit .304, Whitey Witt with .314 and Bob Meusel with .313.

Oddly enough, there was one pitcher in the American League in 1923 that Babe Ruth had a very difficult time hitting: Hub Pruett. In 1923 Hub Pruett was a 22-year-old left-hander for the St. Louis Browns pitching in his second major league season. He threw a screwball that Waite Hoyt stated was better than the one later thrown by Carl Hubbell. Sportsman Park, where the Browns played their home games, was small and Ruth hit with a vengeance when playing in St. Louis. However, using his nasty screw ball when he pitched against the Yankees, Pruett completely put the collar on Ruth, fanning him 13 out of 15 at bats against him in the 1923 season. Hub Pruett only pitched in the major leagues for seven years between 1922–1932, finishing his career with a won-lost record of 29–48 and an ERA of 4.63, but his place in baseball in history was assured with his domination of Babe Ruth. It was Hoyt's belief that the reason for Pruett's short career was that he ruined his arm striking out Ruth with his elbow-bending screw ball. As for Ruth, Hoyt states that he couldn't even remember Pruett's name and simply referred to him as "Prunes." Following his playing days Hub Pruett went on to become a doctor in St. Louis. When he and Ruth met up with each other years later, author Robert W. Creamer contends that Pruett said to Ruth, "I want to thank you for putting me through med school. If it wasn't for you, no one would have heard of me."[16] Ruth supposedly smiled and said to Pruett, "If I helped you get through medical school, I'm glad of it."[17]

Waite Hoyt had an unconventional theory on why the 1923 Yankees were such an excellent team — he felt that the players were able to collar their nervous energy and use it constructively. In a magazine article published in 1938 Hoyt stated, "The Yankees were a great team because they were a nervous team. When the stadium was built in 1923, a clock was put in the clubhouse, and it's a wonder to me that it is still hanging there. I thought our stares had bored it through the wall long ago. Everybody watched it nervously while climbing into their monkey suits, anticipating the time they were to appear on the field. Then, when the others had gone out for batting practice, the pitcher of the day would sit there alone, playing the entire game in his mind, expecting the very worst, watching and listening to the clock tick off the interminable minutes until it was time to go out and warm up."[18]

In the 1923 National League pennant race the New York Giants went wire to wire to win the flag. However, it was not an easy ride for John McGraw as a gritty and determined group of Cincinnati Reds, led by three

Waite Hoyt and Babe Ruth (National Baseball Hall of Fame Library, Cooperstown, N.Y.).

20-game winners in the form of Dolf Luque (27–8), Eppa Rixey (20–15) and Pete Donohue (21–15), kept the pressure on the Giants all the way through the season, finishing just 4½ games behind. Nonetheless, McGraw had won his third straight pennant and thereby set-up the third straight subway series with the intra-city rival Yankees. The 1923 World Series promised to be the most lucrative ever and a record-breaking $200,000 gate was predicted for the first game at Yankee Stadium. If the series was to go the full seven games a million-dollar gate was deemed possible.

On October 10 the 1923 World Series began in the splendid surroundings of Yankee Stadium with a record crowd of 55,307 who paid and another 3,000 who did not. (The gate receipts pulled up a little short of the predicted $200,000 at

$181,912.) Miller Huggins, mindful of the masterful pitching of Waite Hoyt against the Giants in the 1921 World Series, selected him to be the starting pitcher in game one. The Yankees got off to a quick start, scoring one in the first, then two in the second off Giants starting pitcher Mule Watson. The score could have been larger in favor of the Yankees if it were not for some brilliant defensive plays by the Giants infielders Frisch, Kelly and Groh. But Waite Hoyt could not hold the lead and was driven from the box in the third inning after Heinie Groh tripled in two runs during a four-run Giants rally. It was to be Hoyt's only appearance in the series. The Yankees tied the score at 4–4 in the seventh, but the deciding run was scored in the top of the ninth with two outs when Casey Stengel hit an inside-the-park home run off reliever Joe Bush. Stengel took the count to 3–2 off Bush before driving the ball deep to the wall in left center between Whitey Witt and Bob Meusel. Witt chased the ball down, but Casey was off to the races. Running on a bad leg, Stengel lost his shoe rounding second and was rounding third badly winded and hobbling home with the winning margin as Meusel took the relay from Witt and fired the ball toward the plate. The 5–4 loss was the Yankees' eighth straight to the Giants in World Series games.

In the 1922 World Series sportswriter Grantland Rice had narrated games over radio station WJZ in Newark, New Jersey. However, game one of the 1923 World Series was a significant moment in baseball history, being the first to be broadcast on a national radio network. The play-by-play commentary was done by Graham McNamee, a former concert baritone who was aided by baseball writers. Seated in an open box seat at Yankee Stadium, McNamee did his broadcast holding a microphone that was connected to telephone lines feeding the call of the game back to the radio studio of WEAF on Broadway. The game was then transmitted over a hook-up on stations extending from New England to Washington, D.C.

In game two, played at the Polo Grounds, the Yankees finally broke the curse of Giants, beating them 4–2 behind two home runs by Babe Ruth and the pitching of Herb Pennock to even up the series at one game each. Herb Pennock, who had a fine season for the Yankees (finishing with a record of 19–6 and ERA of 3.33) was yet another gift from the Boston Red Sox. While this deal could not be blamed on Harry Frazee who had sold his interest in the Red Sox following the 1922 season, it was still a deal done in the spirit of his previous transactions. Boston sent Pennock to New York in exchange for three little-known players— Camp Skinner, Norm McMillan and George Murray— and of course a wad of Jacob Ruppert's seemingly endless cash in the presence of $50,000.

With the series games rotating between the close proximity of home parks Yankee Stadium and the Polo Grounds, in game three Casey Stengel's home run into the right-field bleachers at Yankee Stadium proved to be the only run that the Giants would need in a 1–0 win. The Yankees evened the series again in game four with a 8–4 win based on a six-run rally in the second and the fine pitching of Bob Shawkey and Herb Pennock. Back in their home park for game five, the Yankees smashed the Giants 8–1 as Joe Dugan led the way with four hits. The Yankees were now out in front in the series three games to two and just one win away from their first World Championship.

That came the next day as the Yankees scored five runs in the top of eighth to defeat the Giants 6–4. Babe Ruth had hit his third home run of the series to give the Yankees an early 1–0 lead. However, by the sixth inning the Giants had taken a 4–1 lead. Then came the five-run outburst by the Yankees in the eighth, keyed by a two-run single by Bob Meusel, to seal the victory as Sad Sam Jones came in to relieve Herb Pennock and shut down the Giants in the eighth and ninth.

Col. Jacob Ruppert had now captured the bragging rights on baseball in New York City. For Babe Ruth it was a sweet redemption from his poor showing in the 1922 World Series as he batted .368 and hit three home runs. While the victory in the final game was a double pleasure coming at the hands of John McGraw in the Polo Grounds—the site of the Yankees' two previous World Series losses to him, this time around the Yankees had really crushed the Giants, scoring 30 runs to their 17 and out-hitting them 60 to 47.

Waite Hoyt's analysis of the Yankees World Series victory was that John McGraw had selected the wrong strategy in which to neutralize the Yankees' power: "McGraw was riding high. He had apparently proved that the science of the Giants could frustrate the sheer strength of the Yankees. But science is not infallible, and perfect theories sometimes boomerang. That, too, was proved in the '23 series when McGraw's insistence on curve balls betrayed the Giants pitchers. The Yankees hit hard throughout the series; by that time we were reasonably certain that almost any given pitch would be a curve, and we were held to less than four runs in only one of the six games. And Bob Meusel got the hit that won the championship for us by calling the turn on one of those inevitable curves. Rosey Ryan struck out Ruth in the pinch, with the bases loaded and the score tied, but Meusel, the next batter, reached across the plate and walloped a Ryan curve on a line over second base to climax an eighth-inning, five-run rally and drive in the winning runs."[19]

Although Hoyt had now cashed three straight World Series checks, he was beginning to ponder the future. He had forgone the vaudeville circuit since getting married and really had no other means of support other than playing ball. Furthermore, during the year he had become a father, with Dorothy giving birth to the couple's first child (son Harry Pyle Hoyt, named after Dorothy's father.) Jacob Ruppert, although extremely wealthy, was tight fisted when it came to salary negotiations with all the players except the Babe. When Joe Dugan went to see Ruppert about getting a raise the Yankees owner browbeat him so badly in his explanation of why he could not afford to raise salaries that Dugan asked Ruppert if he needed a loan. Ruppert was offended by Dugan's remark and never forgot it. Later Dugan was to remark that "Colonel Ruppert owned half of New York. John Jacob Astor owned the other half."[20]

Hoyt once recalled going in to see Ruppert about a new contract and taking notice of all the pictures hanging on his office wall of significant real estate around New York. As the two men sat down to talk, Ruppert with great pleasure began identifying each structure for Hoyt. "That's my office building, 22 stories high in the best location in Manhattan. That's my brewery, the best in the country. That's my mansion, my estate,"[21] said Ruppert. When Hoyt got around to talking salary and asked the Ruppert for a raise, he abruptly jumped up and said, "What do you think I am, a millionaire?"[22]

With a keen understanding of the Colonel's position Hoyt decided it was in his best interest to look elsewhere for the economic security that he deemed necessary in the future. He didn't have to look far, however. He went to see his father-in-law, Harry Pyle, who operated a funeral home in Brooklyn, and asked him about joining him in the business. Harry Pyle was convinced of Hoyt's sincerity to learn the business and thought that it was a win-win situation, as now he would have a successor to carry on his business should he decide to retire. So in early 1924 Hoyt began his venture in the mortuary business and soon was participating in all facets of it other than embalming. After spending a brief apprenticeship in the business under Pyle, Hoyt opened his own funeral parlor on Long Island. Hence the former Schoolboy Wonder suddenly had a new moniker in the press: The Merry Mortician.

Before his formal foray into the funeral business Hoyt had on a least one occasion lent assistance to his farther-in-law. A popular story has it that one day Harry Pyle called him and asked him to pick up a body and transport it to his mortuary in Brooklyn. Hoyt took the hearse and picked up the body as requested, but then drove to the Polo Grounds, parked the hearse in the parking lot there and pitched a game. It was a very hot summer day and by the time he finally delivered the corpse to Pyle later in the day it had started to take on a rather nauseating odor. Pyle was beside himself and livid as he reprimanded Hoyt, using the most uncomplimentary of terms in the process.

The Yankees' string of pennants finally ran out in 1924 as the Washington Nationals won their first American League pennant behind veteran pitcher Walter "Big Train" Johnson. During the season the Yankees had been embroiled in a riot during a game at Navin Field in Detroit. The rivalry between the Yankees and Tigers had become intense and the two teams were the top gate attractions in the American League. On Friday, June 13, 1924, the Yankees were tied for the league lead with the Red Sox, both teams having a record of 26–19. The Tigers were in third place with a record of 28–23.

The Yankees were leading the Tigers in the game 10–6 in the top of the ninth when player-manager Ty Cobb gave a signal from his position in center field to Detroit pitcher Bert Cole to throw at the Yankees hitters. Babe Ruth, who was hitless in the game, was the first batter up and had to duck a pitch thrown near his head by Cole. Ruth then fouled out and that brought Bob Meusel to the plate. Cole immediately hit Meusel in the back with a pitch. Meusel threw down his bat, charged the mound and threw a wild roundhouse punch at Cole that missed. While umpires Evans and Ornsby attempted to restrain Meusel, Ty Cobb came running in from his position in the outfield and got into a confrontation with Babe Ruth as Yankees manager Miller Huggins and umpire Ornsby pushed Ruth away from the melee and toward the dugout. Cole, Meusel and Ruth were ejected from the game by umpire Billy Evans as a Detroit policeman who had been in the stands jumped over the railings onto the field to deter a crisis. However, as Meusel and Ruth gathered up their gloves and started to leave the field the Tiger fans began to hoot and howl from the stands. Suddenly several fans jumped the railing from the stands onto the field. When Meusel and Ruth passed the Tigers' dugout some shoving began; Meusel threw a punch at one of the Tigers players and the unruly crowd sensed that the blood-letting had begun. Hundreds of fans poured onto the field and random fights broke out between the fans and the police all over the stadium. Then it turned into war as 18,000 people flooded the field. The police set up a protective line for the Yankees players to leave the field and threatened to pull their guns to control the crowd. Umpire Evans, seeing that the situation was out of control, declared a forfeit of the game, giving the Yankees a 9–0 win, while under the grandstand Yankees and Tigers were squaring off.

The following day in the aftermath of the ugly incident, 40,000 fans packed into the Detroit ball park for the game. But revenge was nowhere in sight as Waite Hoyt beat the Tigers 6–2, pitching a complete game while giving up just seven hits.

Although the Yankees led the league much of the rest of the season, the Nationals overtook them in mid–September and crossed the finish line two games ahead. The Nationals won 92 games with the 36-year-old Johnson posting a record of 23–7 and relief pitcher Fred "Firpo" Marberry racking up 15 saves. Providing a solid offense was Leon "Goose" Goslin, who hit .344 and led the American League in RBIs with 129. Veteran Sam Rice hit .334 and led the league with 216 hits.

Actually, the Yankees had a solid year offensively as Babe Ruth, despite once again indulging in a steady diet of abundant nightlife, again won two-thirds of a triple crown, this time leading the American League with a batting average of .378 and 46 home runs. It would be the only batting title that Ruth would win his career. Bob Meusel had a fine season as well, hitting .325 with 12 home runs and 121 RBIs. However, other than Herb Pennock, who had a season record of 21–9, the pitching broke down. Waite Hoyt (18–13), Joe Bush (17–16) and Bob Shawkey (16–11) lost nearly as many games as they won. While Sam Jones, after winning 21 games in 1923, could only win 9 in 1924. Carl Mays, who seemed to be on the decline after two mediocre seasons in 1922 and 1923, was traded to Cincinnati, where he suddenly rebounded and won 20 games.

There were cracks in the Yankees armor and Miller Huggins was concerned. Had the Nationals just outdistanced the Yankees in 1924 or had they collapsed? Some moves had to be made, and over the winter Joe Bush was traded to the St. Louis Browns for Urban Shocker. The grumbling among the other players returned to the Yankee clubhouse. And in regard to Babe Ruth, the trouble for Huggins was just beginning. All through the winter of 1924–1925 Babe partied as if there was no tomorrow. By spring training he had ballooned to 270 pounds, his marriage was breaking up and his insatiable appetite for food, booze and sex was out of control. It all came crashing down on the Babe April 7, 1925, when he collapsed in Asheville, North Carolina. He was removed to New York and diagnosed with an intestinal abscess and surgery was performed on April 17. As rumors swirled about Ruth's illness—ranging from too much booze and hot dogs to venereal disease—he would be out of the lineup until June. By then the Yankees were deep in a hole in the pennant race.

As the Yankees struggled, Huggins made changes in the lineup. Shortstop Everett Scott's consecutive game streak came to an end at 1,307 games—the longest on record at that time. He was replaced by Pee Wee Wanninger. On June 1, Babe Ruth returned to the Yankees lineup and Lou Gehrig began his 2,130 consecutive-game streak when he pinch-hit for Wanninger. The next day, first baseman Wally Pipp approached Miller Huggins and told him that he had a headache and asked not to be put in the lineup. (In spring training Pipp had been hit in the head with a ball pitched by ex–Princeton University hurler Charley Caldwell and knocked unconscious. Later an X-ray revealed a brain concussion.) Subsequently, he was replaced at first base by Lou Gehrig and the rest is history. Pipp would finish out the 1925 season with the Yankees primarily sitting on the bench. However, there were other changes taking place in the Yankees lineup. On July 2, in a game against the Philadelphia Athletics, catcher Wally Schang had his right hand severely bruised receiving a fast curve and was replaced in the lineup by Benny Bengough.

As the 1925 season progressed the Yankees just weren't being beaten, they were being humiliated. An example of such is the 19–1 ravaging they suffered on June 17 at the hands of the Detroit Tigers in Yankee Stadium. In the sixth inning of that game three Yankees pitchers had failed to get anyone out and the Tigers scored 11 runs, including a grand slam home run by Ty Cobb. Lou Gehrig provided the Yankees' only tally with a home run. The next day the newspapers reported the score as Tigers 19, Gehrig 1.

On the morning of July 3, 1925, the Yankees found themselves in sixth place in the American League pennant race, 16½ games behind the league-leading Washington Nationals. On July 4 two future Hall of Fame pitchers squared off as the Yankees' Herb Pennock out-dueled the Athletics' Lefty Grove 1–0 in a 15-inning game. Pennock allowed only four hits while walking none. Despite such heroic efforts the season was over for the Yankees.

By that time Babe Ruth had relapsed back into his frolicking ways and once again was burning the candle at both ends. The roof blew off in the Ruth affair later in the season on August 29. The Yankees were playing the St. Louis Browns at Sportsman Park when Ruth came casually sauntering into the clubhouse late from an all-night session at a local bordello. Almost everyone had already taken the field — that is, except for Miller Huggins, who was sitting in a corner waiting for Ruth to appear, and Waite Hoyt. (Hoyt later said that he was to be the Yankees pitcher that day, and was his habit to delay going out on the field.) Huggins had previously given Ruth strict orders to contain his carousing and was extremely agitated.

Hoyt's account of the incident is as follows:

"Suddenly the Babe burst through the door, his coat over his shoulder, his necktie awry. Hug rose to meet him. You don't have to dress today, Babe," said Huggins.[23] "Yeah? And why not?"[24]

"Because I have suspended you. I am fining you five thousand dollars and I am sending you back to New York."[25]

"Suspending me!" Ruth snorted. "That's great stuff. What for?"[26]

"You know what for, Babe."[27]

Hoyt states that all at once Ruth began yelling and screaming at Huggins, calling him a little runt and stating that he would never get away with this. Unbeknown to Ruth was the fact that Huggins had already discussed the matter with Jacob Ruppert.

Ruth then screamed at Huggins, "I made you, you runt, you! I wish you were my size. I wish you weighed 200 pounds. I'd beat your ears off!"[28]

"I wish that I did weigh 200 pounds. I might beat your ears off!" said Huggins.[29]

At that point Hoyt sprinted out of the clubhouse to the Yankees bench to bring the news of what he had just heard to his teammates. Ruth left the team and headed for Chicago in an attempt to discuss the matter with Commissioner Landis. However, Landis was of no mind to intervene and Jacob Ruppert stood firmly behind Miller Huggins. In a state of disbelief and melancholy, Ruth returned to New York, locked himself in his apartment in the Concourse Plaza and spent the remainder of the summer in seclusion. It had been a wasted season for the Babe; he played in only 98 games, hitting .290 with just 25 home runs. Toward the end of the 1925 season Hoyt was pitching in a game against Detroit when Ty Cobb made him an offer that he had to refuse. By 1925 Ty Cobb had become the player-manager of the Tigers and on that particular day was not playing but coaching third base. When Hoyt finished an inning he was walking off the mound toward the dugout. When he crossed the foul line Cobb stopped him. He put his hands on the muscles in Hoyt's arm and said, "I want you to pitch for me next year. I will make a deal for you so that you will. How do you feel about it?"[30] Hoyt immediately turned toward Cobb and replied, "Ty, nothing outside of a national calamity would get me to pitch for you if I didn't have to. I don't like you. Wouldn't like you, and couldn't pitch for you."[31]

Notwithstanding Ty Cobb's offer, the 1925 season had been a miserable affair for Waite Hoyt and the Yankees team as they finished in seventh place with a record of 69–85, 28½ games behind the pennant-winning Washington Nationals. Hoyt had a rather lackluster season, posting a record of 11–14 with an ERA of 4.00. However, there was an enigma among Hoyt's stats for the 1925 season in that he had suddenly become a hitter, batting .304 for the season and getting 24 hits in 79 at bats.

While 1925 had been a disaster, Miller Huggins was confident that he could make the necessary changes in the Yankees and have the team competitive again in the 1926 season. Earl Combs, known as The Kentucky Colonel, had taken over in center field and done a very creditable job, hitting .342. Young Lou Gehrig looked promising at first base hitting .290 with

20 home runs. Joe Dugan, who had been injured during the 1925 season, played in just 102 games, so Huggins was looking forward to a rejuvenated third sacker in the '26 season. To that end the Yankees sold Wally Pipp to the Reds for $7,500 and traded Wally Schang to the Browns for George Mogridge and cash. If the pitching came through in '26 the Yankees could make a run of it.

As for Babe Ruth, after years of irresponsible behavior that included paternity suits, automobile wrecks, drunkenness, orgies, gluttony and his wife, Helen, having a nervous breakdown — Ruth a.k.a. The Sultan of Swat, the Bambino, the Big Bam — decided to make amends and get down to business.

5

Murderers' Row

As spring training in 1926 progressed at St. Petersburg, Florida, most sports writers were not impressed with the rebuilt Yankees. According to Waite Hoyt one journalist (Westbrook Pegler) predicted another seventh-place finish for the Yankees, calling them a collection of misfits who were playing for themselves rather than as a team. There were of course legitimate reasons to question the Yankees competitiveness. Lou Gehrig was still for all intents and purposes a rookie proving himself, there was no reliable catching, the pitching was suspect and the mighty Babe Ruth had totally tanked in the 1925 season.

However, over the winter Babe Ruth had pledged to be all business again; he had been problematic, but in earnest the Babe wanted to win. Also, Miller Huggins had continued to make changes. Gone from the Yankee's starting lineup was shortstop Pee Wee Wanninger, replaced by Mark Koenig. Aaron Ward was replaced by a hard-hitting second baseman from the Pacific Coast League by the name of Tony Lazzeri. In 1925, playing at Salt Lake Lazzeri had hit 60 home runs and driven in an incredible 222 runs. Still further, Pat Collins had replaced Benny Bengough as the regular catcher, while over the winter Joe Dugan had his knee operated on and would return at third. And the Yankees outfield of Ruth, Combs and Meusel potentially smacked of power.

The Yankees finished the 1926 exhibition season with 16 straight wins, 12 at the hands of the Brooklyn Robbins. Babe Ruth, returning in a taxi with Waite Hoyt and Joe Dugan from the ballpark in Birmingham after beating the Dodgers, remarked, "If we keep on beating these guys, we're going to win the pennant."[1] So it was that the Yankees surprised everyone but themselves as they jumped out of the starting gate in front of the pack

Babe Ruth Game

Atlantic Highlands, N.J. Oct 21st, 1926

Waite Hoyt, Herb Hunter, Babe Ruth, Herb Pennock

Waite Hoyt, Herb Hunter, Babe Ruth, Herb Pennock (National Baseball Hall of Fame Library, Cooperstown, N.Y.).

in the 1926 season and by late August seemed to be on cruise control with a 10-game lead. However, that is just when Cleveland, Philadelphia and Washington decided it was time to play ball and the Yankees began to swoon. Shortly after Labor Day, on their last western road trip of the season, the Yankees were beaten in Detroit, Cleveland and Chicago and suddenly their lead over Cleveland was just four games. If they hadn't finally recovered and won the series with the St. Louis Browns, they might have fallen into second place after leading the league all summer. The Yankees held on, though, to win the American League pennant by three games over Cleveland and six games over Philadelphia.

Babe Ruth held true to his behavior-modification pledge and returned to form, once again winning two-thirds of a triple crown by leading the American League in home runs with 47 and RBIs with 145. Ruth was edged out of the batting crown by Detroit's Heinie Manush, who hit .378 to his .372. Newcomer Tony Lazzeri hit 18 home runs while driving in 114. Lou Gehrig set a record for first baseman with 20 triples while hitting .313 with 16 home runs and 107 RBIs. Bob Meusel also had a fine season, hitting .315

with 12 home runs and 81 RBIs, and Earle Combs hit .299. Although the ball club finished with a team batting average of .289—which tied them for third best in the league with Cleveland and Chicago—if anyone in the press would have referred to the Yankees lineup as "Murderers' Row" at that time it would have been considered laughable.

The Yankees' pitching had rebounded too in 1926, with Herb Pennock leading the staff with a record of 23–11 and an ERA of 3.62, while Urban Shocker went 19–11 with an ERA of 3.38 and Waite Hoyt finished 16–12 with an ERA of 3.85 (after being out of action for a month at midseason with a wrenched ligament in his arm). For some reason there is a tendency by historians to downplay Hoyt's contributions to the 1926 Yankees efforts. However, the record shows that Hoyt was the third most effective pitcher on the staff that summer, starting 27 games and completing 12. By contrast, Herb Pennock and Urban Shocker both started 33 games and completed 19 each, while Sam Jones started 23 games and completed six and Bob Shawkey started 10 games with three complete.

In the National League the St. Louis Cardinals—with Rogers Hornsby in his first full year as manager—won the pennant by two games over the Cincinnati Reds. It was the first pennant won by any St. Louis team since 1888 when player-manager Charlie Comiskey led the St. Louis Browns to win the flag in the American Association.

The 1926 World Series was scheduled to begin on October 2 at Yankee Stadium, and Miller Huggins selected Herb Pennock to pitch the opening game. The experts felt that the two teams were pretty evenly matched. The Cardinals were a better fielding team and had Hornsby, but and the Yankees had Ruth. Neither team was particularly fleet of foot, so the edge should go to the Yankees based on their veteran pitching staff of Pennock, Shocker, Jones and Hoyt—all of whom the newspapers were saying had previously thrown some great ball in World Series play and recently had shown a return to form. Also the Yankees had picked up veteran left-hander Dutch Ruether in a late August trade with Washington.

When the first game started there were over 61,000 fans on hand at Yankee Stadium, 20,000 of whom had waited all night to buy bleacher seats for $1.10. After giving up a run in the first inning, Pennock handled the Cardinals with ease the rest of the way, pitching a masterful three-hitter and getting a 2–1 victory. The Yankees scored the winning run off Cardinals starter Bill Sherdel in the sixth inning when Babe Ruth led off with a single and went to second on a sacrifice by Meusel and then scored on a hit by Gehrig. Miller Huggins was pleased with the result: "So far as any deep strategic moves are concerned, there was none. The whole story was written in the pitching box and every move was an open book. And as I see it, there were no breaks except Pennock's wonderful control."[2]

Over in the Cardinals clubhouse Rogers Hornsby wasn't disappointed in the loss: "We don't have to come back in this series, because we haven't gone anywhere to come back from. We just have lost one close game, but we have played so well that we are even more confident than ever."[3]

In game two a couple of veteran pitchers squared off with Grover Cleveland Alexander starting for the Cardinals and Urban Shocker for the Yankees. Alexander had come to St. Louis from the Chicago Cubs in June after being purchased for the waiver price. Now 39 years old and pitching in his 16th season in the big leagues, Alexander had succumbed to alcoholism and was thought to be washed up. Nonetheless, he pitched in 23 games for the Cardinals and finished the season with 9–7 record for them.

In game two Old Pete, as Alexander was called, started out a little shaky, giving up two runs to the Yankees in the second inning when Bob Meusel singled and advanced on an infield out, then scored on Tony Lazzeri's single. However, the run could have been avoided, as Chick Hafey had quickly fielded the ball and made a fine throw to the plate, which was cut off by Alexander. Later in the inning the Yankees attempted a double steal and Lazzeri was trapped between third and home. Instead of simply running Lazzeri down and tagging him, the Cardinals began throwing the ball back and forth. All at once Alexander stepped into the play, took the ball and made a wild throw to third, allowing Lazzeri to cross the plate. After that Old Pete settled down and after giving up a hit to Earle Combs in the third, then retired the last 21 batters while striking out 10 and allowing only four hits in the game. The Cardinals came back to tie the score at 2–2 in the top of the third. They scored the deciding run on a three-run homer by Billy Southworth in the seventh that just made it into the right-field bleachers, eventually winning the game 6–2. Alexander had held both Babe Ruth (0–4) and Lou Gehrig (0–3) hitless. Tommy Thevenow also hit an inside-park home run on a pop fly misjudged by Babe Ruth that hit the ground and went between his feet out of sight. As Ruth desperately looked for the ball, Thevenow rounded the bases.

So with the series tied one game each the teams headed to St. Louis for games three, four and five. For the New York Yankees it would be the first World Series games that they had ever played outside of New York City, having faced the intra-city rival Giants in their previous three trips to the fall classic. The special train bringing the Yankees to St. Louis covered the 1,158 miles in just 23 hours and 30 minutes, breaking a speed record on the route by 15 minutes. All along the route to St. Louis in Ohio, Indiana and Illinois crowds gathered at train stations to get a glimpse of

Babe Ruth and his teammates. When the train made a stop at Uniondale, Indiana, a crowd of 300 had gathered and they refused to let the train leave the station until they could bask in the light of their idol. Without objection, the Sultan of Swat appeared at a window, to the delight of the cheering mob, and then the train was back en route to Missouri.

When the Cardinals arrived home in St. Louis later aboard their own special train, tens of thousands of fans packed the downtown area around Fourth and Washington to greet them. Hundreds of other fans were already in line at Sportsman's Park either waiting to buy tickets or for the gates to open, even though there were still 20 hours to go until game time. The whole city was in a frenzy over the Cardinals. Even the athletic director at St. Louis University announced that the football team, the "Billikens," would discard their traditional blue sweaters in favor of sporting new cardinal-red jerseys to honor the city's favorite baseball team.

In game three at St. Louis Miller Huggins decided to start Dutch Ruether instead of Waite Hoyt, against the Cardinals' Jesse Haines because he felt that Ruether had always pitched well against the Cardinals when he was in the National League with Cincinnati and Brooklyn. Also, Huggins felt that Ruether would have more of a chance at keeping the Cardinals from hitting the notorious long fly balls that seemed to go for home runs in Sportsman's Park. He explained to the press that Hoyt would start in game four. What concerned Huggins more, however, was that fact that the Yankees were not hitting. In the first two games of the series they had only 10 hits; Ruth was batting .143, Gehrig .143 and Meusel .200.

So game three got under way with a record 37,708 fans on hand, the largest crowd to ever witness a baseball game in St. Louis, and the stands were a sea of red. Women wore red hats, men wore red neckties, and red shirts and scarves were endless; it was the only color visible. The game was twice stopped for rain delays. However, the Cardinals prevailed in game three by a score of 4–0, with Haines holding the Yankees to just five hits. The first three and a half innings of the game had been a scoreless duel between Ruether and Haines. Then, in the bottom of the third the Cardinals scored three runs off Ruether. Haines aided his own cause, getting two hits, including a home run.

Down two games to one in the series Miller Huggins was contemplating bringing back Herb Pennock on three day's rest to pitch game four. However, in the end he decided to give the ball to Waite Hoyt. Despite giving up 14 hits to the Cardinals, Hoyt would get the job done in game four. However, he would be assisted by a record-breaking power display put on by none other than Babe Ruth.

To oppose Hoyt, Rogers Hornsby had started Charles Rhem, who had won 20 games during the regular season. In the first inning Rhem started out by striking out both Earle Combs and Mark Koenig. Then Rogers Hornsby walked to the mound and instructed Rhem not to throw anything fast to Babe Ruth, but rather give him off-speed stuff. There exists historical conflict on what Rhem actually threw to Ruth. Rhem maintained that he threw a slow ball to Ruth as Hornsby had instructed. However Hornsby maintained that Rhem ignored his instructions and threw him a fast ball right down Broadway. Regardless, Ruth hit Rhem's first pitch onto the roof of the right-field pavilion for a home run to give the Yankees a 1–0 lead. It was the first run scored by the Yankees in the last 17 innings in the series, having been shut out by the Cardinal pitchers since the second inning of game two at Yankee Stadium. The Cardinals, however, tied the score against Hoyt in their half of the first when Taylor Douthit led off, beating out a hit to deep to the shortstop. Billy Southworth then followed with a single into center, Douthit stopping at third. Rogers Hornsby was next up and he took the count to one ball and two strikes on Hoyt before stroking a single to right, scoring Douthit to tie the score at 1–1.

In the third inning with two out, Babe Ruth came up to bat amidst a mixture of cheers and boos from the fans. Once again Hornsby cautioned Rhem to throw only slow pitches to Ruth. On Rhem's first pitch Ruth drove the ball over the right-field stands into the window of a Chevrolet auto dealership across the street on Grand Avenue. It was Ruth's second home run of the game and it gave the Yankees a 2–1 lead. (Later, the auto dealer, Wells Motor Company, decided to cash in on Ruth's home run by making it part of an advertising campaign to attract customers and proudly displaying the cracked showroom window where Ruth's blast had landed.)

In the top of the fourth the Yankees increased the lead to 3–1, but then the Cardinals got to Hoyt for three runs in the bottom of the inning to take a 4–3 lead. The Cards lead however, was short lived as the Yankees knocked Rhem out of the box in the fifth, scoring four runs to take a 7–4 lead. In the sixth inning, with one man on, Babe Ruth came up against Herman Bell and took the count to 3–2 before he increased the Yankee lead to 9–4 by hitting his third home run of the game. It was the first time that any player had hit three home runs in a World Series game. In the end the Yankees beat the Cardinals 10–5, with Waite Hoyt going the distance for the victory. Notwithstanding Ruth's three home runs, nine World Series records were set in the game and four others tied.

Following the game Rogers Hornsby avoided any hint of wrong doing in his pitch selections for Ruth, preferring to side step the issue: "There's only one thing to be said about the game and that is that you can't win a game that is as badly pitched as this one was. Not once was Ruth pitched to properly and that's the story of the game. We said before this series started that we were going to pitch to Babe Ruth, but when I said that I meant that we would not give him any intentional bases on balls just because he was Ruth and not that we would stick the ball over the plate so he could have a little practice socking the ball over the fence and setting a new record for home runs in a world series."[4]

Although Waite Hoyt gave up 14 hits to the Cardinals, he had better control than the squad of five Red Bird pitchers who attempted to tame the Yankees. In all, Hoyt had made 138 pitches, but he threw only 42 balls. Furthermore, in every inning he threw more strikes than balls. Whereas the five St. Louis pitchers — including Charles Rhem, Art Reinhart, Herman Bell, Wild Bill Hallahan and Vic Keen — had thrown just 102 pitches, with 60 of them off the plate. In all, the Cardinals pitchers issued 10 walks and yielded 14 hits to the Yankees. For Hoyt it was his fourth lifetime victory in World Series competition. John McGraw, who was in attendance and covering the series as a member of the press, stated, "Experience helped Hoyt a lot. He was hit harder than any other New York pitcher, but he managed to hold on to his lead. He was also very fortunate to have the whole club hitting behind him."[5]

The Yankees' victory in game four tied the series at two games each and assured that the series would have to return to New York. Miller Huggins, having exercised a streak of genius by starting Hoyt in game four, now had his ace Herb Pennock available to pitch game five on four days' rest. Opposing Pennock was Bill Sherdel, who had beaten the Yankees in game one. Game five was a scoreless contest until the bottom of the fourth, when the Cardinals scored a run off Pennock to take a 1–0 lead as Jim Bottomley doubled to left and scored on a single by Lester Bell.

In the top of the sixth, however, bad luck began to descend upon Bill Sherdel as Herb Pennock led off, hitting a routine pop fly to left. Chick Hafey — Cardinals left fielder and future Hall of Fame member — misjudged the ball, running in when he should have been running out. When Hafey attempted to recover he slipped and fell, allowing an easy out to go for a double. Mark Koenig then followed with a single to drive Pennock in and tie the score at 1–1. The Cardinals then came back in the bottom of the seventh to regain the lead 2–1 as Lester Bell doubled and then was driven home on a single by Bob O'Farrell.

Bill Sherdel continued to pitch a masterful game, shutting down the Yankees in the seventh and eighth while holding Babe Ruth — fresh off his three-homer game the day before — hitless, throwing him nothing but slow pitches on the inside. Then, in the ninth inning another miscue by the Cardinals outfield put the Yankees back in the game. Lou Gehrig hit a short fly ball to left center and Tommy Thevenow raced back from his shortstop position and seemed to have it for a routine out. However, all at once a stiff wind came blowing in and suddenly Thevenow was racing after the ball as Gehrig raced into second with a double. Tony Lazzeri then laid down a bunt, sacrificing Gehrig to third. Miller Huggins sent Ben Paschal up to pinch hit for Joe Dugan and he singled, driving Gehrig across the plate with the tying run. Herb Pennock held the Cardinals scoreless in the bottom of the ninth and the game moved into the 10th inning tied at 2–2. Leading off in the top of the 10th Mark Koenig singled. Sherdel then pitched to Ruth but walked him. Bob Meusel followed with a sacrifice bunt, advancing both runners, and Sherdel intentionally walked Gehrig to load the bases. However, Tony Lazzeri followed with a sacrifice fly, scoring Koenig with the winning run as Pennock shut down the Cardinals in the bottom of 10th to give the Yankees a 3–2 win and a 3–2 lead in the series.

Back at Yankee Stadium for game six, Miller Huggins decided to start Bob Shawkey. He had Urban Shocker ready to go but decided to hold him back should a seventh game be necessary. During the 1926 season Shawkey had been used primarily in relief, starting only 10 games. Coming down the stretch in the pennant race as the Yankees lead began to shrink from 10 games to five games, it was Shawkey who time and time again was called on by Huggins to put out the fires in late innings and so far he had pitched well in relief during the World Series. Rogers Hornsby selected Grover Cleveland Alexander to oppose to Shawkey.

The selection of Shawkey seemed to backfire on Huggins when the Cardinals came charging out of the gate in the first, scoring three runs as Jim Bottomley doubled home one run and Herman Bell drove in two with a single. The Cardinals carried a 3–0 lead into the bottom of the fourth, when the Yankees scored a run as Bob Meusel hit a triple off Alexander and then scored on a ground-out by Lou Gehrig. In the top of the fifth the Cardinals increased their lead to 4–1 as Tommy Thevenow singled, Alexander moved him along with a sacrifice and he then scored on a single by Watty Holm. In the top of seventh the Cardinals took a 9–1 lead, exploding for five runs off Shawkey and Urban Shocker, who entered the game with one out, one run scored and two men on. Shocker then yielded a two-run single to Rogers Hornsby and two-run homer to Lester Bell. The Yankees added a run in the bottom of the seventh on a single by Earle Combs. However, the Cardinals scored again in the ninth to beat the Yankees 10–2, having tagged Bob Shawkey, Urban Shocker and Myles Thomas for 13 hits, including three by Lester Bell.

Grover Cleveland Alexander had won his second game of the series while throwing only 102 pitches, of which only 29 were balls. He had also held Babe Ruth hitless in three official trips to the plate, although walking him in the sixth. Ruth had not been able to hit the ball out of the infield against Alexander, coming to the plate with runners on base in the third and seventh and on both occasions grounding out on slow rollers. In the 18 innings in the series that Alexander had now pitched, he had walked only three batters while striking out 16. As for the Yankees' pitching in game six, John McGraw felt that Bob Shawkey erred in trying to throw nothing but fast balls past the Cardinals and he wasn't surprised either that the Red Birds teed off on the relief pitching of Urban Shocker: "I did not think that Shocker could beat the Cardinals and said so at the start of the series."[6]

With the deciding game seven of the series at hand, the big question now was who would Miller Huggins use as his starting pitcher? Herb Pennock was a pitcher who needed considerable rest between starts; he had started game five and had only two days rest. Urban Shocker had been shelled in his relief stint in game six. That left Huggins with two choices: Dutch Ruether or Waite Hoyt. When Ruether showed up at Yankee Stadium ill prior to game seven, by default Hoyt became the starter, with Pennock standing by in the bullpen if needed. Rogers Hornsby would send Jesse Haines to the mound to oppose Hoyt in what would become one of the most celebrated games in World Series history.

Game seven was played before only 42,856 fans in cool and misty conditions at Yankee Stadium that saw some fans even wearing overcoats. Waite Hoyt, working like a well oiled machine set the Cardinals down in the first three innings. Then, in the bottom of the third Babe Ruth gave the Yankees a 1–0 lead when he hit a 1–1 pitch off Haines into the right-field bleachers for his fourth home run of the series. In the top of the fourth, however, the Yankees fielding collapsed, allowing three unearned runs to be scored off Hoyt.

The inning started with Rogers Hornsby bouncing the ball back to Hoyt, who threw him out at first. Jim Bottomley was next up and singled over shortstop. Lester Bell then hit a routine grounder to Mark Koenig at short, but Mark fumbled the ball, allowing Bottomley to pull up safe at second with Bell at first. Chick Hafey then dropped a Texas Leaguer between Koenig and Bob Meusel, loading the bases. Next up was Bob O'Farrell, who hit a high fly ball to deep center between Bob Meusel and Earle Combs. Combs could have taken the ball, but was waved off by Meusel, who had the stronger throwing arm to make the throw to the plate. However, either the sun got in Meusel's eyes or he tried to throw the ball before he actually had it. Whatever, the ball hit his outstretched arms and fell to the ground. Momentarily, the Cardinals base runners were stunned and didn't seem to know what to do. Then Bottomley took off for the plate as Bell and Hafey followed suit, advancing to third and second. With the bases now loaded again, Tommy Trevenow singled off Hoyt, scoring Bell and Hafey to give the Cardinals a 3–1 lead. Immediately, the press began conjuring up comparisons of Bob Meusel to Fred Snodgrass of the New York Giants who in the 10th inning of the final game of the 1912 World Series dropped a ball in center field, allowing the Boston Red Sox to eventually overcome a 2–1 lead and defeat Christy Mathewson 3–2 for the World Championship.

Despite the bad breaks, Waite Hoyt kept his composure and continued to pitch great, setting the Cardinals down in order in the fifth. He would have done the same in the sixth if not for a wide throw by Joe Dugan to first on a ground ball by Chick Hafey. Nonetheless, Hafey was then thrown out by Yankee catcher Hank Severeid attempting to steal second. In the bottom of the sixth with two outs, Joe Dugan singled and then was driven home on a double by Hank Severeid to cut the St. Louis lead to 3–2. At that point, with the tying run on second, Miller Huggins sent Ben Paschal up to pinch hit for Hoyt and Spencer Adams in to run for Severeid. However, all of the strategy was futile as Paschal tapped the ball back to Haines, who made an easy throw to first.

In the seventh Herb Pennock became the Yankees pitcher, Pat Collins took over behind the plate and the Cardinals failed to score. The bottom of the seventh is one of those storybook innings lodged deep in the annals of baseball folklore. It all started with Earle Combs leading off against Haines with a single over shortstop. Mark Koenig then laid down a sacrifice bunt, sending Combs to second. Haines walked Babe Ruth on four pitches as the crowd booed his every toss. Bob Meusel then grounded to Bell at third who forced Ruth at second, Combs moving on to third. This brought Lou Gehrig to the plate and Haines walked him, filling the bases with two outs. While Tony Lazzeri approached the plate the St. Louis infield gathered at the mound to confer with Haines. In snapping the curve ball he threw to Gehrig, Haines had opened a blister on the index finger of his right hand. Consequently all the Cardinals infielders were gathered at the mound gawking at Haines' bloody finger.

Out in the St. Louis bullpen no one had been warming up. Flint Rhem was sitting with Grover Cleveland Alexander, who was dozing off with a pint of whiskey in his pocket. Alexander was suffering the effects of a bad hangover, having painted the town the previous evening following his victory over the Yankees. At the mound, all at once Rogers Hornsby turned toward the Cardinals bullpen and signaled for Alexander. Seeing the sign, Alexander handed the pint of hooch to Rhem, and wobbled up and began the trek to the mound. The *St. Louis Post-Dispatch* in its account of the game stated that, "A tall lank figure, with a gaudy red sweater coat, stalked from the bull pen towards the infield."[7] As Alexander approached the mound the crowd in Yankee Stadium began cheering for him. However, Hornsby intercepted him before he reached the mound and explained the circumstances to him: "The bases are filled, Alex. But there's two outs and Lazzeri coming up. Do you feel alright?"[8] Alexander responded, "Sure, I feel fine. Three on, eh. Well, there's no place to put Lazzeri, is there with the sacks all loaded up? I'll just have to give him nothing but a lot of hell, won't I?"[9]

Alexander then took about four warm up pitches and signaled that he was ready to go; the call to play ball was issued and Lazzeri stepped up to the plate knowing that a base hit might mean the difference of $2,000 each for him and his teammates. The first pitch

Grover Cleveland Alexander (National Baseball Hall of Fame Museum, Cooperstown, N.Y.).

to Lazzeri was ball one low. Alexander then threw a fast ball down the center of the plate for one ball and one strike. On the next pitch from Alexander, Lazzeri lofted a long fly foul that curved into the left-field stands. The count now stood at 1–2 as Lazzeri backed out of the box to get the signal. On the next pitch Old Pete threw Lazzeri a curve and he swung and missed — strike three! A great roar of applause went up for Alexander, as the fans began to throw their hats and papers in the air. He had held the Cardinals' 3–2 lead.

In the eighth Pennock held the Cardinals scoreless and Alexander did likewise to the Yankees. In the top of the ninth Pennock set the Cardinals down in order, one, two, three. Leading off for the Yankees against Alexander in the bottom of the ninth was Earle Combs, who on a 2–2 count grounded out to Bell at third. Now the Cardinals were just two outs away from the World Championship. Koenig was next up and also grounded to Bell, for two outs. The next batter was Babe Ruth and Alexander walked him on a three and two count. Bob Meusel was next up. As Meusel swung and missed at the first pitch, Babe Ruth attempted to steal second and was thrown out by O'Farrell to end the game and the series.

The St. Louis Cardinals had defeated the New York Yankees and 39-year-old Grover Cleveland Alexander was the hero of the series, having won two games and lost none while pitching 20⅓ innings with an ERA of 0.89, and throwing 248 pitches, of which 175 (or 71 percent) were strikes. The following season Alexander would post a record of 21–10 for the Cardinals at the age of 40. He would finish up his 20-year big league career in 1930 where it started, with the Philadelphia Phillies. In all, Alexander would win 373 games and lose 208 in his career, including having won 30 or more games in three consecutive seasons. Although he never pitched a no-hitter, in 1915 he had four one-hitters and in two of those games the hit off him came in the ninth inning. He was elected to the National Baseball Hall of Fame in 1938. However, Alexander's legacy would be striking out Tony Lazzeri with the bases full and in the years to come his name would become synonymous with the 1926 World Series. In 1952 his life story was be portrayed on the silver screen in *The Winning Team*, starring Ronald Reagan as Old Pete and co-starring Doris Day. Grover Cleveland Alexander died from alcoholism and other health problems on November 4, 1950, in St. Paul, Minnesota.

The Yankees were of course disappointed with losing the series, but the pain was eased with receiving a losers'-share check of $3,723 each. For Waite Hoyt it was the fourth World Series check he had pocketed in the last six years. He not only pitched masterfully in what would become one of baseball's most famous games, but also pitched well in the series, winning one game and losing one while leading the Yankees pitching staff with an ERA of 1.20 and 10 strikeouts. In regard to Hoyt's efforts, James B. Harrison wrote in the *New York Times,* "Hoyt pitched fine ball all the way through. For a short spell he was again the Hoyt of 1921, when his work against the Giants earned him the brief sobriquet a 'second Matty.' His fast ball was a work of art and his curve the best he has shown in five years — both wonderfully controlled and hopping through like the wind. Hoyt, the staff on which the Yanks leaned in the big test, came through in magnificent style, but it was again his misfortune to be beaten by the breaks of the game. His mind must have wandered back to 1921. In the ill-fated game of that series Roger Peckinpaugh booted a ball away and Hoyt lost 1–0. Once again fate came along to kick him in the shins."[10]

Hoyt refused to criticize Bob Meusel — calling him every inch a gentleman — or his muff of Bob O'Farrell's lazy fly ball in the fourth inning. In fact, in later years Hoyt even defended Meusel, saying that he took his eye off the ball in order to see how much time he had to make the throw home. (However, Hoyt did admit that on occasion Bob Meusel drank too much, but not enough to interfere with play.) As for Babe Ruth, Hoyt—like the rest of the Yankees—felt no ill will toward him either for making the final out in the series attempting to steal second. Hoyt was of the opinion that it made complete sense for Babe to attempt to get the tying run into scoring position.

Also Ruth had contributed mightily to the Yankees cause in the series while setting 10 World Series records, including most series played (7), most home runs in a single game (3), most home runs in a single series (4), most home runs in all series total (8), most total bases in a single game (12) and most bases on balls in a single series (11) Suddenly the press was reporting that Ruth, who had just completed a three-year contract with the Yankees for $52,000 per year, would now ask for $150,000 a year — about $1,000 a game. When Yankee owner Col. Jacob Ruppert was asked what would happen if Ruth demands $150,000 a year, he replied with an explosion, "He won't get it!"[11]

October 10, 1926, at New York
Game Seven

Score by Innings

	1	2	3	4	5	6	7	8	9
St. Louis	0	0	0	3	0	0	0	0	0
New York	0	0	1	0	0	1	0	0	0

Box Score

St. Louis	AB	R	H	New York	AB	R	H
Holm, cf	5	0	0	Combs, cf	5	0	2
Southworth, rf	4	0	0	Koenig, ss	4	0	0
Hornsby, 2b	4	0	2	Ruth, rf	1	1	1
Bottomley, 1b	3	1	1	Meusel, lf	4	0	1
Bell, 3b	4	1	0	Gehrig, 1b	2	0	0
Hafey, lf	4	1	2	Lazzeri, 2b	4	0	0
O'Farrell, c	3	0	0	Dugan, 3b	4	1	2
Thevenow, ss	4	0	2	Severeid, c	3	0	2
Haines, p	2	0	1	Adams*	0	0	0
Alexander, p	1	0	0	Collins, c	1	0	0
				Hoyt, p	2	0	0
				Paschal†	1	0	0
				Pennock, p	1	0	0
Totals	34	3	8		32	2	8

* Ran for Severeid in sixth inning.
† Batted for Hoyt in sixth inning.

October 10, 1926 (*cont.*)

Two-base hit — Severeid
Home run — Ruth
Sacrifice hits— Haines, O. Farrell, Koenig, Bottomley
Left on bases— St. Louis 7, New York 10
Base on balls— off Haines 5 (Ruth 3, Gehrig 2); off Alexander 1 (Ruth)
Struck out — by Haines 2 (Lazzeri 2); by Alexander 1 (Lazzeri); by Hoyt 2
    (Hafey, Haires)
Hits— off Hoyt, 5 in 6 innings; off Pennock 3 in 3 innings; off Haines 8 in
    6⅔ innings; off Alexander none in 2⅓ innings
Winning pitcher — Haines; Losing pitcher — Hoyt
Umpires— Hildebrand (A.L.) at plate; Klem (N.L.) at first base; Dinneen (A.L.)
    at second base; O'Day (N.L.) at third base
Time of game — 2:15
Attendance — 42,856

In early 1927 Babe Ruth signed a new three-year contract with Yankees calling for $70,000 a season through 1929. By comparison Lou Gehrig's contract for 1927 was for $8,000; Joe Dugan's $12,000, Bob Meusel's $13,000; and Earle Combs' $10,500. Tony Lazzeri's contract called for a base salary of $8,000 and Col. Ruppert agreed to pay Pullman expenses and meals to bring Lazzeri and his wife to New York at the start of season from San Francisco and also pay for the return trip home after the season. As for the pitchers, Urban Shocker signed for $13,500 and Bob Shawkey for $10,500; Herb Pennock signed a three-year contract calling for $17,500 a year and a bonus of $1,000 if he won 25 games in any of the years. Waite Hoyt signed a one-year contract calling for $11,000 for 1927 and a bonus of $1,000 if he won 20 games.

Although the New York Yankees were the reigning American League champions, they were not being picked to repeat in 1927. The bookmakers had taken a bath on the Yankees in the 1926 World Series, seeing them lose three games at home. Overall, the Cardinals had played as a team, out-hitting, out-scoring and out-pitching the Yankees. Whereas the Yankees seemed to be dependent on Babe Ruth alone and beat the Cardinals convincingly only one time in the series when Ruth hit three home runs in game four. Consequently, as spring training in 1927 was coming to a close the smart money was going on the Philadelphia Athletics to win the American League pennant. Forty-two baseball experts had been solicited by the Associated Press to give their picks for the 1927 pennant race and 19 of the 42 picked the Athletics, while only nine picked the Yankees.

The Athletics had come on strong in the later part of the 1926 season and Connie Mack had rebuilt the team with some heavy hitters, such as

Jimmy Dykes, Sammy Hale, Mickey Cochran and Al Simmons. Also, over the winter Mack had signed Ty Cobb after he received his release by the Detroit Tigers in the wake of game-fixing allegations levied against him by former pitcher Emil "Dutch" Leonard. Furthermore, the Athletics had been building a formidable pitching staff, anchored by Lefty Grove, along with Rube Walberg and veteran Jack Quinn. Herb Pennock was now the ace of the Yankees pitching staff and the experts didn't really think too much of the rest, including Waite Hoyt.

Hoyt was considered hot headed and not amenable to taking advice from Miller Huggins— or anyone else, for that matter. Huggins felt that if Hoyt could get a grip on his temper he would be a better pitcher. Huggins had long contended that after the quality performance that Hoyt displayed in the 1921 World Series, he should have gone right to the top echelon of pitchers in the major leagues. But at this point there were those who felt that Hoyt was coming up short in his potential.

In early March 1927 Frederick G. Lieb set the concerns about Hoyt down in an article he wrote for *Sporting News*: "Waite never was better than he was in the last game of the 1926 World Series. He had his heart set to win it, was pleased that Huggins entrusted him with the assignment and had his boyish confidence that he would win. Outside of that one disastrous inning, when the Yankee support caved behind him, the Cards got only three men to base on him in six innings, one on an error. However, despite all of Hoyt's bad support in that inning I have contended that his failure to waste a few balls did as much to beat him as anything else. He had two strikes and no balls on Hafey, O'Farrell and Thevenow. At that time it would have been a good plan to pitch a few bad balls. But

Waite Hoyt (National Baseball Hall of Fame Library, Cooperstown, N.Y.).

Hoyt was so confident of his stuff that he put the third one over for each man to hit. It was the old schoolboy attempt of trying to drive them past the batsman. With his natural stuff, Hoyt should be a better pitcher then he is. He is quick to lose his temper, and is inclined to become flighty when things do not break well. He has had his troubles with Huggins, and several have been quite serious ones. They usually started over Hoyt's resentment when he was taken out of a tough game."[12]

Waite Hoyt was well aware of all this criticism and took it to heart. In his later years during his many speaking engagements, Hoyt often gave a rather melodramatic overview of his spiritual awakening in regard to his personality and how it affected his pitching. He contended that during the off-season following the 1926 World Series he went through an intense period of introspection, took a personal inventory and conceded to himself that he had been an egotistical, self-centered, pompous ass who never took anyone's advice but his own. He had battled with John McGraw, Jacob Ruppert and Miller Huggins, dismissing their opinions as trivial. Then, one evening in St. Petersburg, Florida, during spring training in 1927 he took a solitary walk out on a pier and experienced a sort of revelation.

Hoyt stated that he actually felt as if the hand of God had touched him. As a result, Hoyt (now 27 years old), suddenly came to a peace within himself and decided what needed to be done. His first stop in initiating the healing process came the next day went he sought out Miller Huggins and vowed to change his ways and no longer turn a deaf ear to advice. Hoyt had learned the hard way from Huggins the past season when, angry over being taken out of a game, he heaved the ball into the stands, which brought an immediate fine of $200. Huggins, impressed with Hoyt's self-awakening, rewarded his maturation by selecting him to pitch the opening-day game in 1927. Something must have happened out on that pier, because the next two seasons were to be the finest in Hoyt's career, while the relationship between him and Huggins blossomed into a father-son type.

As the 1927 season approached major league baseball was once again filled with anxiety about what the fan reaction would be to the latest scandal. In December 1926 the baseball world was stunned to learn that an allegation had been made by former Tigers pitcher Emil "Dutch" Leonard that Ty Cobb, then player-manager of the Detroit Tigers, and Tris Speaker, then player-manager of the Cleveland Indians, had conspired to fix the last game of the 1919 season so that the Tigers could win the third-place share of the 1919 World Series purse. Despite the fact that Detroit actually finished fourth in the 1919 pennant race, the allegation was taken seriously and an investigation was launched by baseball commissioner Kensaw

Mountain Landis. Furthermore, Leonard had also alleged that former Cleveland pitcher Smoky Joe Wood had placed bets on various games for both Cobb and Speaker.

Leonard's allegations were corroborated by two letters that he sent to the American League office — one written by Cobb, one written by Wood — that discussed the alleged activity. Commissioner Landis held a meeting on the matter, summoning Cobb, Speaker, Wood and Leonard to his office in Chicago. However, Dutch Leonard was so terrified of Cobb that he refused to appear in person. Consequently, Landis had to travel to California take his testimony. At the conclusion of the hearing, Landis was in quandary. Nonetheless, he found that there was nothing in the testimony presented that implicate Cobb and Speaker, two of baseball's biggest stars, in actually placing a bet. Still, Landis found that both may have had knowledge of betting on games taking place. The end result was that Landis swept the whole matter beneath the rug and reinstated both Cobb and Speaker to active-player status, although neither player was rehired by their former team or ever managed a big league team again. Subsequently, for the 1927 season, Cobb signed with the Philadelphia Athletics and Speaker with the Washington Nationals.

When opening day came on April 12, 1927, the fans had apparently forgotten all about the scandals of the past winter as 241,000 showed up around the majors, which was 18,000 more than had attended the 1926 openers. In Chicago a record crowd of 45,000 turned out at Wrigley Field to see the Cubs and Cardinals play. At Yankee Stadium a record crowd of 72,000 was in the stands, with 25,000 more turned away. Every conceivable inch of standing room was occupied in the stadium. Yankee owner Col. Jacob Ruppert had as guests in his box Dr. Wilhelm Cuno, the former chancellor of the German Republic, and his family. Prior to the game the photographers were busy snapping pictures of Babe Ruth and Ty Cobb together. Actually, the photographers were amazed at how fit the Babe was; he had lost a lot of weight! As the two teams paraded to the center-field bleachers for the raising of the Stars and Stripes and the Yankees 1926 American League pennant, the Seventh Regiment Band played the national anthem and Mayor Jimmy Walker threw out the first ball at 3:25 P.M.

Miller Huggins had selected the rejuvenated and born-again Waite Hoyt to oppose Philadelphia Athletics ace Lefty Grove in the opener. Grove, although wild, engaged Hoyt in a scoreless duel for the first 4½ innings. Then the Yankees scored four in the bottom of the fifth to take a 4–0 lead. The Athletics scored two in the sixth, but the Yankees countered with four more of their own in the bottom half of the inning to take an 8–2 lead as Jack Quinn replaced Grove. The Athletics scored one more run off Hoyt in the eighth, but in the end he went the distance, pitching an eight-hitter. Actually, Hoyt had pitched much better than the 8–3 final score indicated. Two of the Athletics' three runs scored on an error and Earle Combs' failure to stop Ty Cobb at third with an easy throw in the sixth. Ty Cobb had bunted his way on to first, then taken third on a single by Sammy Hale. However, Combs' throw was short of the third-base bag, pulling Joe Dugan away from the runner. Cobb then scored on an out by Dudley Branom and Hale scored when Lou Gehrig muffed a throw to first.

The so-called experts in the press had a lot of crow to eat during 1927 in regard to their opinions of the New York Yankees' abilities as a team. After the Yankees won on opening day they never relinquished first place, not even for one day during the entire season, finishing 19 games ahead of the highly touted second-place Athletics. In the month of June the Yankees were 20–4. On July 4 the Washington Nationals arrived in New York, riding high, and manager Bucky Harris was even talking pennant. But the Yankees increased their lead to 11½ games over second-place Washington when they destroyed the Nationals in a doubleheader 12–1 and 21–1. In a doubleheader following Labor Day they did the same to the then second-place Athletics, sweeping a twin-bill from them 10–5 and 18–5. At the season's end the Yankees had won 110 games—an American League record that would stand until the Cleveland Indians won 111 games in 1954. During the season the Yankees were shut out just one time — that coming at Shibe Park in Philadelphia on September 3 when the Athletics beat them 1–0.

The 1927 Yankees were such an awesome offensive ball club that when the season ended they occupied the leadership in eight out of the 10 individual batting and base-running titles, including home runs (Ruth, 60), RBIs (Gehrig, 175), hits (Combs, 231), home run percentage (Ruth, 11.1); doubles (Gehrig, 52), slugging average (Ruth, .772), total bases (Gehrig, 447); base on balls (Ruth, 138), runs scored (Ruth, 158) and triples (Combs, 23). In addition, Gehrig occupied second place in home runs (47), hits (218), home run percentage (8.0); slugging average (.765) and runs scored (149), while Bob Meusel finished second in stolen bases (24) and Babe Ruth finished second in RBIs (164).

Four Yankees finished with more than 100 RBIs—besides Ruth and Gehrig, Bob Meusel knocked in 103 and Tony Lazzeri 102. Waite Hoyt silenced a few of his critics too, as he compiled a season record of 22–7, his first 20-game win season, while leading the American League in wins (22), winning percentage (.759) and earned run average (2.63).

Waite Hoyt contended that the 1927 Yankees were an almost perfect ball club that seldom if ever beat themselves. Nineteen twenty-seven was in fact the dawn of the so-called "Yankee tradition." "We concocted two slogans," said Hoyt.[13] "One was the "Second time around." Meaning if a pitcher retired the Yankee batters the first time around the batting order, beware the "Second time around." In those days the games at the (Yankee) Stadium started at 3:15. The eighth inning usually arrived around 5 o'clock. Earle Combs invented the slogan "Five o'clock lightning." If the Yanks were behind it was usually in the eighth, when the "Five o'clock lightning struck. The team had good pitching and great fielding — and the combination of everything gave rise to fabled stories. The Yanks began to believe in themselves as something apart from the other teams."[14]

New York Yankees
1927 Home and Away Record

	Won	*Lost*	*Percentage*
Home	57	19	.750
Away	53	25	.679
Total	110	44	.714

While the Yankees were all business on the field, they were still a frolicking bunch at night. That was, everyone but Babe Ruth and Bob Meusel. Ruth had now become a loner and stayed out of the limelight at night. The Yankees provided him with a suite in the hotel on the road where he ate his meals and entertained. After games he would retire to the suite, cloak himself in a red dressing gown and red Moroccan slippers and light a cigar. On some occasions the Babe would have the bathtub filled up with ice and illegal bottles of beer, then hold court with his public as if he were some sort of foreign diplomat. When Ruth did go out he usually went to places were his privacy could be assured. In St. Louis, according to Hoyt, the Babe went to a restaurant owned by a rotund German lady, where the specialty of the house was spareribs and the Babe could gorge himself to his heart's delight. At home in New York he often traveled to a bar located across the Hudson River in New Jersey, where the owner had even built a private entrance for him. As for Bob Meusel, he didn't chase women, drank some, roomed with Herb Pennock and preferred to be alone much of the time.

On the other hand, there was still a considerable amount of public partying going with the other Yankees players. Waite Hoyt, Joe Dugan and Herb Pennock regularly enjoyed nights out on the town and once in a while they could even convince the solitary man Bob Meusel to join them.

On a road trip to Chicago, Hoyt and his Yankee buddies were living it up one evening at a restaurant when one of them asked the waiter if they could see Big Al, meaning notorious Chicago gang chieftain Al Capone. Gangland violence in Chicago had been capturing national headlines for two years now, with Capone attempting to consolidate his South Side bootleg empire with that on the North Side. In fact, just last fall (the day after the World Series had concluded) noted gangsters Earl "Hymie" Weiss and Paddy Murray and three others were killed in a hail of machine-gun fire in front of Chicago's Holy Name Cathedral, leaving the facade of the church raked with bullets and five men lying in a huge pool of blood. Weiss had been a gunman working for murdered North Side gang boss Dion O'Banion, who had been ambushed himself and gunned down near the same spot three years before. Al Capone of course was a suspect in planning these murders.

But it so happens that Capone was an ardent baseball fan and often went to White Sox games at Comiskey Park, sometimes even taking his son Al Jr. along. To everyone's surprise, one of the restaurant employees made a phone call and within a short time a limo arrived to take the party to see Big Al. The limo took them to the Lexington Hotel, where Capone had his South Side headquarters, and they were directed to a room upstairs. Outside the room there was stationed a rather ominous, watchful lieutenant who met Hoyt and his party, then proceeded to frisk them. Seeing that they were "clean," they were admitted. There, sitting behind a rather large desk, was none other than Al Capone. Hanging on the wall behind Capone were two large portraits—one of George Washington, the other of Abraham Lincoln. Gazing upon the quasi-patriotic setting moved Hoyt's roommate Joe Dugan to remark, "Three great guys—George, Al and Abe."[15] Less than two years later on February 14, 1929, Al Capone's gang would murder six members of the rival Bugs Moran Gang inside a garage on North Clark Street in what became commonly known as The Saint Valentine's Day Massacre and Capone would be in complete control of Chicago's bootleg alcohol industry until Prohibition was repealed.

Waite Hoyt rationalized the Yankees' penchant for partying to being a factor of the times in which they lived: "Don't forget this: When the Yankees first became a dynasty, it was in the middle of the Roarin' Twenties. It was the birth of something new and everybody from the Astors to gangsters wanted to meet baseball players. It was fashionable to say, 'I met so and so last night at such and such night club.' Another thing that is forgotten: Then we played strictly day baseball and we had ample time at night to go here and there. Also the schedules were different. You'd stay in one city at least four days."[16]

The defining event in the 1927 season for the Yankees was the home run race between teammates Babe Ruth and Lou Gehrig. Babe Ruth had led the major leagues in home runs for six out of the past eight years. The years that he did not win the home run title (1922 and 1925), it was because he was either ill or suspended and didn't play the full schedule. By 1927 Ruth had already become legendary in the minds of his fans and was expected to swat huge totals of round-trippers every year now. However, what was not expected is that the Babe would stand such a stiff challenge for the home run leadership in 1927 as the year before. In 1926, when Ruth had hit 47 home runs, the second place challenger in the American League had been Al Simmons with 19, while over in the National League Hack Wilson had hit 21.

Joe Dugan (National Baseball Hall of Fame Library, Cooperstown, N.Y.).

But in 1927 the challenge came from teammate Lou Gehrig, who all at once began to pound the ball out of the park with authority. While Ruth got off to a fast start in the home run derby, hitting 22 in the first 55 games, Gehrig stayed close to him and by late July they were hitting home runs at an even pace. On August 10 Gehrig was in the lead 38–35. On August 16 the Yankees were playing in Chicago. The White Sox had just built a second deck on the right-field stands and everyone felt fairly sure that no one would ever clear the roof with a batted ball. But that's exactly what happened when Babe Ruth launched a towering home run off of Chicago pitcher Tommy Thomas that cleared the roof as the Yankees won 8–1. It was Ruth's 37 home run of the season and from that point on until the end of the season he battered American League pitching, hitting 23 more home runs—including a total of 17 in the month of September.

When the Yankees arrived into Boston for a doubleheader on Labor

Lou Gehrig (National Baseball Hall of Fame Library Cooperstown, N.Y.).

Day, September 6, Ruth and Gehrig had hit 44 home runs each. However, when the day was over Ruth had hit three home runs, Gehrig none. The next day Ruth hit two more. The home run chase was over. Suddenly Ruth had 49 home runs, Gehrig 44. On September 11 Ruth hit a home run against St. Louis and then on September 13 hit two against Cleveland to bring his total to 52. Now Ruth had a shot at breaking his major league record of 59 home runs in a season set in 1921. On September 27 at Yankee Stadium he hit number 57, a grand slam off Lefty Grove of the Athletics. Now he needed only three more homers to break the record. With three days left in the season on September 29 at Yankee Stadium playing against Washington, Ruth hit home run number 58 off Hod Lisenbee and then hit number 59, another grand slam, off Paul Hopkins, who was pitching in his second major league game. Ruth now needed just one home run in the final two days of the season to set the new record.

In Waite Hoyt's remembrances of that next to the last day of the season on September 30, 1927, he states that in the Yankees clubhouse prior to the game Ruth was trying to find a way to motivate himself for the challenge of getting that last round-tripper he needed for the record. He told Tony Lazzeri, "Jeez, I'm tied with myself. Guess I'll hit one."[17] Lazzeri responded, "I'll bet you ten bucks you don't."[18] That being done, Ruth hit a slow curve ball from Washington pitcher Tom Zachary down the line into the right-field bleachers for number 60. Zachary argued with the umpires that the ball had been foul, but to no avail. In the clubhouse following the game the Babe was jubilant, jumping up and down yelling, "Sixty, count 'em, sixty! Let's see some other son of a bitch match that!"[19] Ruth would play the final day of the season in game number 154, but go 0–3 at bat.

In subsequent years others would challenge the Babe's single season home run record, including Jimmie Foxx (1932) and Hank Greenburg (1938). However, it would be 34 years before the actual next son of a bitch, Roger Maris, would hit 61 home runs in 1961. Maris' quest occurred simultaneously with his hair falling out from the tension associated with challenging the Babe's record during a controversial 162-game season mandated by expansion. Ironically, in that 1961 season Maris would take part in a home run contest reminiscent of the Ruth-Gehrig contest, with Yankees teammate Mickey Mantle hitting 54 before succumbing to a painful hip injury.

The defending World Champion St. Louis Cardinals failed to win the National League pennant in 1927 finishing 1½ games behind the Pittsburgh Pirates. Earlier in the season the pennant race had been between the Pirates and Chicago Cubs. The Cubs maintained the lead through August, but in early September the two teams squared off a in crucial series at Forbes Field, with the Pirates prevailing and taking over the lead. With the Cubs reeling, the Cardinals and Giants made a run at the Pirates, but both came up short.

The Pirates were led by right fielder Paul "Big Poison" Waner, who won the National League batting crown with an average of .380 and also led the league in RBIs (131), hits (237), triples (17), runs scored (133) and total bases (338). Supporting Waner's efforts were his brother, rookie center fielder Lloyd "Little Poison" Waner, who hit .355, and veteran third baseman Pie Traynor, who hit .342. All three players would eventually be elected to the National Baseball Hall of Fame. Also, future Hall of Fame member Kiki Cuyler was on the team, but was in manager Donie Bush's dog house after being benched following a confrontation during the season. He did not play in the World Series. Following the 1927 World Series Cuyler was traded to the Chicago Cubs. As for pitching, the Pirates mound staff included Carmen Hill, who won 22 games and lost 11, and a pair of 19-game winners in Lee Meadows (19–10) and Ray Kremer (19–8).

One of the myths that has grown out of the 1927 World Series is that when the Pittsburgh Pirates saw the New York Yankees take their initial batting practice at Forbes Field they were ready to throw in the towel. Unfortunately, this is not historically accurate, although this type of diamond fable does become perpetuated in the sport from time to time. Now it is a fact that the powerful reputation of the Yankees lineup did precede them to Pittsburgh. It is also a fact that the Pirates were quite interested in seeing what the Yankees hitters looked like and hung around Forbes Field with many other onlookers from the press, major league managers in town for the series, etc., to get a glimpse of the Yankees power hitting machinery. The Yankees took batting practice in the order of their lineup with Earle Combs hitting first, then Mark Koenig, Babe Ruth, Lou Gehrig, and others. Ruth didn't disappoint anyone, as the solid crack of his bat could be heard throughout Forbes Field as he sent several drives into both decks of the right-field stands. As Ruth left the batting cage and headed toward the dugout, he smiled and said, "That's easy. They can leave the stand right where it is, as it is just right."[20] Gehrig, on the other hand, wasn't so impressive, but did drop a couple of balls into the lower deck. Both Meusel and Lazzeri had to settle for long fly balls to the outfield.

The *Pittsburgh Post-Gazette* summarized the Yankees workout in the following manner: "The Yankees, like the Pirates, who preceded them in the workout, kept the outfielders busy chasing their drives to the fences. Aside from the smashes of the two left-handers, Babe and Lou, the Yankees did not show any apparent advantage over the Buccos, excepting that their wallops bonded greater distances and made it evident that the official ball of the American League must be more elastic than that of the Heydler (National League) circuit."[21] (For the record, it was a common theory in the late 1920s that the ball used in the American League was more lively. In fact, one of the major proponents of this theory was the Pirates captain and third baseman Harold "Pie" Traynor.)

The Pirates weren't showing any signs of anxiety, however, over playing the Yankees. Prior to game one manager Donie Bush stated, "We're not afraid of any batter or any pitcher on the New York team and we'll just go in there and win. All of our players are in the best possible condition and I've never seen any more pep or fighting spirit in all my life. Our right-handed pitchers are going to fool the Yankees and our own hitters will cross up the Yankee pitching."[22] Pie Traynor was not only predicting that the Pirates would win the series in six games, but also that Paul and Lloyd Waner would out-hit Babe Ruth and Lou Gehrig. (Furthermore, Traynor stated that he could eat Babe Ruth under the table. When Ruth, a true masticating machine, was informed of Traynor's later comment he just grinned.)

The starting pitchers for game one were to be Waite Hoyt for the Yankees opposing the Pirates Ray Kremer. For Hoyt, it would be his eighth start in a World Series game; for Kremer, his third. Hoyt's eight starts in World Series games by comparison put him in some very elite company, as Christy Mathewson had started in 11 series games, Rube Marguard in eight, Eddie Plank and Wild Bill Donovan in six, and Stan Coveleski, Grover Cleveland Alexander and Walter Johnson each in five games.

While an estimated 20 million fans listened on radio broadcasts by NBC and CBS over 63 stations nationwide and with 41,467 fans on hand at Forbes Field, game one of the 1927 World Series got underway. As circumstances turned out the Pirates beat themselves in game one, allowing the Yankees to score three runs in the third inning with just one hit, while being aided by two Pirates errors and two base on balls. In the first inning, with two outs Babe Ruth singled to right, then scored on a triple by Lou Gehrig to give the Yankees a 1–0 lead. However, the Pirates came right back in their half of the inning to tie the game. Lloyd Waner led off and was hit by a pitch from Hoyt that just nipped the sleeve on his uniform. After Clyde Barnhart lined out to Ruth in right, Paul Waner then swung at the first pitch from Hoyt and doubled to right, sending Lloyd Waner to third. Only a rapid return of the ball from Ruth in right field prevented Lloyd Waner from scoring. Moments later, however, Lloyd Waner scored on a sacrifice fly to right by Glenn Wright to tie the score at 1–1, with Paul Waner advancing to third. Hoyt then got Pie Traynor to fly out to Ruth to end the inning.

In the bottom of the second Tony Lazzeri and George Grantham nearly came to blows. Grantham was on first base after being walked by Hoyt when Joe Harris hit a ground ball to Lazzeri. The Pirates had a reputation for rough-and-tumble play and as Lazzeri fielded the ball, Grantham ran into him at high speed. Lazzeri tagged Grantham and was able to hold on to the ball and throw to first to complete the double play. However, immediately following the play Lazzeri argued with Grantham that he had used unnecessary roughness on the play and the two started to advance towards each other. Moments later, as Lazzeri threw out Earl Smith to end the inning, the crowd booed him loudly as he came into the dugout.

In the third inning the Pirates staked Hoyt to a three-run lead when with one out Grantham muffed a grounder by Mark Koenig. Babe Ruth followed with a single to right, sending Koenig to third. Ray Kremer then walked Lou Gehrig to load the bases and followed with another walk to Bob Meusel to force in a run, giving the Yankees a 2–1 lead. Lazzeri then forced Meusel at second, but Ruth scored on the play to increase the Yankees lead to 3–1. Then the Yankees attempted to pull off a double steal, with Gehrig scoring and Lazzeri going to third when Smith let Traynor's throw go between his legs. The official scorer, however, ruled no stolen bases, issuing an error to the Pirates catcher on the play. The Yankees took a 4–1 lead into the bottom half of the inning, but the Pirates fought back against Hoyt and scored a run. Ray Kremer started the rally against Hoyt with a ground-rule double. Then, after Hoyt got Lloyd Waner to fly out, Bob Meusel — who was rapidly getting a reputation for miscues in big games — dropped a lazy fly ball hit by Barnhart. Kremer did not advance, however, holding on second. This brought Paul Waner to the plate and Hoyt began throwing him low curve balls. Waner singled into center, scoring Kremer to make the score 4–2 Yankees. Barnhart halted at second. Moments later Wright forced Waner, with Barnhart going to third. The inning ended when Hoyt got Pie Traynor to hit into a force-out of Wright.

In the top of the fifth Mark Koenig led off with a double off Kremer, advanced to third on a ground ball by Ruth and scored on a sacrifice fly by Gehrig to make to score 5–2 Yankees. But once again the Pirates came back in the bottom of the inning, scoring a run off Hoyt to make the score 5–3 when Lloyd Waner doubled and scored on a single by Barnhart. The rally came up short, though, when with two outs and a runner on third Hoyt got Pie Traynor to fly out to Combs to end the inning. In the top of the sixth Tony Lazzeri led off with a double that hit the left-field fence. At that point, Pirate manager Donie Bush replaced Kremer on the mound with Johnny Miljus. Joe Dugan then laid down a sacrifice bunt, sending Lazzeri to third. Miljus walked Yankee catcher Pat Collins on four pitches. This brought Waite Hoyt to the plate with a chance to help his own cause but he quickly hit into a double play to end the inning.

In the bottom of the eighth with the Yankees still leading by a score of 5–3, Paul Waner led off against Hoyt and lined out to Meusel. Glenn Wright followed, however, with a single to right. Then Pie Traynor followed with a single over second, with Wright holding at second. At this point the game was halted and Miller Huggins headed for the mound. Waite Hoyt had developed a painful blister under the nail on the second finger of his right hand and as a result was having trouble with his control. In fact, for the last few innings he had been throwing the ball with one finger. Consequently, Hoyt was relieved by Wilcey Moore, a thirty-year-old rookie who had been brought up by the Yankees from the Sally League in 1927 and had posted a 19–7 record (with 13 of his wins coming in relief in which he also accumulated 13 saves). With two men on and Moore now pitching, Grantham forced Traynor, Gehrig to Koenig, with Wright going to third. However, Traynor went into second high and knocked Koenig over. Koenig, shaken up on the play, needed a few moments to collect himself. When play was resumed Wright scored on a single by Joe Harris to make the score 5–4 Yankees. Moore then got Smith on a ground ball to Gehrig to end the inning. In the ninth, with the pitcher Miljus due up first, the Pittsburgh fans by the thousands pleaded for manager Donie Bush to send the banished Kiki Cuyler up to pinch hit. Bush ignored the yells for Cuyler and sent up reserve outfielder Fred Bricknell to hit. Moore got the Pirates out in order to end the game and give the Yankees a 1–0 lead in the series.

There was jubilation in the Yankee clubhouse as Babe Ruth entered swinging the bat that he had used in the game to get three singles. "It won't be long now,"[23] bellowed Ruth. "Say, I was sure due for a homer if Kremer had only stayed in the Pirate box. The first two hits clicked just right, but I slipped as I slugged the third one at Grantham. I had the range and that next time up the ball would have made the bleachers if Donie Bush hadn't yanked Kremer."[24]

Waite Hoyt came over to Ruth and said, "Nice hitting Babe."[25]

"Nice hitting, my eye; only three singles," responded Ruth.[26]

All that Hoyt could say was, "What a man!"[27] (Actually, a great deal of the Pittsburgh fans left Forbes Field disappointed that Ruth did not hit a home run. The disabled war veterans of Pittsburgh had even sent a basket of flowers to Ruth in his room at the Roosevelt Hotel in honor of his record-breaking 60 home runs.)

There was also some discontent with the game expressed by the sports writers. For one, Ring Lardner wrote in his column, "Early in the morning a dense fog hung over Pittsburgh and in the afternoon, some of the ball players acted like they were still in it. A good many of we experts thought that the two clubs wasn't Pittsburgh and New York at all, but the Phillies and Browns disguised as Lon Chaney. Waite Hoyt and Ray Kramer seemed to be betting on each other. Both these gents are a whole lot better than they looked in this battle. If they ain't, I am going to take up pitching."[28]

Regardless, Waite Hoyt got the win in game one and it was the fourth World Series win in his career. The difference, however, in the game he pitched and the one pitched by his opponent Ray Kremer was the fact that Yankees fielded behind him. Hoyt had given up eight hits in clusters, only to see his teammates bail him out with extraordinary fielding. Hoyt was aware that Lady Luck had been on his side that afternoon: "If I had been pitching against the Detroit Tigers or the Philadelphia Americans I would have been knocked out in two innings," remarked Hoyt.[29] Nonetheless, Hoyt had retired Pie Traynor as the last out in three critical innings in the first, third and fifth. Also, his win was preserved by the best relief pitcher in baseball, Wilcey Moore, in the final 1⅔ innings.

When Hoyt left the game in the eighth he went to the clubhouse, where the Yankee trainer had to puncture the nail on his blistered finger to treat it. Still, Hoyt was hopeful that he could be ready to pitch on Sunday in New York if needed. Hoyt told reporters that he realized being knocked out of the box was part of the game and he was aware of the fact that he was having problems. "Some one told me to feed the Waners nice curve balls, high on the inside,"[30] said Hoyt. "I did and those boys were laying back waiting for them. They won't get four hits between them the next time I pitch. I'll wager on that."[31] Then Hoyt turned prophetic. George Pipgras had been chosen by Miller Huggins to oppose the Pirates in game two. "I'll just bet," declared Hoyt, "that Pipgras, if he's as good as he was in his last start, he will shut out the Pirates with no more than five hits"[32]

Hoyt was not far off in his prediction as the following day George Pipgras, pitching in his first World Series game with a fast ball and superior control, pitched a complete game, beating the Pirates 6–2 while yielding seven hits. The Yankees took a 2–0 lead in the series back to New York. Although Pipgras gave up seven hits, he never allowed more than one in a single inning and only twice did the lead-off man get aboard in the game. In the clubhouse Babe Ruth grabbed George Pipgras by the hand and shook it. "Great work, kid," said the Babe,[33] "You showed them a real fast ball today, and they didn't like it either. Allowing seven hits in your first world's series games is something you should be proud of. I was just as happy as you are right now when I won my first world's series game with the Red Sox. I don't think you'll get another chance though, for we're going to end this thing in four games."[34]

However, for the second straight game the Yankees had failed to hit a home run. In five times at bat Babe Ruth struck out in the first, hit a sacrifice fly that scored a run in the third, walked on four pitches in the fifth, grounded out in the seventh and with the bases full in the eighth grounded out, forcing a runner at the plate.

With the Yankees back in New York, Tony Lazzeri stated, "Our traveling for 1927 ended yesterday in Pittsburgh. Herb Pennock, with his left-hand assortment, will probably go against the Pirates today. He'll beat them. He is the greatest money pitcher in the business. Then we have Wilcey Moore and Hoyt to go back in the box again. I have all the confidence in the world in Hoyt, if he performs again."[35] However, Waite Hoyt never got another chance to pitch in the 1927 World Series. In game three at Yankee Stadium Herb Pennock absolutely dominated pitching a three-hitter and beating the Pirates 8–1. Pennock retired the first 22 men in succession before Pie Traynor touched him for a single with one out in the eighth and then scored on a double by Clyde Barnhart. In the seventh inning Babe Ruth hit the first home run of the series with Combs and Koenig on base.

In game four Miller Huggins decided to start Wilcey Moore instead of Waite Hoyt. Moore had made a significant contribution to the Yankees pennant efforts with his brilliant relief pitching in 1927 and it seemed only fitting that he have the opportunity to finish the series in four games. The Yankees did just that, beating the Pirates 5–4 with Moore going all the way for the victory. Babe Ruth hit a two-run home run in the game and the Yankees' scored the winning run on a wild pitch by reliever Johnny Miljus in the bottom of the ninth inning with the bases loaded and two outs. The Yankees share of the 1927 series pot was $167,765.97. That meant a full share to each eligible Yankee of $5,592.17, which raised Waite Hoyt's total post-season earnings for playing in five World Series to $21,888.41. (While an extra five grand was a lot of loot for a ballplayer to rake in back in 1927, it pales in comparison to the World Series shares of today. In the 2003 World Series the Florida Marlins defeated the New York Yankees 4–2. The payout for a full share of series winnings to each eligible Marlins player was $306,150.00 — nearly double what the entire pot was for the 1927 New York Yankees team.)

The Yankees had swept a star-studded Pittsburgh Pirates team whose lineup included three future Hall of Fame members in Lloyd Waner, Paul Waner and Pie Traynor. Immediately the press began calling the 1927 New York Yankees baseball's greatest team ever — a debate that continues until this very day. Unfortunately for the Pittsburgh Pirates, the 1927 World Series would be their last appearance in the fall classic for the next 33 years. However, the Pirates would have their revenge against the Yankees of another era when Bill Mazeroski hit a home run in the ninth inning of the seventh game to win the 1960 World Series. It would be a bitter loss for the Yankees and Mickey Mantle would state that the flight back to New York that night after losing the 1960 World Series was the longest of his career.

The 1927 season had been the most successful one to date in Waite Hoyt's career. Of course later he attributed that success to the personal inventory of his behavior that he had taken in spring training. However, if Hoyt had implemented behavioral modification inside the ballpark, he still had some work to do outside of it. In early November Hoyt's explosive temper finally caught up with him when he became abusive with a New York City traffic policeman and was arrested. On the evening of November 6, as Hoyt was driving in the Bronx, he failed to keep to the right and drove through a safety zone at 156th Street and Westchester Avenue. When he was stopped by New York City police officer Andrew Dolan, Hoyt verbally abused him. Following the outburst Dolan immediately informed Hoyt that he was under arrest; he was taken to the station house and summarily charged with disorderly conduct. Released on $500 bail, and facing Magistrate Rosenbluth the following day in court, Hoyt apologized to officer Dolan and was given a suspended sentence.

During the off-season Hoyt continued to work in the mortuary business and did a little vaudeville. In late January 1928 Ed Barrow, the Yankees business manager, mailed out contracts for the coming season. When Hoyt opened his and saw that he was being offered a modest raise over his $11,000 salary for the previous season, he promptly sent it back to Col. Ruppert unsigned. Using the marketing training that he had been tutored in by his father Ad Hoyt, he went public, explaining to press his reasoning for not signing. "I rated first in winning percentage and second to [Wilcey] Moore in the earned run column, with 2.64 runs per game. I worked in 36 games a total of 256 innings and if the records speak the truth I did pretty well. I figure that I am reaching the peak of a career and should be even better within the next three years."[36] Hoyt now knew how the game was played and was aware of the fact Ed Barrow knew that with the success he and the team had had in 1927, in order to negotiate effectively he would have to leave plenty of room in his initial offers. Hoyt was also aware of the fact that Lou Gehrig, who played the 1927 season for $8,000, had just signed a new three-year deal calling for a rising scale that would net him $75,000 over the life of the contract. Subsequently, Hoyt informed Barrow that he wanted a three-year contract calling for $20,000 a year. The Yankees took it personally for a while and even indicated that perhaps his vaudeville appearances were affecting his pitching and he should choose between the stage and the mound. But when all was said and done, Hoyt signed a two-year contract for $20,000 a year. However, to earn the full amount in the first year he would receive a bonus of $2,500 if he won 22 games again.

The defending World Champion Yankees got off to fast start in the 1928 season and built an early lead that promised to leave every other team in the American League in their dust. On May 24 at Shibe Park in Philadelphia, the first-place Yankees and the second-place Athletics were scheduled to play a doubleheader. The first game was scheduled to begin at 1:30 P.M. However, by 10:30 A.M. when the ticket windows opened, thousands were already waiting to enter the park. The parking lot at 21st and Lehigh was filled by noon with over 500 cars bearing license plates not only from

Pennsylvania, but also Delaware, New York, New Jersey and even Maryland. The attendance was estimated at 42,000 inside the Shibe Park with another 5,000 or so fans attempting to watch from the roof tops of houses along Twentieth Street.

The Yankees won the first game 9–7, defeating Lefty Grove. Waite Hoyt, the third Yankee pitcher, entered the game in the ninth inning in relief of Wilcey Moore and after walking two batters got Ty Cobb out on a hot grounder back to the box to end the game. The Athletics won the second game 5–2 behind the pitching of rookie Ossie Orwoll.

No one knew it at the time, but in years to come the first game of that doubleheader would become a most memorable event. The significance of the first game was not that the Yankees won or that Waite Hoyt pitched in it, but the incredible circumstances that occurred with 13 future Hall of Fame members playing in the game. For the Yankees: Earle Combs, Leo Durocher, Babe Ruth, Lou Gehrig, Tony Lazzeri and Waite Hoyt. For the Athletics: Ty Cobb, Tris Speaker, Mickey Cochran, Al Simmons, Eddie Collins, Lefty Grove and Jimmie Foxx. While these 13 players played in the game, two future Hall of Fame managers— Miller Huggins and Connie Mack — were in the dugouts, as were two future Hall of Fame pitchers in Herb Pennock and Stan Coveleski. Also, two of the umpires in the game — Tom Connally and Bill McGowan — were also future Hall of Fame members.

By the Fourth of July the Yankees had built a 13½-game lead over the Philadelphia Athletics despite experiencing a series of injuries to key players such as Joe Dugan, Tony Lazzeri and Mark Koenig, and also having problems with the pitching staff. Dutch Ruether had retired after the 1927 season, Urban Shocker became seriously ill during spring training and Wilcey Moore had suddenly lost the touch coming out of the bullpen. But by mid–July the Yankees lead was in jeopardy. Connie Mack had made some changes in his lineup and the Athletics suddenly went on a tear, eventually posting a record of 25–8 in the month of July.

Still the Yankees fought on. On July 25 in Detroit, Tiger rookie right-hander Vic Sorrell and Waite Hoyt hooked up in an 11-inning 1–1 duel. Then in the 12th the Yankees scored 11 runs on 12 hits and two walks to win the game. Following the Detroit series the Yankees opened a four-game set in Cleveland. After losing the first three games of the series on July 31, a trio of Yankee pitchers including Waite Hoyt, Wilcey Moore and Herb Pennock finally got the Yankees back on the winning track with a 12–9 win over the Indians. However, the Yankees could not shake loose the hard-charging Athletics as the Mackmen beat the St. Louis Browns 8–4 behind Lefty Grove to cut the Yankees' lead to 5½ games.

Although Waite Hoyt, George Pipgras, Herb Pennock and Hank John-son were doing a creditable job on the mound, Miller Huggins believed that he needed help in the pitching department for the stretch drive and obtained a pair of journeyman left-handers to bolster the staff. On August 9 the Yankees acquired Freddy Helmach, a former Athletics and Red Sox hurler from St. Paul of the American Association, and then on August 23 bought Tom Zachary from Washington for the waiver price. Zachary was of course the pitcher that had served up Babe Ruth's record-breaking 60th home run the year before. On August 10, Helmach paid immediate divi-dends, pitching a four-hitter against Boston in a 7–1 triumph. Still, the Athletics kept the pressure on and by August 30 the Yankees lead had been cut to 2½ games.

On September 1 at Washington Waite Hoyt kept the Yankees in the lead as he beat the Nationals 8–3 with a little help from Bob Meusel, who went 4-for-4 with three RBIs. But on September 7 the Athletics swept a doubleheader from Boston and moved into a tie with the reeling Yankees as they lost a doubleheader to the Nationals. The Nationals won the first game 11–0 behind the pitching of Bump Hadley, who also had three hits in the game. In the nightcap the Nationals Firpo Marberry beat Waite Hoyt 6–1. The next day on September 8 the Athletics swept another dou-bleheader at Boston and vaulted over the Yankees into first place by one half game. Consequently, the stage was set for a crucial four-game show-down between the Yankees and Athletics at Yankee Stadium on Septem-ber 9–12.

While the Yankees seemed to be faltering on the eve of the big series with the Athletics, they also had several things going for them. For one, Babe Ruth at this point in the season had hit 48 home runs and was bat-ting .330. Second, although Lou Gehrig was not hitting home runs at the same pace as the previous year, he was leading the American League in hitting with an average of .376, having just edged by Goose Goslin of Washington (who had led the league most of the season and was currently hitting .374). Third, Waite Hoyt was the leading pitcher in the American League with a won-lost record of 17–4 and winning percentage of .810. Fourth, the Athletics' best pitcher Lefty Grove who was second in the league behind Hoyt with a record of 21–6 and a winning percentage of .778), was on a 14-game winning streak, but seemed to be able to beat every team in the American League but the Yankees.

The first two games of the showdown series with the Athletics were scheduled as a doubleheader to be played on Sunday, September 9, 1928. The closeness of the pennant race had generated massive fan interest in New York and the surrounding area in New Jersey and Connecticut. As a result, a record crowd of 85,265 on hand for the twin bill was the most ever at that point in time to witness a major league game. George Pipgras pitched the first game for the Yankees and shut out the Athletics 5–0 on a nine-hitter.

In the second game Al Simmons gave the Athletics a 2–0 lead in the sixth when he hit a home run with Mickey Cochrane on base. The Mackmen added another run in the seventh to take a 3–0 lead. Rube Walberg, the Philadelphia pitcher, had been breezing along through the first six innings. Then, in the bottom of the seventh, the Yankees came to life and scored two runs. With the bases loaded Walberg walked in the tying run to make the score 3–3. At that point Connie Mack summoned Eddie Rommel from the bullpen and he extinguished the Yankee rally. However, in the eighth the Yankees smothered Rommell. Mark Koenig singled, Lou Gehrig followed with a double and Babe Ruth was given an intentional pass to load the bases. That brought Bob Meusel to plate, who took Rommell to a full count and then slammed the ball into the left-field stands for a grand-slam home run to give the Yankees a 7–3 lead. After using two pitchers in the game, Miller Huggins took no chances with the heavy-hit-

ting Athletics lineup in the ninth and sent his leading pitcher, Waite Hoyt, out to mound. It was Hoyt's 29th birthday; he celebrated it by quickly shutting down the Athletics and with a sweep of the double-header the Yankees were back in first place by 1½ games. Nonetheless, however victorious the day had been for Hoyt and the Yankees, it was also a bittersweet one as they learned that earlier teammate Urban Shocker, who had suffered with a serious illness since March, had died at the age of 38 in Denver, Colorado.

In game three of the series Connie Mack sent his ace, Lefty Grove, to the mound to face the Yankees, but in the end it was Waterloo for Grove as he saw his 14-game winning streak come to an end in a 5–3 loss. The Athletics actu-

Bob Meusel (National Baseball Hall of Fame Library, Cooperstown, N.Y.).

ally staked Grove to an early lead, scoring three runs off Yankees starter Hank Johnson. However, with the Athletics leading 3–1 in the eighth, Grove uncorked a wild pitch, allowing Earle Combs to race home and make the score 3–2. Then, with Mark Koenig and Lou Gehrig on base, Babe Ruth belted his 49th home run of the season to deliver the coup de grace to the Athletics' pennant hopes. The win increased the Yankees' hold on first place by 2½ games.

In the fourth game of the series, which happened to be the final game of the regular season at Yankee Stadium, 40,388 fans attended to bring the total attendance for the big series to 177,113. Connie Mack chose Howard Ehmke to start for the Athletics and Miller Huggins sent Waite Hoyt to the mound. In the eighth inning, with Yankees trailing 3–2 and the bases loaded, Ehmke wrenched his knee pitching to Tony Lazzeri. Connie Mack quickly called for Ossie Orwoll out of the bullpen to replace Ehmke and he walked Lazzeri, forcing in the tying run. With the score 3–3 Hoyt went to the mound in the ninth and without delay got the first two outs. Now he was facing Max Bishop, who took the count to 2–2, then drove the next pitch from Hoyt over Ruth's head right into the stands for a home run. In the bottom half of the ninth, Mack sent Rube Walberg to the mound, and he closed the Yankees down to secure the 4–3 win and reduce their lead to 1½ games. Now both teams were heading on a final western road trip to close out a season that had seen the Yankees play 15 games and the Athletics 13. The Athletics fought hard down the stretch but the Yankees never looked back.

Coming down the stretch, Waite Hoyt was still attempting to win those 22 games he needed for the $2,500 bonus and he also found himself confronted with another dilemma. Still operating his funeral business in Larchmont in the off season, he had been preparing to take the New York State examination for a license to practice as a journeyman embalmer. In between starts Hoyt would take both his glove and a bound black volume of New York State embalming regulations and questions and seek the seclusion of the bullpen to study for his upcoming exam. The exam was scheduled for September 29 in Buffalo and the Yankees had given him permission to leave the team and participate, provided that they had clinched the pennant by September 28. As things turned out Hoyt never got the chance to take that exam. Had he taken the exam and passed, it is possible that his future following his career in baseball might have taken a very different course and a broadcasting legend might have been lost in a vocational void.

On Saturday, September 28, the second to last day of the season in Detroit, the Yankees clinched the 1928 American League pennant. Back at the hotel Babe Ruth rented four rooms with adjoining doors and the Yankees participated in a wild celebration throughout the night. Waite Hoyt had pitched the first game of the series in Detroit and won. By his count it was his 21st win of the season. Therefore, he still needed another win to get the $2,500 bonus that was promised to him by Col. Ruppert if he won 22 games. Now it was too late to get the train for Buffalo so the embalming exam was off. Hoyt went to Miller Huggins and asked to pitch the last game of the season. Several of his teammates, knowing that he needed an assist for the bonus, went to see Huggins as well. Hoyt had pitched brilliantly down the stretch and his efforts had a lot to do with the fact that the Yankees were able to stave off the ever-menacing Athletics. After considering the matter Huggins said why not and penciled Hoyt in as the starting pitcher for the final game of the season.

The following afternoon one by one the Yankees players began to arrive at the ballpark, mostly hung over. Later, Waite Hoyt remarked, "Nobody was overly interested in baseball when we got to the park the next day. Our catcher had his uniform on backwards."[37] The Yankees then went out and proceeded to play very sloppy ball that day. According to Hoyt, the guys frittered away runs in the early innings. With the game in the late innings and the Yankees down 6–4, Hoyt sat down next to Babe Ruth on the bench and said, "This is costing me $2,500."[38] Ruth grunted and replied, "Why didn't you say so?"[39] The next inning, and with two men on base and with Ruth badly hung over himself and seeing more than one ball coming out of the pitcher's hand, he hit his 54th home run of the season over the left-field wall to give Hoyt a 7–6 win.

There is, however, a couple of postscripts to this infamous incident. First, in telling this story over the ensuing years, Hoyt neglected to mention that he had some help that day from Lou Gehrig too. Gehrig, who was not hung over, hit his 27th home run and finished the season with a .378 batting average, just one point behind the league leader (Goose Goslin of Washington). Also, as Hoyt told and retold the story of that day in ensuing years he never mentioned the fact that the Yankees almost lost Lou Gehrig for the World Series in that final game of the season when in the seventh inning he was struck in the face by a batted ball and collapsed. However, Gehrig recovered and was able to walk off the field without assistance. The loss of Gehrig would have been devastating to the Yankees, who had already been badly crippled by injuries to Dugan and Lazzeri during the season, and now Herb Pennock and Earle Combs.

The second postscript to the incident is a calamity in that, when Hoyt went to the mound in the final game of the season, he already had a season record of 22–7 and the win that day was actually his 23rd. Hoyt stated that he didn't learn that was his 23rd win until he returned to New York. "That taught me a lesson to keep a closer check on statistics, especially wins and losses, because that Sunday game was a real struggle for me as well as the rest of the team," said Hoyt.[40]

No one was using the term *dynasty* yet, but for the third straight year and sixth time in the last eight years the New York Yankees were in the World Series. Their opponents in the 1928 fall classic would be the St. Louis Cardinals, who had opposed them in the 1926 series. The Cardinals had won the National League pennant by two games over John McGraw's New York Giants. The Pittsburgh Pirates had won the pennant the previous year. However, in 1928, despite having the league's best team batting average (.309) and leading the league with 100 triples, the Pirates fell to fourth place finishing nine games behind the Cardinals. The Giants had trailed the Cardinals throughout most of the 1928 campaign, then caught fire in September, winning 25 games to chase them neck and neck down to the wire before St. Louis finally clinched the pennant on September 29.

The 1928 Cardinals were led by first baseman Jim Bottomley, who led the National League in RBIs (136), triples (20) and total bases (.362). Bottomley also hit 31 home runs to tie for the league lead with Hack Wilson of the Chicago Cubs. The pitching staff was anchored by Bill Sherdel (21–10) and Jesse Haines (20–8). Also, they still had the Yankee-killer 41-year-old Grover Cleveland Alexander (16–9), on the team. The Cardinals were now managed by Bill McKechnie, who had managed the Pittsburgh Pirates to a World Championship in 1925.

Former manager Rogers Hornsby, now with the Boston Braves, won the National League batting title in 1928 with an average of .387. Following the 1926 season he had been part of a controversial blockbuster trade that saw the Cardinals and Giants swap second basemen, with Hornsby going to New York for Frank Frisch and pitcher Jimmy Ring. Hornsby had been having troubles with the St. Louis franchise's majority stock owner Sam Breadon. Likewise, Frank Frisch despised playing for Giants manager John McGraw. The trade was of course a shock and widely unpopular with Cardinals fans, but Frisch played hard in St. Louis, hitting .337 in 1927 while leading the league in stolen bases with 48. Then in 1928 he hit .300 and was second in the league in stolen bases with 29. As one writer later stated, Frisch didn't make the St. Louis fans forget Hornsby, but he made them remember Frisch.

Hornsby hit .361 for the Giants in 1927. However after filling in as manager for an ailing John McGraw part of the season, it is widely believed that he fell into disfavor with several Giants players, including Bill Terry, Edd Roush, Travis Jackson and Fred Lindstrom, who allegedly told Giants owner Charles Stoneham they wouldn't play if Hornsby did anymore managing. While this scenario remains as speculation today, it seems that Stoneham sided with his players and Hornsby was traded to Boston for catcher Shanty Hogan and outfielder Jimmy Welsh.

The Yankees were picked as underdogs by the oddsmakers and approached the 1928 World Series with a degree of caution. Despite the fact that they had outlasted the hard-driving Philadelphia Athletics, they were injury plagued going into the series. First big game ace Herb Pennock (17–6) had developed a sore arm. Then lead-off hitter Earle Combs (who had hit .310 and led the league in triples) was out of the series with a broken finger. Also, Babe Ruth was nursing a bad ankle and Tony Lazzeri (who had missed 38 games during the season) had a sore throwing arm. While Tom Zachary, acquired from Washington in late August, was being counted on to make up for some of slack in the Yankees' pitching rotation, Miller Huggins was counting on Waite Hoyt (23–7) and George Pipgras (24–13) to do the majority of the heavy lifting on the mound.

Game one took place October 4 at Yankee Stadium before a crowd of 61,000 plus fans. The starting pitchers were Bill Sherdel for the Cardinals and Waite Hoyt for the Yankees. Hoyt was at his finest in game one as he pitched a three-hitter, defeating the Cardinals 4–1. Pitching a complete game, he struck out six and walked three. In the fourth inning he set down three left-handed Cardinals hitters in a row by striking out Andy High, fouling out Frank Frisch to the catcher and then taking Jim Bottomley on a hot grounder to Gehrig. The only run scored off Hoyt was on a solo home run by Jim Bottomely in the seventh inning into the right-field seats. Bottomley seemed to be the only Cardinal who could figure out Hoyt's pitches, getting two of the three Cardinals hits and also drawing a walk. The first of the Yankee's four runs was scored in the first inning on a pair of doubles by Ruth and Gehrig. Then, in the fourth inning Ruth doubled, and one batter later Bob Meusel drove the ball into the right-field seats to give Hoyt and the Yankees a 3–0 lead. The additional insurance run came in the eighth on singles by Koenig, Ruth and Gehrig.

In game two 60,714 fans showed up at Yankee Stadium as George Pipgras opposed Grover Cleveland Alexander. However, the Yankees apparently solved the mystery of Old Pete as they battered the Red Birds 9–3. The Yankees took a 3–0 lead in the first when Cedric Durst, filling in for the injured Earle Combs, led off with single. Alexander then got Koenig to fly out, but followed with a walk to Babe Ruth on four pitches, bringing up Lou Gehrig — who hit the first pitch deep into the right-center-field bleachers 423 feet from home plate. The Cardinals came back to tie the game at 3–3 in the second, but the Yankees regained the lead 4–3 in the bottom half of the inning. Then, in the third the Yankees finished off Alexander, scoring four more runs to take a 8–3 lead.

The St. Louis Post-Dispatch eulogized Alexander's performance the following day: "In 1926 it was just a breeze for Old Pete, but in 1928 it was a shower. It was tragic the sight of old Alexander knocked out."[41] Clarence Mitchell had replaced Alexander on the mound and held the Yankees until the seventh, when they scored their final run. Although George Pipgras was a little wild, he went the distance, holding the Cardinals to four hits, striking out eight — including Jim Bottomley three times — while issuing four walks.

In the first two games the Cardinals had managed just seven hits and four runs off Hoyt and Pipgras, while striking out 14 times. The St. Louis press was high in its praise of the Yankees hurlers: "Waite Hoyt and George Pipgras have turned in wonderful performances. Hoyt, winner of 44 games and loser in but 14 in his last two major league campaigns, figured to be tough. He was worse than that. He was poison as a three-hit battle attests. And Pipgras, supposed to be inconsistent, was right behind with a four-hit battle. He was inconsistent at the start of his battle, being rather wild. But put out in front for the second time, he came through with a sensational effort."[42]

The Cardinals, however, were complaining about not being able to see fast balls from Hoyt and Pipgras against the backdrop of the fans' white shirts in the center-field bleachers. During the regular season at Yankee Stadium a green canvas had usually been stretched out in the bleachers, allowing the hitters a better vision of the ball. However, with high demand for seats the Yankees ownership stripped away the canvas and sold tickets. One anonymous Cardinals player told the press, "Huggins' pitchers knew what they were doing. They knew about those shirts and moving fans out there. If they pitched in the middle or lower part of the strike zone we were not bothered. But when they pitched high, the ball slipped right out of some bleacher fan's ear and whisked into Bengough's glove. Why, they were pitching letter high to all of us."[43]

White shirts or not, playing on bad legs and not yet having had a home run Babe Ruth was coming close to matching the entire St. Louis offensive output for the first two games, hitting .714 with five hits and four runs scored.

With Herb Pennock out, Miller Huggins handed the ball to left-hander Tom Zachary for game three in St. Louis, with the oddsmakers still calling the Cardinals a remarkable 5–2 choice to win the series. Zachary would be opposed by Jesse Haines, who had who beaten the Yankees twice in the 1926 World Series. While the Cardinals were starting to privately admit that they thought the wounded Yankees might be easy to handle in the series, they were confident that Haines would get them back on track. New York Giants manager John McGraw, no friend of the Yankees, was also confident that the Cardinals would come backs. "In 1921, the Giants lost the first two games of the world series to the Yankees, both being shutouts. The Giants came right back and forced the fight down to the seventh game and won. With Jess Haines opening for the Cardinals in St. Louis, there is an excellent chance of them getting back in the series."[44]

Babe Ruth had a slightly different take on the series so far: "We've got two victories. We'll win the championship as sure as fate. But if we clean up in four games, and I hope we can do it, it will be because we get a lot of breaks along with our good playing. Winning that second game meant a lot more to us than winning the first one. We figured to win that first one and the Cardinals, down in their gizzards, figured us to do it. They were afraid of Hoyt. They figured he might beat them and they weren't down-hearted when he did. But winning that second one was the big thing. That hurt them. To have Alexander knocked out of the box and at the same time to have Pipgras hold them to four scattered hits was a blow that they won't get over for a long time."[45]

In game three Jesse Haines held the Yankees scoreless in the first inning for the first time in the series. The Cardinals, on the other hand, jumped on Tom Zachary for two runs. However, Lou Gehrig got one of the runs back in the second with a tremendous home run off Haines that landed on the roof of the right-field pavilion. Then, in the fourth with a runner on base, Gehrig sent a line drive past diving St. Louis center fielder Taylor Douthit and raced around the bases for a two-run inside-the-park home run to give the Yankees 3–2 lead. The Cardinals scored a run in the fifth to tie the game at 3–3 when Zachary hit Douthit with a pitch and then scored on a double by Andy High. However, the turning point in the game came in the sixth as the Yankees came back and scored three unearned runs. Two of the runs came as a result of errors by Cardinals catcher Jim Wilson. With one out in the sixth, Babe Ruth on second and Lou Gehrig on first, Bob Meusel hit a slow roller to third baseman Andy High, who threw to Frisch at second to force Gehrig. Frisch, then attempting to double up Meusel, threw wide to Bottomley at first. Ruth, noticing the wide throw, broke for the plate as Bottomley threw a bullet to the plate. However, Ruth crashed into Wilson like a pile driver, knocking the ball out of his hand, and was safe. Wilson, knocked flat by the 225-pound Ruth, got up and quickly made a throw to second in an attempt to get Meusel, who had rounded first and was heading for second. However, there was no one at second to take Wilson's throw and the ball shot into center field as

Meusel sprinted around second and into third. Then Bob Meusel and Tony Lazzeri pulled off a double steal with Meusel scoring. Finally, Gene Robertson singled, scoring Lazzeri with the third run of the inning. The Yankees added another run in the seventh to make the score 7–3 and give the New Yorkers a 3–0 advantage in the series. While Tom Zachary pitched a complete game to notch the win and was nearly always ahead of the Cardinals hitters in the count, he worked hard, throwing 134 pitches.

Following the game the Yankees were jubilant in the clubhouse with Tony Lazzeri again predicting a series sweep. The Cardinals, however, were furious. "They didn't beat us. We beat ourselves,"[46] said manager Bill McKechnie. Jim Wilson had a few comments too. "I want to have the ball in my duke, and be ready for Mr. Ruth if he gets a chance to come tearing into the plate tomorrow."[47]

Miller Huggins was humble in victory and was deeply contemplating who would be his starting pitcher in game four. He knew that Waite Hoyt could wrap up the series. However, with the Cardinals hitting a weak .167 for the first three games, he was curious as to what young Henry Johnson could do under World Series conditions. The 22-year-old Johnson had been the Yankees' fourth leading hurler in 1928, posting a record of 14–9. His fast ball was as good as that of Hoyt and Pipgras and he had pitched some important games for Huggins during the season. Also, starting Johnson would give Hoyt an extra day of rest. "I'm not sure what I will do," said Huggins.[48] "I may start Hoyt and I may start Henry Johnson. Henry is a young fellow and I would like to see him get the experience of world series pitching and he is the sort of fellow who if he is right would give the Cardinals all sort of troubles. Hoyt is ready to pitch too, and anxious to wind things up. And if I go with Hoyt I am sure he can win, but as yet I am undecided and I may not make up my mind definitely until the boys warm up before the game."[49]

Bill McKechnie, however, with his back to the wall had only one choice in a starting pitcher; he would have to go with his ace Bill Sherdel. But soon it started to rain in St. Louis and by the next morning the outfield at Sportsman's Park was soaked and muddy in places. At about 10:00 A.M. Cardinals owner Sam Breadon called baseball commissioner Landis at the Hotel Jefferson and informed him of the circumstances. Landis immediately called the game off. When play was resumed on October 9, Miller Huggins abandoned his experiment with Johnson and instead sent him out to pitch batting practice, then sent Waite Hoyt to the mound in game four.

With a total attendance of 37,331 on hand at Sportsman's Park, Hoyt pitched a complete game, beating the Cardinals 7–3. However, as had happened so many times before, he was upstaged by his famous teammate, Babe Ruth, as the Bambino swatted three home runs in the game. The game started out with Sherdel and Hoyt each holding the other's offense scoreless for the first two innings. In the first inning Hoyt started the game by striking out Ernie Orsatti. The next batter, Andy High, then hit a high fly to right that went for a double when Ruth lost it in the sun. Hoyt then struck out Frisch for the second out. After walking Bottomley, Chick Hafey hit a little tapper back to the mound and Hoyt was out of the inning unscathed. However, in the Cardinals half of the third Hoyt was touched for a run. Ernie Orsatti, playing instead of Taylor Douthit as Bill McKechnie loaded up his lineup with seven left-hand hitters against Hoyt, doubled to center. He went to third on a safe bunt by High and then scored on a sacrifice fly by Frank Frisch. Nonetheless, Hoyt was pacing himself, taking plenty of time between pitches, and seemed to be in no hurry.

The Yankees tied the score at 1–1 in the fourth as Babe Ruth led off with a home run over the right-field pavilion. The Cardinals took back the lead 2–1 in their half of the fourth, aided by two Yankee errors. Earl Smith led off against Hoyt with a single. Rabbit Maranville then forced Smith. However, after he stepped on the bag, Lazzeri's throw to first was wide and the alert 36-year-old Maranville scampered down to second. Bill Sherdel flied to Paschal in center field and Maranville took second. Moments later Maranville scored as Hoyt threw wild attempting to pick him off at second. The Cardinals maintained their 2–1 lead as Sherdel got out of jams in the fifth and sixth.

In the seventh, "five o'clock lightning" struck early. Mark Koenig led off and popped up to Maranville. Babe Ruth then hit the ball over the right-field pavilion for the second time in the game to tie the score at 2–2. However, Ruth's home run was not without controversy. Sherdel had two strikes on Ruth when Ruth momentarily turned his head to chat with Cardinal catcher Earl Smith. Sherdel delivered the ball without a windup for strike three. While quick pitches were legal in the National League, they were ruled out by Commissioner Landis in World Series play. Subsequently, Ruth protested to home-plate umpire Cy Pfirman and it was ruled no pitch. Sherdel was outraged and stormed off the mound to protest. With the crowd booing and littering the field, Bill McKechnie charged out of the dugout to join the dispute. Miller Huggins also came out to take care of business and make sure that the umpire stood by his call. Ruth kept out of the argument. Eventually peace was restored and the call stood. Ruth and Sherdel exchanged a few words, the next pitch was delivered and Ruth hit it out of the park.

Lou Gehrig followed with another blast that landed on the roof of the

1928 New York Yankees (National Baseball Hall of Fame Library, Cooperstown, N.Y.).

pavilion to give the Yankees the lead at 3–2. After Bob Meusel singled off Sherdel, he was replaced on the mound by Grover Cleveland Alexander. Tony Lazzeri hit a long fly ball to center that was dropped by Orsatti. Meusel sprinted around second and took third on the error. Miller Huggins, smelling victory, sent Gene Robertson up to hit for the ailing and slumping Joe Dugan. Robertson hit the ball to Frisch at second and Meusel took off from third and beat the throw to the plate to give the Yankees a 4–2 lead. Earle Combs then batted for Bennie Bengough and hit a sacrifice fly, scoring Lazzeri to increase the lead to 5–2. The inning ended as Waite Hoyt bounced out to Alexander. As Babe Ruth trotted out to assume his position in left field following the Yankees half of the seventh, the fans in the bleachers booed him loudly and some even tossed a few soda bottles onto the field. Ruth simply pointed to the right-field wall where his home runs had passed over.

In the eighth the Yankees added a couple of insurance runs on back-to-back home runs off Grover Cleveland Alexander. Cedric Durst led off with a home run into the right-field pavilion to make the score 6–2 Yankees. Babe Ruth then followed with his third home run of the game — a shot that also landed in the right-field pavilion to make the score 7–2.

Hoyt then held the Cardinals scoreless in the eighth and Alexander did likewise to the Yankees in the top of the ninth. The Cardinals opened the bottom of ninth with Earl Smith touching Hoyt for a single to right field. Pepper Martin was sent in to run for Smith and stole second without Hoyt paying any attention to him. Maranville then popped up to Koenig for the first out. Wattie Holm pinch hit for Alexander and grounded out Koenig to Gehrig. However, Martin scored on the play, once again taking bases without any concern from the Yankees, to make the score 7–3. Orsatti followed with a single and High did the same. Then Frisch flied to Ruth along the left-field foul line to end the game. Ruth grabbed the ball with his glove hand and ran into the dugout waving it high above him.

Sam Breadon, the Cardinals owner, was so outraged by the Yankees sweep of the series that he demoted Bill McKechnie to manager of the AAA farm club in the International League at Rochester, replacing him with Billy Southworth. On the other hand, the New York Yankees for the second year in a row were World Champions. The Yankees had now won eight straight world series games. The train ride back to New York was a wild affair and the celebration lasted all night long.

Waite Hoyt gave a magnificent performance in the series, winning two games and losing none; he pitched 18 innings, allowing 14 hits, struck out 14, walked 6 and led all pitchers in the series with an ERA of 1.50. Nonetheless, the headlines went to Ruth and Gehrig. Babe Ruth had set a new World Series record, hitting .625 with 10 hits in 16 at bats and also hit three home runs. Ruth's .625 batting mark still stands to this very day as the highest ever in World Series competition. Lou Gehrig had hit .545 with six hits in 11 at bats. Also, Gehrig had set a new World Series record of nine RBIs and tied Ruth's record of four home runs in a series.

While the New York Yankees had now played in three straight World Series for the second time in the decade of the 1920s, time and fortune were about to run out for Murderers' Row. The Philadelphia Athletics had been making loud footsteps that the Yankees could hear behind them and suddenly they seemed to be getting closer. By 1929 Connie Mack's second dynasty was about to begin, with Jimmie Foxx, Al Simmons, Mickey Cochran, Lefty Grove, Rube Walberg and George Earnshaw coming of age. For the next three years the Athletics would reign supreme as American League champions.

6

Good-bye, Walter

Back at Yankee Stadium a few days after winning the 1928 World Series the players cleaned out their lockers, said their good-byes and went their separate ways for the winter. Waite Hoyt pocketed his most recent World Series winner's share of $5,531.91 and began to prepare for a brisk winter of activity. In late September, with the pennant on the line, he had been gunning for his 22nd win of the season in order to achieve the $2,500 bonus from Jacob Ruppert. While Hoyt had missed the New York State embalmers exam in Buffalo, he and his partner were still running their funeral parlor up in Westchester County and now he had made a decision to cash in on his World Series notoriety by returning to vaudeville during the off-season for a full slate of performances.

In early November Hoyt made his debut at Proctor's Eighty-Sixth Street Theatre in a three-a-day, split-week performance singing in his fine baritone voice, accompanied on the piano by songwriter J. Fred Coots ("Sally, Irene and Mary," "Gay Paree," "Love Letters In The Sand," "Artists and Models," etc). On Sunday, November 18, he and Coots moved on to the Prospect Theatre for a four-day engagement the pair titled "A Battery of Fun." In his performance Hoyt would often make comedic references to his funeral business: "[Here I am] knocking 'em dead on Seventh Avenue, while my partner is laying 'em out up in Westchester."[1] Also while doing his Shtick, Hoyt would also take pot shots at baseball. "Wives of ballplayers, when they teach their children to pray, should instruct them to say: "God bless mommy, God bless daddy, God bless Babe Ruth! Babe has upped daddy's pay check by 15 to 40 percent !"[2] A typical review of the Hoyt and Coots act of the time described it as "Ball Player and Song Writer offer mildly diverting entertainment." It was during this period that Hoyt officially received his second nickname, The Merry Mortician, courtesy of a New York City newspaper reporter by the name of John Kieran. Later that year Hoyt shared the bill with a young upcoming comedian by the name of Jimmy Durante.

On April 16, 1929 the Yankees opened the season with numbers on their uniforms, the first major league team to do so. There were other changes too. Over the winter Joe Dugan had been sold to the Boston Red Sox on waivers and Gene Robertson would start the season at third. Mark Koenig was replaced as the starting shortstop by the good fielding but light-hitting Leo Durocher, and Bill Dickey was now the starting catcher. While Bob Meusel was visibly coming to an end in his career, hitting just .261 with 10 home runs, several of the Yankees would have outstanding seasons in 1929. Babe Ruth hit .345, led the American League in home runs again with 46, and had 154 RBIs. Lou Gehrig finished second behind Ruth with 35 home runs. Tony Lazzeri hit .354, Earle Combs .345 and Bill Dickey .324. But it would not be enough to overcome the Philadelphia Athletics, who outdistanced the second-place Yankees by 18 games in winning their first pennant since 1914.

On the mound the Yankees had some problems. Tom Zachary was 12–0 and had an ERA of 2.48, while George Pipgras led the Yankee hurlers with a season record of 18–12 and had a 4.23 ERA. However, two others who had won a combined total of 40 games in 1928 won only 19 in 1929. Herb Pennock had a sore arm and finished the season at 9–11 with an ERA of 4.90 and Waite Hoyt, who just a year ago had been the kingpin of the Yankees staff, was out sick for five weeks and also had a sub-par season, finishing 10–9 with an ERA of 4.24. Hoyt's season had actually started out rather well. On May 9 he beat the St. Louis Browns, throwing a five-hitter for his fourth win in five tries, with no defeats. However, for the balance of the season he went 6–9.

During the season Miller Huggins had developed erysipelas, an acute disease of the skin and subcutaneous tissue caused by streptococcus, and was ailing constantly. In mid–September at Yankee Stadium Hoyt was pitching against Cleveland, when in the fifth inning Huggins suddenly left the bench and went to the clubhouse. About the same time Joe Hauser, the Indians reserve first baseman, hit a home run off Hoyt, knocking him out of the game. Hoyt stormed from the mound into the clubhouse and angrily threw his glove at his locker. Huggins was lying on the training table in agonizing pain, with a wet towel pressed against the growth on his cheek. He looked up and said to Hoyt, "What happened?"[3]

"Hauser hit a long one and here I am," said Hoyt.[4] "I pitched where I always pitch to him — high outside — but he hit this one."[5]

Huggins was silent for a moment then said, "How old are you?"[6]

"I was 30 this month," replied Hoyt.[7]

Huggins nodded his head, then said, "Well, I'll tell you this. You're getting older. After 30, you can't do what you did when you were 25 and 26. You can't come back as fast. You've got to take better care of your condition. The season is over for you now. We've got two weeks to go. Go down and get your check — go home. I'll see you next spring — but stay in shape this winter. That's my advice to you."[8]

That was the last time Hoyt ever saw Huggins alive. Later that afternoon Huggins entered the hospital and died on September 25. Hoyt always maintained that the conversation that Huggins had with him in the locker room that day was the last he had with any of his players.

When the news of Huggins' death reached the Yankees they were playing in Boston. After the fifth inning players from both teams gathered at home plate and observed a minute of silence in tribute to Huggins. Following the game the tears flowed freely in the Yankees clubhouse. Waite Hoyt had lost his best friend in baseball and was one of the most visibly shaken people that attended Huggins funeral. Following funeral services in New York, Huggins' body was taken by Herb Pennock and Yankees coach Charlie O'Leary to his hometown in Cincinnati and buried at Spring Grove Cemetery.

Years later in an interview, Hoyt would state that Huggins was more like a father than a manager to his players. "Nice pitching,' or 'Good going,' generally was the extent of his compliment to one of his players after a good day. Yet he always had our best interest at heart. I can still hear him telling us before the stock market crash in 1929 to 'get out of the market right now while you can still get your money back with a profit because it's going too high — and something is going to happen.' As usual Hug was right, although I never did know how many players followed his advice."[9]

That winter Hoyt was back on the vaudeville circuit. A woman by the name of Selma Waldman had been part of his act from November 13, 1929, to January 10, 1930. Ten months later in November 1930 Miss Waldman filed suit in Central Municipal Court in New York for breach of contract against Hoyt and Harry Romm, who arranged the bookings for the act. Miss Waldman contended that she had a verbal agreement with Hoyt to pay her a $100 a week until March 5. While Hoyt denied that there was any such agreement, Justice Kunstler reserved decision on a motion to set aside the verdict and Hoyt was ordered to pay Miss Waldman $800 in damages.

With the death of Miller Huggins, Bob Shawkey — who had pitched for the Yankees from 1915–1927 — was named the new manager. Shawkey had been one of Waite Hoyt's first roommates in New York. As the 1930 season approached, Hoyt sensed that with Huggins gone, his days with the Yankees were numbered. Also, Hoyt seemed to be focusing more on his personal appearance than his conditioning for the forthcoming campaign. Hoyt had been known in the past to break camp to get haircuts and in late March he got two haircuts in two days. Before the Yankees left St. Petersburg on March 28, he got a haircut. However, he quickly decided he didn't like it and when the train pulled into Jacksonville, he headed immediately for the nearest tonsorial parlor to get another. It was seemingly little insignificant things like this that Bob Shawkey noticed and he began to wonder if Hoyt was really focusing on pitching.

When the season began the Yankees seemed to be going nowhere. The players had become accustomed to playing for Miller Huggins; they were losing and morale on the team was waning. It seemed like 1925 all over again. The Washington Nationals were now being managed by Walter Johnson; they came charging out of the pack and quickly took the American League lead with the Philadelphia Athletics nipping at their heels. While the Yankees were getting some great run production out of Babe Ruth, Lou Gehrig, Earle Combs and Bill Dickey, their pitching was always on the verge of collapse and by the end of the season the Yankees hurlers would rack up a team ERA of 4.88 — the second highest in the American League.

A tense relationship between Shawkey and Hoyt had been simmering since spring training, but in mid–May it boiled over. Hoyt was pitching against the Philadelphia Athletics when Al Simmons took him downtown with a powerful upper-deck home run. When Hoyt got out of the inning and came into the dugout Shawkey approached him and asked what pitch Simmons had hit. "A fast ball," said Hoyt.[10]

Shawkey then quickly snapped at Hoyt, "Well, don't do that again. After this make him hit your curve ball."[11]

"If I ever threw him the curve ball,"[12] said Hoyt, "he'd hit it over the stand. Don't tell me how to pitch to Simmons. I'll go on pitching to him my own way."[13]

"You'll pitch the way I tell you to, or you won't pitch for me at all," replied Shawkey.[14]

Whether or not Hoyt had reneged on his personal St. Petersburg accord of 1927 is not known. A few days later a reporter asked Hoyt what was wrong with the Yankees. His immediate response was, "The trouble with this club is that there are too many guys on it who aren't Yankees."[15] While he was referring to the lackluster play of the club, it was a statement that left a bad taste in Bob Shawkey's mouth. Two weeks later — on Memorial Day, May 30, 1930 — with the Yankees in third place behind Washington and Philadelphia, Hoyt was traded along with Mark Koenig to the Detroit Tigers. The Yankees received three players in the deal: pitcher Ownie Carroll, infielder Yats Wuestling and outfielder Harry Rice. Rice replaced Bob Meusel who had been sold on waivers to Cincinnati following the 1929 season, in the Yankees outfield. In 1930 Rice would play 100 games for the Yankees and hit .298. The 1930 season was to be the last for Wuestling in his two-year big league career; he would play in 25 games for the Yankees and hit .190. Carroll would pitch in 10 games for the Yankees, going 0–1, before being sold to Cincinnati later in the season on September 13. He would wind up his nine-year big league career in 1935 with Brooklyn.

In 1948, looking back on the day he was traded, Hoyt stated, "It was tough leaving the team on which I had enjoyed so many happy years. Intuition told me the best had passed. Common sense told me that with Ruth facing me, instead of backing me, things were going to be mighty different. A reporter once asked me to what I owed my pitching success. I had a ready reply: playing with Babe Ruth on my side."[16]

The following day, after being traded to Detroit, Hoyt and Koenig arrived at the Yankees clubhouse to gather up their things and say goodbye to everyone. As Hoyt worked his way down the row of lockers shaking hands with Lou Gehrig, Tony Lazzeri, Herb Pennock and others, he arrived at what he describes as "Ruth's sanctuary" over near the door. Babe Ruth actually had two lockers, one for his baseball gear and one for his various paraphernalia, souvenirs, mementos, gifts from fans, stacks of letters, drawings of himself made by fans, odd bats, whatever. Seeing Hoyt approaching, Ruth turned around, grasped his hand and said, "Good-bye Walter. Take care of yourself."[17]

It wasn't unusual for Ruth to forget people's names and it made no difference that he had known Hoyt since 1919; that was simply Babe Ruth. In spring training that year at a train station, Tony Lazzeri, seeking a good laugh, had brought pitcher Myles Thomas over to where Ruth was standing and introduced him as a new pitcher. "Hi, Keed," said Ruth.[18] "Glad to have you on the club."[19] The fact of the matter was that Thomas had been on the Yankees pitching staff since 1926.

The first time Hoyt faced his old Yankees teammates pitching for the Detroit Tigers, they quickly knocked him out of the box. He appeared in 26 games for the Tigers in 1930 and finished with a record of 9–8. The Tigers as a ball club finished in fifth place in the American League, 27 games behind the pennant-winning Philadelphia Athletics—who had finally caught up with the Nationals in mid-summer and bolstered by the strong pitching of Lefty Grove (28–5) and George Earshaw (22–13), rolled on to the pennant.

When the season ended, Tigers manager Bucky Harris sat down and had a talk with Hoyt. He was optimistic about next season and told Hoyt that he was counting on him to pitch the Tigers back into the first division in 1931. Then he told Hoyt, just as Miller Huggins had the year before that he was not getting any younger and that he needed to report to spring training in shape. In December Harris ran into Hoyt in Detroit and was amazed at what he saw. Suddenly Hoyt had become very lean. Hoyt told Harris that since the end of the season he had made no vaudeville bookings, had been living on one meal a day and now weighed less then he had for years. Harris was ecstatic and told reporters that with Hoyt in such good shape he didn't see why he couldn't win as many games for the Tigers as he did when he was with the Yankees. In fact, Hoyt told Harris that he felt like he could win as many as 15 games next season. Hearing that, Harris told Hoyt that if he did the Tigers, who were a young ball club, would be in the pennant race. However, the hopes of Harris and the Tigers in 1931 were but a pipe dream as they finished in seventh place, a distant 47 games behind the pennant-winning Philadelphia Athletics. Waite Hoyt saw his weight rebound to over 200 pounds and he pitched in only 16 games with Detroit before being sold to the Philadelphia Athletics on June 30 with a record of 3–8.

In 1931 Connie Mack's Philadelphia Athletics were gunning for their third straight World Championship. The Mackmen started off the season slow, but by the end of June had caught the Washington Nationals and moved into first place. Connie Mack had a formidable pitching staff in Lefty Grove, George Earnshaw and Rube Walberg. Nonetheless, when Mack learned that Hoyt was available from the Tigers, he opened his wallet immediately and brought him to Philadelphia. Joining the Athletics brought Hoyt yet another opportunity to play for a legendary manager in Connie Mack. In Hoyt's opinion, "I played for him in 1931—and during the brief space of one season, I discovered Connie Mack was a person apart from any manager I had ever played for. First of all—and perhaps representative of his character, he calls most of his ball players "Mr." When he gets excited—which is seldom—he drops the formality. I remember the first day I was to pitch for him. It was the afternoon game on the Fourth of July 1931. Most managers would say—'Hoyt, you're workin'.' Or, 'You're the pitcher.' But not Connie. In the most fatherly way, he quietly said, 'Mr. Hoyt, I'd like you to pitch this afternoon.' That 'Mr.' floored me."[20]

Mr. Hoyt made his debut for the Mackmen pitching in the afternoon game of a doubleheader in Philadelphia on July 4, 1931, against the Boston Red Sox. In the morning game, played before 10,000 fans at Shibe Park, the Athletics scored seven runs in the first inning. However, by the end of the second inning the Red Sox had narrowed the gap to 7–4 and Lefty Grove came in to relieve Eddie Rommel, the second Athletics' pitcher. Grove went on to pitch seven innings, strike out 10 batters and notch his 16th win of the season as the Athletics prevailed 9–7. The afternoon game was played before 20,000 fans. Connie Mack had asked Waite Hoyt to give him a good six innings. Hoyt did better than that, pitching a complete game while allowing the Red Sox just eight hits in a 6–2 victory. Besides pitching a fine game, Hoyt also starred at bat, scoring a run while getting a single, and a double and also laying down a perfect sacrifice bunt.

With the Independence Day sweep of the doubleheader from Boston and the sweep of a doubleheader by the Yankees over the Nationals, the Athletics pulled out in front of Washington by four games. Streaks seemed to be an important part of the Athletics strategy for 1931. At various points during the season the Athletics would put together winning streaks of 17 and 13 games. Waite Hoyt would win the first six straight games he pitched for Connie Mack and finish the season with a record of 10–5 for the Ath-

Connie Mack (National Baseball Hall of Fame Library, Cooperstown, N.Y.).

letics. However, his win streak would be eclipsed by Lefty Grove, who would win 16 straight games in route to posting an incredible season record of 31–4 with an ERA of 2.06.

As the season progressed, time and time again Connie Mack surprised Hoyt. Later in the season the Athletics were playing in Washington. Firpo Marberry, the great Senators relief pitcher, had been having a competitive feud with Al Simmons all season long. Every time Simmons came up to hit against Marberry, he knocked him down with a pitch or Simmons would strike out. At this point Simmons was fuming and wanted to punch Marberry in the nose. The Philadelphia players were deeply in support of Simmons. With Marberry on the mound sending one Athletics hitter after another sprawling in the dirt with knock-down pitches, the bench was in a rage and everyone wanted a piece of Marberry. Hoyt later said that around the sixth inning Connie Mack had enough of the emotional estrangement of his players to the score of the game and said, "Now look here gentleman — your actions do not measure up to your baseball standards. Instead of threatening Marberry with your fists — perhaps you could do a little better with your bats. I'd appreciate it, if you'd try to score a run or two."[21] Hearing the edict from the Old Man, as the Athletics players referred to Mack, most of them began to calm down. However, as the Athletics took the field Simmons was boiling mad! He was slow getting to his position in left field, then he kicked his glove in the air and strolled around in the outfield without paying much attention to proper position. As Mack observed this odd behavior he sat up very straight, then turned to the players on the bench and said, "You know gentleman — sometimes Simmons believes he's Ty Cobb."[22]

On August 23 Philadelphia played a doubleheader with St. Louis. In the first game Lefty Grove was going after his 17th consecutive win against the Browns. However, Grove lost the game 1–0 when Jimmy Moore, who was playing in left field, misjudged a routine fly ball hit by Sky Melillo that went for a two-out double scoring a run. Following the game Grove was furious — not over Moore's misjudging the ball, but rather over the fact Al Simmons, the regular Athletics left fielder, had not played. (However, Simmons proved his worth to the club over the long run of the season as he won the 1931 American League batting crown with a .390 average. Finishing behind Simmons was the Yankees' Babe Ruth, who hit .373.) In the second game Waite Hoyt pitched a six-hit shutout beating the Browns 10–0.

On Labor Day, September 7, the Yankees came to Philadelphia to play another one of those morning-afternoon doubleheaders at Shibe Park. In the morning game the Yankees beat the first-place Athletics 15–3. In the afternoon game Waite Hoyt was selected by Connie Mack to oppose his old teammates and Hoyt got a firsthand education of what it is like to face the Yankees when they are hot. For the first six innings Hoyt pitched shutout ball against the Bronx Bombers. Then, in the sixth inning he was roughed up. First he got a re-education on how not to pitch to the Bambino. Hoyt knew that if the Ruth hit the ball to right field, that is where he did the most damage, so his strategy was to pitch him high and outside. However, as Ruth took his stance he was leaning inside toward the plate, so Hoyt thought that he could pitch him inside, handcuff him and pop him up. Hoyt delivered an inside fast ball. Hoyt was to say later, "Behind the right-field wall, in Philadelphia, there's a street. On the far side of the street stand a row of houses, and behind them another row of houses, and still another street. Somewhere along that street they found my carefully planned inside fast ball where the Babe had put it."[23] Circumstances didn't get any better for Hoyt as Lou Gehrig followed with another home run. Then, in the ninth Ruth homered off Hoyt again; it was his 40th of the season and the Yankees won the game 9–4 and swept the doubleheader.

The double beating the Athletics suffered that day didn't matter much, though as they came down the stretch to win their third straight American League pennant, finishing 13½ games in front of the second-place New York Yankees. For the seventh time in the last 11 years, Waite Hoyt was in the World Series.

The Athletics' opponents in the 1931 World Series were the St. Louis Cardinals whom they had beaten in six games for the World Championship the previous fall. The Cardinals, like the Athletics, were virtually the same team that had played the year before, with one notable exception in the St. Louis lineup — hard-playing outfielder Pepper Martin. While Martin had first arrived in the big leagues in 1928, he played in just 13 games in the regular season and appeared in only one game in the 1928 World Series, then returned to play in six games for the Red Birds in the 1930 campaign. So 1931 was Martin's rookie season and he hit .300, playing in 123 games. When the Athletics scouted the Cardinals as a possible World Series opponent in September they focused on Jim Bottomley, Chick Hafey and the pitching staff. Ignoring Pepper Martin in their intelligence exercise turned out to be fatal for the Mackmen. In the World Series The Wild Hoss of the Osage, as Martin was known, ran roughshod over the Athletics, batting .500 with 12 hits, 5 stolen bases and 5 scored runs. Martin's 12 hits tied the World Series record held by Charles Herzog (New York Giants, 1912), Shoeless Joe Jackson (Chicago White Sox, 1919) and Same Rice (Washington Nationals, 1925). However, Herzog and Jackson achieved their 12 hits in eight-game series.

The series began in St. Louis on October 1 with the Athletics' Lefty Grove defeating the Cardinals' Paul Derringer 6–2. In the game Grove scattered 12 hits, three of them to Pepper Martin. In game two the Cardinals evened up the series at 1–1 as Wild Bill Hallahan shut out the Athletics 2–0. Pepper Martin had two hits, two stolen bases and scored both St. Louis runs. Game three, played in Philadelphia, saw the Cardinals win 5–2 as veteran Burleigh Grimes lost a bid for a shutout, yielding two runs to the Athletics in the ninth. With St. Louis in the series lead 2–1, game four saw George Earnshaw shut out the Cardinals 3–0 to even the series up at 2–2.

In game five Connie Mack handed the ball to Waite Hoyt. Hoyt, pitching in his seventh World Series, was touched for a run in the first inning.

Sparky Adams led off with a clean single to left, then limped off the field after making the turn at first and aggravating a previous injury. He was replaced by Andy High. Frank Frisch then singled to center, sending High to third. Pepper Martin was next up and hit a liner to left that was caught by Al Simmons. However, it allowed High to tag up and scamper home, giving the Cardinals a 1–0 lead. In the fourth Hoyt had a close call. Pepper Martin dragged a bunt toward first and beat it out for a single when neither Hoyt or second baseman Mark Bishop covered first. This brought Chick Hafey to the plate. As Hoyt watched the speedy Martin at first closely, he fanned Hafey for the first out. Jim Bottomley was next up and in the hole with a

Waite Hoyt (National Baseball Hall of Fame Library, Cooperstown, N.Y.).

count of 0–2 when he drilled a single to right, sending Martin to third. Hoyt got out of the inning, however, when batter Jimmie Wilson hit the ball on a line to Bishop, who snagged it and quickly doubled up Bottomley before he could get back to first.

While Hoyt held St. Louis to one run through the fifth inning, the Athletics could not score on Cardinal pitcher Wild Bill Hallahan. Hoyt took the mound in the top of sixth still trailing 1–0. However, after Frank Frisch doubled and Hoyt retired the next batter, it brought Pepper Martin to the plate. Martin quickly deposited the ball into the upper deck of the left-field stands for a home run to make the score 3–0. Interestingly, Connie Mack allowed Hoyt to be the lead-off batter in the seventh and he hit a small fly ball to Frisch. Mack then sent up Eric McNair to bat for Bishop and he fouled out to Wilson. Then Jim Moore pinch hit for Mule Haas, who had hit .323 during the regular season, but who was slumping terribly in the series. Moore, facing Hallahan, lined to Watkins. As the seventh began Waite Hoyt was replaced on the mound by Rube Walberg, who held the Cardinals in the seventh and then gave up a run in the eighth on a walk to Watkins and a single by Martin. The Athletics finally scored a run in the bottom of the seventh to make the score 4–1 St. Louis. In the ninth Connie Mack sent Eddie Rommel to the mound and he gave up three singles and the final St. Louis run.

Waite Hoyt was the losing pitcher in the game, giving up seven hits and three runs in six innings. It would be the last World Series appearance for Hoyt in his career. The *Philadelphia Inquirer* summarized Hoyt's appearance in game five as follows: "Waite Hoyt, who boasts a record of six World's Series wins against two defeats [actually three], two scored over the Red Birds in the 1928 series when pitching for the Yanks, proved no enigma for the Streetmen [reference to St. Louis manager Gabby Street]. While they did not hit him to any alarming extent his failure to pitch to and baffle Pepper Martin, with a few other slight lapses from peak efficiency, sent him off the field a beaten man. It was Martin's timely hitting, naturally aided and abetted by some of his pals, which put Hoyt behind from the first inning, and he was never up to par there after."24

The series returned to St. Louis for game six and the Athletics won 8–1 behind the pitching of Lefty Grove to even up the series. However, in the seventh game the Cardinals prevailed, staving off a ninth-inning rally by Philadelphia to win the game 4–2 and the World Championship. It would be the last appearance for the Athletics in a World Series while playing in Philadelphia. The next appearance of the Athletics in the World Series would come 41 years later in 1972 after the franchise had hop-scotched across the country from Philadelphia to Kansas City in 1955 to Oakland in 1968.

The following winter would be a particularly difficult time for Hoyt. It all had started in September while Hoyt was pitching for the Athletics in the heat of the stretch drive in the American League pennant race. His wife, Dorothy Pyle Hoyt, had packed up the kids and left the Hoyt home in Larchmont and moved into an apartment in Garden City, Long Island. Hoyt's difficulties had begun when he took the side of his former team-mate and drinking buddy Jumping Joe Dugan in a marital spat of his own. With Waite and Joe the best of friends, likewise the players' wives had also formed a bond. Mrs. Dugan had recently sued for separation, charging that Joe was irresponsible as a husband, going out often at night and returning home intoxicated. Well, Joe — who was now out of baseball after being dropped by the Detroit Tigers earlier in the season — took counter action by obtaining affidavits from various people alleging that in fact it was Mrs. Dugan who was the irresponsible party in the marriage. Waite Hoyt signed one of the affidavits in support of Dugan and it caused

Dorothy Hoyt to go ballistic! She championed Mrs. Dugan's cause and thought that Waite had been terribly chauvinistic in the matter. Furthermore, having a little experience with a free-spirited husband of her own, she took the kids and moved out, but didn't stop there. She then filed an affidavit on the part of Mrs. Dugan, alleging that in her experiences with Joe Dugan, he was off the wagon on many occasions.

In mid–January Waite and Dorothy began to appear in public together again leading to speculation in the press that a reconciliation might be occurring between the two. In fact, Dorothy did move back into the Hoyt's household in Larchmont, but the bliss was only temporary. The nightlife and Hoyt's carousing was continuing to take a toll on his marriage. Consequently, on April 1, 1932, Waite and Dorothy were divorced in Reno, Nevada. The 10-year marriage ended with Dorothy, a former Flatbush debutante, issuing an allegation of incompatibility and cruelty. Hoyt was ordered to pay $25 a week to support the couple's two children, Harry Pyle (9) and Doris Arlene (7).

As Hoyt's world suddenly began to crumble, on February 8, 1932, Connie Mack came to the conclusion that he could also use a professional divorce from Hoyt and gave him his unconditional release. In part Mack released Hoyt — often referred to in the press as "the plump playboy of the American League" — because he didn't care for his training methods, which included his nights out on the town. Now, the fact of the matter was that Hoyt had resumed his one-meal-a-day diet and was shedding pounds. In early February Hoyt had boarded a train and headed down to Florida, where he was working out with the Athletics. When he got his release, he packed his gear and headed over to the Yankees camp, where as a free agent Yankees manager Joe McCarthy allowed him to work out with the team. On February 28 Hoyt drifted over to Clearwater, where he sought out Brooklyn Dodgers manager Max Carey and the two talked contract. Carey felt that Hoyt was sincere in his comeback effort, and suddenly Hoyt was going home to Brooklyn.

Now, if Waite Hoyt had not been signed by the Brooklyn Dodgers, then one of the oldest baseball jokes about "Daffy Town" might never have been told. This ancient joshing, which takes a poke at the lexicon of the infamous Brooklyn accent, goes as follows: Waite Hoyt is pitching for the Dodgers and is hit by a line drive. *The Brooklyn Eagle* headline proclaims: HOYT HURT! A fellow notices the headline and walks into a bar. He says to the bartender, "Did you see the headline on the *Eagle*?" The bartender says, "No, what did it say?" The fellow says, "Hurt Hoyt!"

Meanwhile, down in Florida, Hoyt's diet was catching on. Hoyt's latest convert was Hack Wilson, the former stout slugger of the Chicago Cubs who was now playing for Brooklyn. Wilson professed that he hit better while on the diet. By the time the season started Hoyt himself had lost 28 pounds on the diet, and with the press printing stories about it, he had received over 1,000 letters from people requesting the regimen. Hoyt stated that he had been given the diet courtesy of former Washington Nationals pitcher Al Schacht.

However by April 28 Hoyt was through with the pursuit of "thindom." The Associated Press reported that Hoyt was going from group to group in a hotel lobby looking for Al Schacht. "Just let me find that guy," said Hoyt.[25] "I want to tell him what I think of that diet of his. It'll be plenty."[26] What had happened was that Hoyt felt the loss of weight (30 pounds) had caused him to lose his effectiveness on the mound. He was trying to gain weight back and couldn't gain a pound: "My stomach's shrunk and so has my appetite. I'm trying to eat steak and things and can't get them down."[27] Something indeed had happened. Hoyt was not effective, appearing in eight games with a record of 1–3. His one victory had come in a relief role over the New York Giants. On June 7, the Dodgers gave Hoyt his unconditional release. His homecoming had been short. But the supreme disappointment of his release came as a result of him receiving the news of being cut by the Dodgers from the clubhouse boy Babe Hamberger.

Two weeks later, on June 23, he was signed by the New York Giants, returning to the team who had originally signed him as The Schoolboy Wonder in 1915. However, John McGraw was not there to greet Hoyt. He had been ill and resigned after 30 years as manager of the Giants, turning over the responsibilities to Bill Terry. For Hoyt the return to the Polo Grounds was far from a triumphant encore and quickly became another rough ride.

Then, on Tuesday, August 9, 1932, Hoyt's world was suddenly shattered. He received the news that his father, Addison W. Hoyt, had died of a heart attack. Ad Hoyt was 60 years old and had been working on assignment in Detroit as an auditor for Swift & Company when he was fatally stricken. The next day his body was brought to Brooklyn for funeral services. On Saturday, August 13, although distraught and grieving, Waite Hoyt took his place in the Giants pitching rotation and started the second game of a doubleheader against the Dodgers. Perhaps—and understandably so—his mind wasn't really in the game as he was tagged for home runs in the first inning by Joe Stripp, Lefty O'Doul and Tony Cuccinello as the Giants went down to defeat 5–4. The following Monday, August 15, Hoyt, along with his mother, ElLuise, and sister, Peggy, buried Addison Hoyt in Brooklyn. Waite Hoyt had not only lost his father, but his mentor, his best friend and inspiration. Throughout the remaining years of his life Hoyt would talk openly about almost every aspect of his existence, but seldom, if ever, did he mention a word in regard to the loss of his father. The pain he experienced in the loss of Ad was just too overwhelming. He finished that dismal season appearing in 18 games for the sixth-place Giants with a record of 5–7. Having no further plans for the 33-year-old Hoyt, on November 29, 1932, the Giants released him.

Hoyt may have been down, but he was not out, and 1933 was destined to be a far better year for him in every regard. It all began on January 21, 1933, when he was signed to a contract by the Pittsburgh Pirates. The Pirates had actually been hoping to sign a left-hander, but when all the deals didn't materialize they went for Hoyt. Pirates manager George Gibson thought that Hoyt might provide some useful experience in the bullpen and as a spot starter on a team loaded with hitters, but with a weak pitching staff. Club president William E. Benswanger told the press, "We have a young pitching staff and we believe that Hoyt will add experience and poise to our twirling department. I believe he still is a good starting pitcher. At least we felt it would be wise to give him a trial and see if he can stage a comeback."[28]

Meanwhile, in New York, Hoyt's old buddy Babe Ruth was in a hot contract dispute with Yankees owner Jacob Ruppert. Ruth was coming off a very good year in 1932 that saw him hit 41 home runs, lead the league in RBIs with 130 and hit for a .341 average. Then, in the 1932 World Series he hit .333 against the Cubs. Now, with the depression in full swing, Ruppert wanted to cut the Babe's salary by $25,000 to $50,000 a year. Ruth was having none of it. A reporter caught up him with in New York and asked the Babe what he thought of the $25,000 cut. Ruth responded, "It's the biggest since the Panama Canal."[29] When the reporter asked him if he was going to sign, Ruth responded, "Not unless they give me ether."[30] The reporter was somewhat perplexed with his response and couldn't comprehend the reference to anesthesia in Babe's remarks. So he asked for a clarification. "Yes, ether my 1932 contract or one with a fair reduction."[31] Babe eventually signed for $52,000, but it was the beginning of the end for him in pinstripes as he hit 22 home runs in the 1933 season — his lowest season total since 1918.

On Friday May 12, 1933, the Pirates were in New York to begin a series with the Giants. That evening, in a very secret ceremony in Montclair, New Jersey, Waite Hoyt was married for the second time. The bride was Ellen Burbank, a prominent lady in the Garden State social circles who had attended the Ogontz School in Philadelphia. The ceremony was held at the home of the bride's parents and Hoyt's teammate Fred Lindstrom attended with him. However, there was no best man and no maid of honor. It was the second marriage for both parties. Hoyt, ever the perfectionist, had been very distraught over the breakup of his first marriage, so as he and Ellen moved into the Schenley Apartments in Pittsburgh to begin their new life together, he vowed that this marriage would succeed. As for the ultimate success of the marriage, that would be a matter for the future.

However, in 1933 Hoyt succeeded on the mound and staged a remarkable comeback. Closing in on 34 years old, Hoyt still commanded respect from opposing teams. In one game during the season Hoyt was pitching against the Chicago Cubs, who had just been swept by the New York Yankees the previous fall in the 1932 World Series. (According to baseball folklore that was the series in which Babe Ruth called his shot, hitting a home run off Cubs pitcher Charlie Root.) Nonetheless, at one point during the game the Chicago bench began to relentlessly heckle Hoyt on the mound. He took it for a while, then when he decided he had had enough, he stepped off the mound walked toward the Chicago dugout, stopped short of going in and said, "If you guys don't shut up, I'll put on my old Yankees uniform and scare you to death."[32] As strange as it may be, the Cubs bench became silent.

On September 12, with the Pirates tied for second place with the Cubs in the National League race 7½ games behind the Giants, Hoyt made one of his occasional starts in the second game of a doubleheader against Brooklyn. In just one hour and 28 minutes he pitched a four-hit, 2–0 shutout. It was the 200th victory in his career and his first victory since July 18, when he had beaten the Cubs in relief. For 16 years in the major leagues Hoyt now had a lifetime record of 200–147. By reaching the 200-wins plateau, it placed him among an elite group of six active pitchers in 1933 that had posted 200 or more career victories: Eppa Rixey (Reds, 266), Burleigh Grimes (Cardinals, 265), Urban "Red" Faber (White Sox, 252), Herb Pennock (Yankees, 236) and Sam Jones (White Sox, 221).

The Pirates finished in second place in 1933, five games behind the New York Giants. Hoyt had a season record of 5–7 with an ERA of 2.86, appearing primarily in relief. The first All-Star game had been played during that summer of 1933 at Comiskey Park in Chicago, with the American League defeating the National League 4–2. (The first home run in the mid-summer classic was hit by — who else — Babe Ruth). Of course Hoyt was on a comeback when the game was initiated and with his best years already behind him, he was not selected to the National League squad.

One footnote of sorts on the 1933 season for Waite Hoyt should be added regarding his unintended contribution to American popular culture. Although at the time it was totally insignificant, Hoyt was to be included in the distribution of the 1933 GOUDEY bubblegum cards set produced by the Goudey Gum Company of Boston. Today collectors have designated the 240-card set that includes 41 Hall of Fame players as the beginning of modern baseball card collecting. The 1933 GOUDEY Big League gum cards were distributed one to a pack of gum and the set is regarded as the prototype of the baseball cards being produced today. (While the 1933 set contained 240 cards, for some reason the manufacturer did not include card #106 Nap Lajoie in the distribution, therefore making the number of cards in the set actually 239. Some collectors were outraged by the omission of the Lajoie card and those who wrote to the manufacturer were sent the card in the mail.) The Waite Hoyt card is #60 in the set and regularly sells on such outlets as eBay for $10–$75, depending on the condition of the card. Other players in the set include Dizzy Dean, Carl Hubbell, and Rogers Hornsby. The Babe Ruth cards include four different poses. Lou Gehrig has two cards in the set. An entire set of the 1933 GOUDEY cards in extra-mint condition (without card #106) can fetch upwards of $20,000–$30,000.

In the 1934 season Hoyt showed baseball that there was still a lot of life left in his right arm as he had his best year since 1928. Midway through the season George Gibson was fired as manager of the Pirates and replaced by Pie Traynor. One of the first things that Traynor did was move Hoyt out of the bullpen and into the starting rotation. In his first start against the Cubs he was knocked out of the box. Then, in his next start he lost to the Giants, but pitched well. Pie Traynor was still confident in Hoyt. He kept him in the starting rotation and in his next start on July 15 — in the first game of a doubleheader against the Braves — he responded by pitching a one-hit shutout, beating Boston 5–0. The only hit off Hoyt was a single by Tommy Thompson in the third inning. *The Boston Globe* described Hoyt as "practically unhittable." Facing 30 hitters in the game Hoyt only allowed one man to reach second base, while walking three and striking out seven. At this point his season record was 5–3.

Thirteen days later on July 28, Hoyt beat the St. Louis Cardinals 5–4, stopping Dizzy Dean's consecutive win streak at 10. Hoyt actually got off to a rocky start when in the first inning he gave up a triple to St. Louis lead-off hitter Burgess Whitehead, who later scored on a sacrifice fly by Frank Frisch. Then, after Joe Medwick reached first on an error by Cookie Lavagetto, Ripper Collins homered to give the Cards a 3–0 lead. However, the Pirates battled back against Dizzy Dean, scoring a run in the first, then adding two more in the third to tie the game at 3–3 (on a single by Lloyd "Little Poison" Waner and a home run by Paul "Big Poison" Waner). In the sixth the Pirates took the lead 4–3 when Earl Grace took Dean deep, hitting a home run into the upper deck of the right-field pavilion. Meanwhile, Hoyt shut down the Cardinals from the second through the sixth. In the seventh the Cardinals scored a run off him to once again knot the game at 4–4. However, in the bottom of the seventh the Pirates regained the lead and then Hoyt cruised the rest of the way for the 5–4 victory.

In late August Hoyt pitched another shutout against Boston. He finished the 1934 season with a record of 15–6 with an ERA of 2.93. His .714 winning percentage was the second best in the National League to that of Dizzy Dean, who finished with a record of 30–7 and a winning percentage of .811. In New York, Detroit, Philadelphia, etc., Hoyt had thrown a fast, curve and palm ball. When he joined the Pirates he added a slider to his pitching repertoire, which undoubtedly aided his comeback.

Another important factor in Hoyt's comeback was the domestic bliss that he had found with Ellen at his side. Hoyt saw Ellen as a source of inspiration, and she had traveled regularly with him on road trips during the 1934 season. In the off-season he gave up the bright lights of the Palace stage and sold out his interest in the funeral home business in Westchester County, New York. Baseball was now his full-time job. In September 1934 Hoyt, a well-known man about town, proudly boasted that he had not had a drink in 20 months. Waite Hoyt was now a homebody. So dramatic was the change in Hoyt that it prompted newspaper writer C. William Duncan to write in his column, "I see a different Hoyt when the Pirates come to town. Waite now talks and thinks baseball. His one burning ambition is to enter another World Series and win two more games. He seldom goes out at night and if he does, is accompanied by Mrs. Hoyt."[33] The pinnacle of Hoyt's sudden new lifestyle, however, occurred during the

Waite Hoyt (National Baseball Hall of Fame Library, Cooperstown, N.Y.).

winter when he and his new bride headed to Bermuda and Waite took up playing polo to stay in shape.

As the 1935 season opened it was apparent that the Pirates were going nowhere in the pennant race. Yet on Saturday, May 25, at Forbes Field they would play host to the last hurrah of the great Babe Ruth. Ruth, now 40 years old, was at the end of his storied playing career and harbored a strong ambition to manage. With Joe McCarthy solidly entrenched as the Yankees field general, it frustrated Ruth and caused tension between the two. Often he second-guessed McCarthy and quarreled with him as he had done in earlier years with Miller Huggins. It was at that point in time that Ed Barrow, still serving as the Yankees general manager, issued his famous edict in regard to Ruth's managerial ambitions: "If he can't manage himself, how can he manage twenty-five players?"[34] In the 1934 season, the 39-year-old Ruth had played in 125 games and hit .288, with 22 home runs and 84 RBIs, while packing stadiums all over the American League. However, in February 1935 the New York Yankees—the team that Ruth had established and whose stadium bore the moniker "The House That Ruth Built"—handed him his unconditional release.

Up in Boston, Judge Emil Fuchs, the owner of the Boston Braves, offered to help out in the matter and made an offer to Ruth to become the assistant manager and vice president of the Braves, with the stated intent to move him into the managerial role at some point during the season. In reality Judge Fuchs had no intention of appointing Ruth as manager of the Braves, then or at any time in the future, and was simply attempting to milk whatever escalated attendance figures he could by exploiting Ruth's fame.

By 1935 Ruth was really packing on the pounds and his abilities were in sharp decline. Waite Hoyt later said of Ruth at the time, "Babe was a sorry spectacle that season. His eyes were bad—his legs tottering—and his bay window took on extended proportions. Babe was about as comfortable with the second division Braves as a seal in the desert."[35] Nonetheless, Ruth started the season playing for the Braves, but quickly became totally disenchanted with his role with the club and with his relationship with Fuchs. On May 12, Ruth announced to Fuchs that he no longer wanted to be an active player and asked to be put on the voluntarily retired list. However, at the time the Braves were about to make their first western road trip of the season and Fuchs informed Ruth that ball clubs in St. Louis, Chicago, Pittsburgh and Cincinnati had sold huge numbers of tickets in anticipation of his appearance with the Braves. In fact, in Cincinnati a Babe Ruth Day had been planned to honor The Sultan of Swat. Reluctantly Babe agreed to make the trek west.

As the road trip began in St. Louis the Braves were in last place in the National League and Ruth was hitting a paltry .155. He was complaining about a cold causing his eyes to water, making it difficult to see the ball coming out of the pitcher's hand. When the Braves rolled into Chicago he showed some resemblance to the Ruth of old, hitting a home run (his third of the season) and playing well in the outfield. Playing for the Cubs at first base during that series at Wrigley Field was a young Phil Cavarretta. By virtue of Ruth agreeing to make the road trip with the Braves, Cavarretta thus became the only player in major league baseball history to have played against both Babe Ruth and Henry Aaron in his career.

When the Braves arrived in Pittsburgh, Ruth told the press that he intended to play in at least 100 games this season. "My logs are OK now," said Ruth.[36] "I have no thoughts of quitting. Reports that I will hang up my playing glove after this western trip are all wrong and you can say for me that I am feeling better now than I have been the past four years."[37] The Pirates pitchers were all career National Leaguers, with the exception of Waite Hoyt, and clueless as to how to pitch to Ruth, despite the fact that he wasn't even hitting his weight. Hoyt of course found this all to be very amusing. Nonetheless, Pie Traynor held a clubhouse meeting on the matter and Hoyt told the Pirates pitching staff, "The best way to pitch to Ruth is to pitch behind him. He has no weaknesses except deliberate walks. You have your choice — one base on four balls, or four bases on one ball."[38] This analysis of the Big Bams capabilities didn't set well with the other members of the Pirates pitching corps. Guy Bush, who had been with the Chicago Cubs and faced Ruth in the 1932 World Series, remarked, "I pitched against him in the '32 series. I got him out throwing sinkers."[39] "So did Charlie Root,"[40] said Hoyt. "Charlie Root threw the Babe a sinker that the Babe dropped into the center field bleachers."[41] Hoyt stated some years later that as he left that meeting, for the first time in his life he didn't really care if the other team won or not. He just wanted to see Babe hit one.

In the first game of the series in Pittsburgh, on Thursday, May 23, with just 10,000 fans on hand, Babe Ruth made his first appearance in Forbes Field since the 1927 World Series. The Pirates beat the Braves 7–1. Bill Swift was the Pirates pitcher and throwing sinkers to Ruth seemed to work as he went hitless in the game. However, in the sixth inning Ruth was robbed of a home run when Paul Waner made a great catch by leaping high against the wall and making a one-handed catch.

That night the Pirates held a huge testimonial dinner at a Pittsburgh hotel to honor Rabbit Maranville. The retiring Maranville, playing in the last year of his 23-year big league career with the Braves, had played for the Pirates in the years 1921–1924. Following the dinner, Ruth, along with Maranville and a few others, went out on the town and didn't stop partying until the sun came up. Regardless, Babe played on Friday and had one hit in four at bats.

On Saturday, May 25, a crowd of only about 10,000 showed up for the game at Forbes Field. Red Lucas was the starting pitcher for the Pirates. In the first inning the crowd gave the Babe a huge standing ovation as he came to bat with a runner on base. He acknowledged their respect by taking a few pitches, then driving the ball into the right-field seats for a two-run home run. On the bench, Hoyt began to razz the other Pirates pitchers, telling them they should have listened to him. When Ruth came up in the third inning Lucas was already taking a shower, so he faced Guy Bush on the mound. Bush stood firm on his strategy and threw Ruth a sinker. Ruth hit the ball into the extreme corner of the right-field pavilion for his second home run of the game, giving the Braves a 4–0 lead that they would not be able to hold.

When Ruth again faced Bush in the fifth inning with Les Mallon on second base, the Pirates pulled shortstop Arky Vaughan directly back of second base to play. Ruth then deliberately stroked a single into left field, driving home a run. Later in the inning, Ruth on his suspect legs put on a burst of speed and sprinted around second, then made a hook slide into third past Tom Thevenow that was cause for a rhubarb when he was called safe by umpire Charlie Moran. Guy Bush was still on the mound in the seventh inning when Ruth came to bat for the fourth time in the game. This time Arky Vaughan played at his usual position at shortstop. Bush got behind Ruth with a 3–0 count, then whipped a fast strike by him. Then, on the next pitch Ruth connected again, sending the ball over the top of the right-field pavilion for his third home run in the game. It was the first home run ever hit over the right field pavilion in Forbes Field. For Ruth it was the 714th home run in his career and his last one. Ruth then trotted around the bases, tipped his cap to the fans, crossed the plate and shot through the Pirates dugout to the clubhouse to sit the rest of the game out. Ruth's third blast had cut the Pirates lead in the to game 7–6.

Although Ruth had hit three home runs in the game it only tied the modern National League record. The feat had been accomplished three times before. George Kelly of the Giants had hit three home runs in a National League game twice, first on September 17, 1923, and then on June 14, 1924. Rogers Hornsby hit three homers in one game playing for the Cubs against the Pirates on April 24, 1931. The major league record was held by Lou Gehrig, who had hit four home runs in one game on June 3, 1932. However, in the 1890s two National League players had hit four home runs in one game — Robert L. Lowe of the Braves hit four homers on May 30, 1894, and Edward J. Delehanty of the Phillies hit four home runs in a game played on July 13, 1896. Nonetheless, Babe Ruth had become the first player to ever hit three home runs in a game in both the American and National Leagues. (Ruth of course not only hit three home runs in a game during the 1926 and 1928 World Series, but hit three in a regular season game on May 21, 1930, in the first game of a doubleheader.)

As irony would have it the next Pittsburgh pitcher to see action in the game after Ruth had departed was Waite Hoyt in relief of Bush. After allowing the Braves to tie the game at 7–7 on a sacrifice fly, Hoyt proceeded to set the Braves down during the remainder of his stint to become the winning pitcher as the Pirates beat the Braves 11–7. For the Pirates, Tommy Thevenow drove in five runs with a triple and double. For the Braves Babe Ruth had gone 4–4, with three home runs and a single with six RBIs. A few years later Ruth told Hoyt, "That's the day I should have quit. That was the end."[42] The *Pittsburgh Press* wrote of Ruth's heroics that day, "George Herman Ruth — the Great Man of Baseball — lighted the twilight of his career with a fantastic display of home run hitting at Forbes Field yesterday — a gaudy exhibition that was dimmed not one whit because his Boston mates could not prevent the Pirates from winning 11 to 7."[43]

Ruth continued on the road trip, keeping his commitment to Judge Fuchs, and played in Cincinnati, where he looked terrible. On May 27 a near-capacity crowd of 24,361 turned out at Crosley Field to see the Babe play. Prior to the game the fans besieged the Babe for autographs. He signed nearly everything that was pushed in front of him, with the exception of score cards; he just felt that there were too many of those to attempt taking on. In the game the Reds beat the Braves 6–3. Ruth went 0–4, striking out three times against starting pitcher Si Johnson, who would only have 40 strikeouts for 130 innings in the entire 1935 season. Ruth then went on to Philadelphia and went hitless. Finally on June 2, 1935, he called it quits. Suddenly, after all those glorious seasons in the sun, all that remained of Babe Ruth for the baseball world was his legend. Its radiance would be eternally sustaining to the game.

Meanwhile, a frustrating season continued for Waite Hoyt. On July 10, at Forbes Field he threw his glove in the air after being knocked out of the box by the Giants. At this point in the season his record was 6–7. Then, on August 9 in Pittsburgh, a young woman was struck by Hoyt while driving his car. Twenty-two year old Anna Belasco was en route to Bettis Field to catch a plane to Detroit for her father's funeral when she was hit by Hoyt. According to the United Press, Hoyt was arrested and placed under $1,000 bond. Miss Belasco was taken to a local hospital and treated for a dislocated foot and contusions of the scalp. However, Hoyt was eventually cleared of any wrongdoing in the matter when it came to light that the woman had stepped directly into the path of the car.

The Pirates finished in fourth place in 1935, although Arky Vaughan led the league in hitting with a .385 average. Hoyt finished the season with a record of 7–11, posting an ERA of 3.40 while working in 39 games both as a starter and out of the bullpen. Still, in one category he was among the pitching leaders in the National League, as his six saves tied him for second place among relief pitchers.

Approaching the 1936 season Hoyt was 37 years old and hanging on as a major league pitcher. He endured a split season that year when on May 16 he had an emergency appendectomy. The Pirates were in New York to play a series against the Giants when Hoyt was stricken and taken to Mountainside Hospital in Montclair, New Jersey, near the home of his in-laws. The loss of Hoyt left Pirates manager Pie Traynor in dire straights as his pitching staff had been lackluster since the start of the season — with the exception of Hoyt, who had been coming into games in tight spots and getting the job done. At this point in the season Hoyt had pitched in eight games, going 24⅔ innings with a won-lost record of 2–2.

On July 20, after convalescing for two months Hoyt returned to the Pirates and pitched in an exhibition game against the New York Yankees at Forbes Field with 2,500 fans looking on. The Pirates beat the Yankees 7–2 and Hoyt pitched six strong innings, giving up just one run and five hits. The only run given up by Hoyt was on a home run by his old teammate Lou Gehrig in the sixth. However, Hoyt had no trouble retiring the Yankees highly touted rookie, Joe DiMaggio, throwing a hard-called third strike past him the first inning and then getting him to ground out the next two trips to the plate. Hoyt completed the 1936 season pitching in 22 games, starting 9 with a record of 7–5, while the Pirates finished in fourth place, eight games behind the pennant-winning Giants.

Hoyt started the 1937 season with the Pirates but was not effective. In the early part of the season the Pirates were leading the league and in mid–May were wrapping up a highly successful eastern road trip. Then on May 13 at the Polo Grounds the Pirates lost to the Giants and Carl Hubbell by a score of 5–2, with Waite Hoyt taking the loss in relief. Hoyt had entered the game in the third inning in relief of Ed Brandt with men on second and third, no outs and the Giants leading 2–1. He preceded to get Mel Ott to pop out. He then walked Lou Chiozza to fill the bases, but got out of the inning when Gus Mancuso fouled out and Johnny McCarthy flied out. The Pirates scored a run off Hubbell in the fourth on a home run by Arky Vaughan to tie the game at 2–2. However Hoyt got into a jam in the fifth. Jim Ripple started the rally, beating out a slow roller to Vaughan. Then Kiddo Davis sacrificed with Ripple taking second. Hoyt then struck out Mel Ott for the second out. Then the flood gates opened, and four straight singles and an error later the Giants had a 5–2 lead and all the runs that King Carl Hubbell, a.k.a. The Meal Ticket, would need to send his lifetime record against the Pirates to 31–12. It was also Carl Hubbell's 21st consecutive win going back to the previous season when on July 17, 1936, he beat Pittsburgh 6–0.

As the first place Pirates returned home to open a series against the Cardinals a drenching rain poured down on Pittsburgh. Waite Hoyt's future with the team now looked rather dim. After appearing in just 11 games with a record of 1–2, Hoyt was released. In four and half years with the Pirates Hoyt had won 35 games and lost 31; his overall major league record stood at 230–175 and he longed to continue his career.

Still, Hoyt was openly talking about quitting as an active player at the end of the season when in June the big break came, with the Brooklyn Dodgers offering him a contract for the second time in his career. The Dodgers, now managed by Burleigh Grimes, were stuck in the cellar in the National League pennant race and could use any help that they could get. On August 20 Hoyt pitched them out of last place with a 3–0 shutout in the first game of a doubleheader with the Philadelphia Phillies. It was Hoyt's third victory since joining the Dodgers and the 233 of his career. However, the Dodgers dropped the nightcap as Van Lingle Mungo was shelled 7–5 by the Philadelphians and faded back into the cellar. Eventually Brooklyn rallied and finished in sixth place one game ahead of seventh-place Philadelphia and six games ahead of the last-place Cincinnati Reds. Hoyt appeared in 27 games, compiled a season record of 7–7 for the Dodgers and was looking forward to returning the following season.

After 21 years the 1938 season would be the last appearance in a big league uniform for Waite Hoyt. Several dynamics occurred to hasten his retirement. First, the Brooklyn Dodgers had not finished in the first division since 1932 and not won a pennant since 1920. By 1938 the franchise, near bankruptcy, was simply tired of playing third fiddle to the Giants and Yankees. To that end the Dodgers hired Larry McPhail away from Cincinnati to run the team and opened their check books for him to spend $200,000 on renovations at Ebbets Field, not including an extra $72,000 for lights for night baseball and $50,000 to buy first baseman Dolph Camilli. McPhail also hired additional scouts and hired Red Barber away from WLW in Cincinnati to broadcast the Dodgers games on the radio.

McPhail was serious about his intentions in Brooklyn and as he left his job in Cincinnati he told traveling secretary John McDonald, "I am going to be president of the Daffiness Boys. I'm going to turn Brooklyn inside out, upside down, and win pennants every year."[44]

The second aspect leading to Hoyt's departure from major league baseball occurred when he put himself in a vulnerable position by collaborating on a controversial magazine article, "Why The American League Wins," with writer Stanley Frank that was published in the April 2, 1938, edition of *The Saturday Evening Post.* In the lengthily article Hoyt told Frank that the National League suffered from the ghostly influence of deceased manager John McGraw, who put the emphasis on low-scoring games. In his opinion, that was still the modus operandi of the league, as opposed to the free-scoring methods advocated by Miller Huggins and the American League clubs. "In sharp contrast, American Leaguers are permitted to exercise their initiative, can play the game as flesh-and-blood individuals rather than robots who are pulled by strings tied to tradition. This stifling of initiative by the National League is, I'm convinced, the reason for American League supremacy."[45] Hoyt also stated in the article that he didn't discover how the other teams lived until he left the Yankees. "I discovered other teams, particularly those in the National League, had a sense of disbelief in their own ability. When a team won, the players were inclined to attribute their success to the breaks, their luck in avoiding injuries to the defections of the opposition. When the Yankees won, they accepted success as their heritage. The loss of a pennant was a terrible shock to them. I discovered in the National League that I had lost my identity as an individual."[46]

All of this stream-of-consciousness rhetoric lent itself to a view of pure skepticism about Waite Hoyt as he prepared for the coming 1938 season in a Brooklyn Dodger uniform. Hoyt now appeared to most National League executives as rather disingenuous. There was a general feeling that after being drummed out of the American League by Connie Mack following the 1931 season Hoyt had found refuge in the National League and was given the opportunity to continue his major league career by several years. A newspaper editorial, responding to Hoyt's remarks in the magazine article, stated in part, "To say the least, the article sponsored by Waite Hoyt came as a surprise. Here is a man who in the sere and yellow of his pitching career, has found a haven in the National League. Why, then, attack that haven? Some critics say he has shown the courage of his convictions. But to us, it seems he showed ingratitude."[47]

When Hoyt got of to a rocky start in the 1938 season, posting a 0–3 record with the stigma of the article in *The Saturday Evening Post* hanging over his head, Larry McPhail lowered the boom on him in what became publicized as the Dodgers' big house cleaning on May 16, 1938. With a week still to go before the major league clubs were required to reduce their active rosters to 23 players, Larry McPhail started early. He demoted pitcher George Jeffcoat to the minors in Kansas City, and gave unconditional releases to Roy Spencer, Heinie Manush and Waite Hoyt.

When Hoyt arrived at Ebbets Field on May 16 he found Heinie Manush not yet dressed in his uniform and asked him what was up. Manush whispered to Hoyt that he had just been released. Hoyt proceeded to his locker where he found a Western Union telegram lying on a chair. Upon opening it, he discovered that it was from John McDonald the Dodgers traveling secretary who McPhail had brought with him from Cincinnati. The message read: "BURLEIGH [Grimes] ASKED ME TO ADVISE YOU HE IS GIVING YOU UNCONDITIONAL RELEASE TODAY STOP HE WILL SEE YOU AT CLUBHOUSE BUT WE DID NOT WANT YOU TO READ IT IN PAPERS FIRST AND COULD NOT REACH YOU ON TELEPHONE = JOHN MCDONALD."[48] Hoyt then yelled out to Manush, "I just joined you. Wait a minute and we'll leave together."[49]

Hoyt had a brilliant career during his 21 years in the big leagues, but now it was over and the newspapers were not sympathetic. A New York newspaper stated, "Just as soon as Hoyt's outspoken, frank, informative, but decidedly ill-advised article had gained circulation it became quite apparent that he had outstayed his welcome in the National League. The front office of the Dodgers insists that only technical and physical consideration prompted the unconditional release of the veteran. But those on the sidelines are inclined to believe that Hoyt's holding up the old circuit to a poor comparison with the American League in methods and results certainly furnished the impetus to Hoyt's good-bye."[50]

Hoyt later stated that he left the clubhouse that day and then stood outside Ebbets Field looking up at the ballpark in disbelief that his career had suddenly come to an end: "Then is when I realized this was the end of a very vital part of my life. I'd seemingly lost my reason for living the full life I had enjoyed so much. Suddenly the glamour and enthusiasm were gone. It just didn't seem possible this could happen to me at age 38."[51] Then the man who had held Ty Cobb to a paltry lifetime batting average against him of .168 (8-for-48) began to ponder the future. It was May, nearing summer and standing on the outside of Ebbets Field looking in, he still wanted to play ball. So he signed on to pitch for the semi-pro Bushwicks in Brooklyn for the remainder of the season, then hung up his glove for good.

Waite Hoyt
Career Pitching Statistics

Year	Team	League	W	L	Pct.	ERA	G	SO	BB
1916	Mt. Carmel	PA State	5	1	.833	—	6	—	—
1916	Hartford-Lynn	Eastern	4	5	.444	—	10	22	24
1917	Memphis	Southern Assn.	3	9	.250	3.23	17	41	25
1917	Montreal	International	7	17	.291	2.51	28	65	78
1918	Nashville	Southern	5	10	.333	2.73	19	51	35
1918	New York	National	0	0	.000	.000	1	2	0
1918	Newark	International	2	3	.400	2.10	5	25	9
1919	Boston	American	4	6	.400	3.26	13	28	22
1920	Boston	American	6	6	.500	4.39	22	45	47
1921	New York	American	19	13	.594	3.10	43	102	81
1922	New York	American	19	12	.613	3.43	37	95	76
1923	New York	American	17	9	.654	3.02	37	60	66
1924	New York	American	18	13	.581	3.79	46	71	76
1925	New York	American	11	14	.440	4.00	46	86	78
1926	New York	American	16	12	.571	3.85	40	79	62
1927	New York	American	22	7	.759	2.63	36	86	54
1928	New York	American	23	7	.767	3.36	42	67	60
1929	New York	American	10	9	.526	4.24	30	57	69
1930	2 teams NY — A (8G 2–2) Detroit — A (26G 9–8)								
total	NY–Detroit	American	11	10	.524	4.71	34	35	56
1931	2 teams Detroit — A (16G 3–8) Philadelphia — A (16G 10–5)								
total	Detroit — Phila.	American	13	13	.500	4.97	32	40	69
1932	2 teams Brooklyn — N (8G 1–3) NY — N (18G 5–7)								
total	Brooklyn — NY	National	6	10	.375	4.35	26	36	37
1933	Pittsburgh	National	5	7	.417	2.92	36	44	19
1934	Pittsburgh	National	15	6	.714	2.93	48	105	43
1935	Pittsburgh	National	7	11	.389	3.40	39	63	27
1936	Pittsburgh	National	7	5	.583	2.70	22	37	20
1937	2 teams Pittsburgh — N (11G 1–2) Brooklyn — N (27G 7–7)								
total	Pitts.— Brooklyn	National	8	9	.471	3.41	38	65	36
1938	Brooklyn	National	0	3	.000	4.96	6	3	5
Major League Totals	21 years	237	182	.566	3.59	674	1206	1003	
American League Totals	14 years	189	131	.591	3.68	459	851	816	
National League Totals	7 years	48	51	.485	3.31	216	355	187	

World Series Record

Year	Team	League	Won	Lost	Pct.	ERA	G	SO	BB
1921	New York	American	2	1	.667	.000	3	18	11
1922	New York	American	0	1	.000	1.13	2	4	2
1923	New York	American	0	0	—	15.43	1	0	1
1926	New York	American	1	1	.500	1.20	2	10	1
1927	New York	American	1	0	1.000	4.91	1	2	1
1928	New York	American	2	0	1.000	1.50	2	14	6
1931	Philadelphia	American	0	1	.000	4.50	1	1	0
World Series Totals	7 years		6	4	.600	1.83	12	49	22

Waite Hoyt All-Time World Series Statistical Ranking

Wins 6 (5th)
Losses 4 (7th)
Strikeouts 49 (8th)
Games 12 (7th)
Innings Pitched 84 (5th)

7

Hitting Bottom

By the late 1930s radio was in major league baseball to stay and Waite Hoyt, now unemployed, longed to be part of it. He was intelligent, loquacious and possessed the necessary skills and knowledge to handle the task. However, the radio broadcasting industry in baseball had a rough start. During the Great Depression of the 1930s, 4.5 million Americans were unemployed. Consequently, major league baseball was hit hard economically. Total attendance for the 1933 season was 6.3 million, with only an average of 393,750 seats sold per team. Most clubs in the American League were losing money (the exceptions being the New York Yankees and Detroit Tigers, who were making a modest profit.) There was even talk of moving the struggling St. Louis Browns franchise to the west coast. Likewise, in the National League there was only a handful of clubs barely keeping their heads above water (such as the Chicago Cubs, Cincinnati Reds, St. Louis Cardinals and New York Giants). To compensate, team owners were slashing salaries and some began selling off their star players.

In Washington, Calvin Griffith, in order to reduce his payroll and bring in some cash, sent Goose Goslin and another player to the St. Louis Browns for three little-known players and $20,000. In Philadelphia Connie Mack dismantled the engine that drove his second dynasty that had won three consecutive pennants (1929–1931) by arranging deals that sent perennial ace Lefty Grove to the Boston Red Sox for $125,000, catcher Mickey Cochran to the Detroit Tigers for $100,000 and Al Simmons, Jimmy Dykes and Mule Hass to the Chicago White Sox for $100,000. In St. Louis during the World Championship season of 1934, the Cardinals had only drawn 325,000 fans through the turnstiles. However, due to an extensive farm system that had been developed by Branch

Rickey, the Red Birds were able to sell a lot of promising players and still remain competitive.

By 1935 attendance in the major leagues began to recover, fueled by the innovative vision of some team executives. Some clubs expanded concessions and the return of beer with the repeal of the Volstead Act (prohibition) provided a great opportunity for increased sales. Still other clubs went beyond attempting to mine as much revenue out of pockets at the gate and began creatively marketing their teams. In the early 1930s night baseball had been successfully introduced by teams in the Negro Leagues such as the Kansas City Monarchs and Pittsburgh Crawfords. Larry McPhail, the general manager of the Cincinnati Reds, saw the enormous potential in night baseball and on July 31, 1935, introduced it into the major leagues as President Franklin D. Roosevelt threw the switch from the White House that turned on the lights at Crosley Field. Night games were an instant success in Cincinnati, with the Reds drawing 30,000 fans for the inaugural nocturnal contest and a total attendance of 130,337 fans for the seven games under the lights on the schedule. In fact, the Reds' total attendance for those seven night games exceeded the total attendance for some major league clubs' entire 77 home games schedules in 1935. However, in New York Ed Barrow called night baseball a passing fad and said that it would be frivolous for the Yankees to spend $250,000 to install lights on the stadium.

Larry McPhail also realized that even during the Depression there was a tremendous growth industry occurring in the country — radio. By 1933 annual sales of radios in the USA were over 4 million and over half the families in the country had one in their homes. Not only did radio provide a remarkable outlet to market a team, but also generated revenue through the sale of broadcasting rights. While radio broadcasts of the World Series had been occurring for over a decade by the early 1930s, the individual ball clubs were slow to accept radio as an asset. Some teams, such as the New York Yankees, were adamant in their belief that putting their games on the airwaves was tantamount to giving their product away free.

Nonetheless, in Cincinnati McPhail went full-steam ahead putting together his radio broadcast format of Reds games. Reds owner and industrialist Powell Crosley Jr. just happened to manufacture radios and personally called the play-by-play on the ball club's first broadcast from Crosley Field. McPhail negotiated a contract with the 50,000-watt giant WLW in Cincinnati to broadcast the Reds games and the station hired a young college drop-out from the University of Florida for $25 a week by the name Lanier "Red" Barber to broadcast the games. The broadcasting of Reds games never hurt the gate and, in fact, by the late 1930s plans were being drawn up to expand the upper grandstand at Crosley Field.

By 1938 the Brooklyn Dodgers were one million dollars in debt and close to going out of business. To help rebuild the franchise Larry McPhail was hired away from Cincinnati to be general manager. Among the plans McPhail had to rejuvenate the Dodgers was to introduce radio broadcasts of their games. Upon arriving in Brooklyn McPhail learned that the three New York teams (Dodgers, Giants and Yankees) had agreed to a five-year ban on radio broadcasting of their games. McPhail, knowing that broadcasting games actually improved attendance rather than diminished it, chose to ignore the ban despite threats from the Giants and Yankees.

For the 1939 season McPhail negotiated a contract with General Mills, maker of Wheaties, to sponsor the Dodgers radio broadcasts. He then induced Cincinnati Reds radio broadcaster Red Barber to join him in Brooklyn to broadcast the Dodgers games over the 50,000-watt station WOR. The radio broadcasts of Dodgers games were an instant success. So successful were the radio broadcast of Dodgers games in 1939 that the attendance figure for the club actually increased. By the end of the season the Dodgers had a total attendance of 955,000, far outdistancing both of their inter-city rivals at the gate, with the pennant-winning Yankees seeing only 855,000 fans go through the turnstiles while the Giants drew only 705,000.

Now, the financial aspects of baseball broadcasting have changed pretty much since Cubs owner William Wrigley extended an invitation in 1925 to Chicago radio stations to broadcast all the Cubs games for free. Soon after, money began to matter to baseball in the area of broadcasting and in 1935 baseball commissioner Judge Kenesaw Mountain Landis signed a $400,000 deal with three networks to broadcast the World Series. By 1946 the Gillette Safety Razor Company had signed a 10-year $14-million deal to broadcast the World Series. Today the figures for broadcasting rights with major league baseball are over 1.5 billion dollars. In the period of 1996–2000 major league baseball signed contracts with FOX for $575 million, NBC for $400 million, ESPN for $440 million and Fox/Liberty Media Cable for $172 million.

Waite Hoyt had been casually considering a future in broadcasting for some time as his major league career wound down. In the late 1920s, while still pitching for the Yankees, Hoyt had even made brief appearances on WNEW. After getting his walking papers from McPhail and the Dodgers in May 1938, by the fall Hoyt was broadcasting on New York station WMCA as a master of ceremonies for a sports quiz show. However, he quickly grabbed another opportunity at WNEW for a program called *Grandstand and Bandstand*.

In 1939, with the success of the Dodgers games on radio the previous season, the Yankees decided to get in on the action and began broadcasting their games on WABC. Hoyt really wanted the play-by-play job with the Yankees. However, the sponsor (Wheaties) wouldn't let him audition: "I knew my real goal was to be a baseball announcer. I really pushed. But Wheaties wouldn't even let me take an audition because they didn't think we baseball players had enough of a vocabulary to do a decent job."[1] Therefore, Arch McDonald was hired to call the play-by-play. Nonetheless, they also hired Hoyt to air a ten minute pre-game show called *According to Hoyt* where he would talk about baseball, past and present. A typical script for the program written by Hoyt is presented in the following excerpt where he discusses Ty Cobb's personality and eventually recalls an encounter that Cobb had with Yankee catcher Wally Schang.

"It was Cobb's turn to bat. He was coming to the plate. When he finally did it was amid wild acclaim from the home admiring fans of Detroit. Cobb approached the plate swinging three bats. He condescendingly bowed in three or four directions. He acknowledged the applause for his individual greatness. Evidently, he was so overcome by his unstinted welcome, he forgot the evident prowess of the opposition. He strode to the plate with a wild look in his eye, a wild valiance and a daredevil spirit. In his unbrooked eagerness he reached out and knocked the cap off of the head of our bald-plated friend — Wally Schang. Schang, one of the strongest men in the league, with muscles like Atlas, and a fellow you couldn't tip over even with a head-on rush, stood nonchalantly at the plate, reached out and grabbed Cobb with his left hand with a stiff catching glove held thereon. Cobb's head and feet suddenly took a decided turn for the worse. His posterior hit the ground with an abrupt period to all there gone before. His hat flew one way. His bats flew another. And, you never saw a more disappointed or a more embarrassed American baseball star in the history of the entire game. Cobb, the Great Cobb; Cobb, the Holy; Cobb, who could do no wrong was thoroughly humbled before forty thousand people with one deft jab of Wally Schang's catcher's glove."[2]

The early press reviews on Hoyt's broadcasts were favorable and Alton Cook of the *New York World Telegram* stated in his column, "In his early days on WNEW Hoyt sounded like a hopeless case. He read haltingly in a flat voice. Lately he has asserted ease, poise and a script writer — all of which have added liveliness and an air of authority to his programs. He prefaced yesterday's game with a dramatic story of what a baseball pitcher thinks about when trouble develops. His opinions and reminiscences carry a ring that the announcer cannot get into pre-game preliminaries about the lineups and averages."[3]

Unfortunately, the program was cancelled after just three weeks, as Hoyt's show was local and the ABC network — having priority over its affiliate WABC — wanted to switch to a national program. However Hoyt, was now honing the skills that would eventually make him a baseball broadcasting legend. It was about this same time that Hoyt decided to drop by and visit his old friend Babe Ruth. The two hadn't seen each other since they were part of a ceremony to honor Lou Gehrig at Yankee Stadium on July 4, 1939. It was the day that Gehrig, now stricken with amyotrophic lateral sclerosis, gave his infamous 25-second "Today, I consider myself the luckiest man..." speech. Since retiring from major league baseball the Babe had been waiting for the call that never came to manage a big league team. Meanwhile, he tried to keep busy with golf, playing in a few exhibition games, and when his health was up to it, quaffing beer and scotch to numb the pain caused by the rejection that baseball had cast upon him. During the 1938 season Larry McPhail talked Babe into putting on a Brooklyn Dodgers uniform, signing him to a one-year $15,000 contract and acting as if he were a coach. In reality, it was another one of McPhail's publicity stunts to beef up the Brooklyn gate and he milked every once of revenue out Ruth possible by putting his image in a Dodger uniform on everything, including exhibition game score cards.

Leo Durocher, an old adversary of Ruth's from the Yankees Murderers' Row teams, was now a shortstop on the Dodgers. Peter Golenbock states in his book *Bums: An Oral History of the Brooklyn Dodgers* that Durocher felt pity for Ruth's status on the Dodgers, knowing that "he had been hired only as a freak to hit home runs during batting practice to draw fans."[4] As the 1938 season progressed, Ruth started to have visions of displacing current Dodgers manager Burleigh Grimes. However, Durocher took steps to block the "coup de tat," — for it was he that had designs on that job for himself.

Then Ruth started to believe that he could play again. But Grimes was well aware of Ruth's falling eyesight and blocked that move. At the end of the season, Larry McPhail fired Grimes and replaced him with Durocher. Babe Ruth then went back into retirement.

Upon arriving at Ruth's apartment on Riverside Drive that day and pressing the intercom button, Ruth's wife, Claire, immediately told Hoyt to come on up. He found the Babe in his study, nattily dressed in a silk robe covering his shirt and trousers. He was surrounded by many of his trophies and sitting in a big leather armchair puffing on a pipe with Claire seated off to the side. Babe had become somewhat domesticated. His annual income was provided from a trust fund he had established with an insurance company and he was living comfortably. It turned out to be a casual evening and loads of fun as the Babe and Hoyt discussed the past and present. On occasion Ruth would point to one of the many pictures hung on the wall and comment. One of the pictures was of Ruth and about a half dozen Filipinos. "See that picture over there?" said Ruth,[5] "That was taken in Manila. We had a time over there. Those Hawaiians tried to give me the business."[6]

Claire broke in, "Filipinos, Babe."[7]

"Yeah — Filipinos. Well, anyway, there must have been 30,000 people out there that day. All you could see was heads jammed together. They tried to tell me there were only 10,000 in the park. I stood to lose a bundle of dough. I said 'No money — me no play.' I've been looking at crowds all my life. I know 30,000 when I see them. So this Hawaiian says...."[8]

Again Claire interceded, "Filipino Babe."[9]

"— Filipino says, 'Me no-un'ers'an'." I picked up my glove and started for the gate. They guy understood that all right. We played and got paid. So we played an all-star team and beat them 35 to nothing or something. Tough people, those Hawaiians."[10]

"Filipinos," said Claire.[11]

"Aw, what the hell," said Babe.[12] "Make it Eskimos. We beat' em!"[13]

It was a great evening for Hoyt, the Babe and Claire. Over the ensuing years Hoyt would see the Babe again on several occasions at banquets, benefits, golf outings and the like. However, he always felt that Babe should have had his chance at managing a big league team. But the team owners and executives stood fast and united by the line that Babe should start in the minors and work his way up the baseball food chain. In reality, it was double talk. Ty Cobb, Rogers Hornsby, Bill Terry, Pie Traynor and many others including Leo Durocher did not have to earn their stripes toiling in the minors to manage in the major leagues. Even today it seems like an enormous injustice for major league baseball to have turned their back on the man that gave so much to the game when it needed it the most.

In 1940 Hoyt landed a job with WOR, the station that was broadcasting the Brooklyn Dodgers games with Red Barber doing the play-by-play. His task was to do pre- and post-game commentary. The post-game commentary was a unique challenge in that Hoyt was expected to fill the airtime at the end of the Dodgers game broadcast until the next quarter hour. Therefore if a Dodgers game was over at 20 minutes before the hour, he had five minutes broadcast time. If the game was over at 14 minutes before the hour then that was to be the length of his commentary. Surprisingly, Hoyt did a remarkable job at keeping his commentary new and crisp and his stint on WOR was enormously popular in New York. He wrote his own scripts and talked about a variety of subjects ranging from

Ty Cobb to Rogers Hornsby to the balk rule in baseball, and of course Babe Ruth.

Red Barber harbored a personal disdain for former athletes attempting to be broadcasters. However, he freely admitted that Waite Hoyt was a natural at broadcasting, especially baseball. But while Hoyt had quickly established an audience with his commentary on WOR, he was far from pleased with his status. He did a second season with WOR in 1941, but deep in his heart he wanted to be where the real action was, doing the play-by-play. "I enjoyed those programs with the Dodgers, but I still wanted to be the big—cheese—I wanted to do balls and strikes,"[14] said Hoyt. To expedite the process, Hoyt moved his family from their New Jersey home back across the Hudson River into an apartment in New York City and signed on with the prestigious William Morris Talent Agency.

In Cincinnati, the Reds, led by a dynamic duo of pitchers in Bucky Walters and Paul Derringer, along with future Hall of Fame catcher Ernie Lombardi, had won back-to-back National League pennants in 1939 and 1940, then defeated Hank Greenberg, Charlie Gehringer and the Detroit Tigers in the 1940 World Series. Although the team finished third in 1941, the Reds had firmly established their broadcasting market and games were being aired on WLW and WSAI, with Dick Bray and Roger Baker (who had replaced Red Barber after he left for the Dodgers broadcast job). Both of these stations were controlled by Reds owner Powell Crosley Jr. At the same time, another Cincinnati station (WKRC) had decided to enter the market, gained broadcasting rights with the Reds and established a sponsorship with Burger Beer. Subsequently, WKRC—which was controlled by the family of former United States President William Howard Taft—began its search for an outstanding announcer to do the play-by-play of its games. The sponsor Burger Beer wanted that person to be a creditable spokesman for their product.

When the William Morris Agency first approached Hoyt about the WKRC opportunity he balked: "An agency man came to me and asked if I'd consent to going out of town. I asked him where. He said Cincinnati. I laughed and told him that when I was playing Cincinnati was the only town in the majors where there was no place to go out after a game."[15] True, Cincinnati in 1941 was and probably still is—when compared to other major league cities in terms of night life—a conservative town. But here was the opportunity that Hoyt so coveted to begin his play-by-play broadcasting career staring directly at him with the same intensity of standing on the mound and seeing Al Simmons or Babe Ruth at the plate. For the moment he set aside his petty social opinions of the Cincinnati

Red Barber (National Baseball Hall of FameLibrary, Cooperstown, N.Y.).

community, let better judgment guide him and asked the William Morris Agency to audition for the job.

Waite Hoyt was no amateur when it came to auditions. As a child he had watched his father Addison Hoyt audition for jobs on the vaudeville stage. He too had faced the rigors of selling himself not only in the performing arts, but early on in baseball at 15 years old auditioning as a pitcher for John McGraw at the Polo Grounds. He was determined to not the let this opportunity wind up in the hand of his competitors. To that end Hoyt put together a two-point strategy to win the Reds broadcasting job. First he took a unique approach to making his audition disc. He was convinced that his competitors would make their audition discs doing hypothetical play-by-plays of games. Hoyt felt that doing a play-by-play scenario would be slow and simulating game action would come off as contrived and even a bit silly. Hoyt was already a consummate story teller and decided that he would feature his skills as such. So he wrote a script about a little boy that he recorded.

Author Ellen Frell, also a niece of Hoyt's, stated in her work *Waite Hoyt: The Broadcast Years in Cincinnati* that, "He went into the studio, marked his script for pauses, and began. On the disc was Hoyt's rich, energetic voice, telling a story full of emotion and interest, sending a clear message to the Burger Brewing Company: they had found their man. Bud Koons, former president of the Burger Brewing Company, clearly remembered Hoyt's audition disc. "When all of them had been reviewed, Hoyt's stood out a mile from the rest."[16] With a superb job done on the audition disc, Hoyt sealed the deal when he got J. G. Taylor Spink (publisher of *The Sporting News*, 1914–1962) to speak to the Reds and Burger Beer on his behalf. In late November 1941 Hoyt was offered the job at WKRC in Cincinnati. Hoyt stated, "When they offered me the job of play-by-play, it took me about half-a-second to yell yes."[17]

On November 28, 1941, Hoyt's appointment to broadcast the play-by-play of the Reds games in the 1942 season was formally announced in *The Cincinnati Enquirer*. While Hoyt was still reveling in his selection to Cincinnati, his colleague at WOR, Red Barber, came to him with some heartfelt advice to ensure his success in the new venture. Barber's assessment of Hoyt's demeanor was that "he was a drinker and a pretty rough guy."[18] Although feeling a little trepidation, on a Saturday he approached Hoyt in his office at WOR and said, "Waite, you haven't asked me for any advice, but I'm going to give you some and you won't like it. Now stay in your chair. You are a hard drinker." He turned red in the face. "Cincinnati is a small town and you can't go there and drink as hard as you drink. It'll get around."[19] Barber then exited the office quickly.

In a way Barber, thought he was returning a favor to Hoyt. When Barber had become the Reds broadcaster in 1934, Larry McPhail assigned him the task of getting some of the visiting Pittsburgh Pirates to interview before the game. Therefore, Barber went to the hotel in Cincinnati where the Pirates were staying, saw Pirates manager George Gibson in the lobby and asked him to provide a couple of players for his program. Gibson's reaction was a crude one, as he began yelling and peppering Barber with profanity. When Gibson walked away, Barber wondered what he would tell McPhail; he was without any program material. He was a rookie at his craft and felt threatened. At that moment two men who had been watching Gibson's disgusting tirade got up from a sofa in the lobby and approached Barber. One said, "Son, I'm Waite Hoyt and this is Freddie Lindstrom, and we'll be glad to go the ballpark and go on your program."[20] With Hoyt's natural ability for the art of glib, the show turned into a one-hour production instead of the anticipated 15 minutes. Barber felt that Hoyt may have saved his job and he was grateful. Whether or not Barber's blunt advice, administered to Hoyt seven years later was appropriate or not is really academic, but it did give Hoyt something to think about.

Hoyt did his best to prepare his wife, Ellen, and young son, Chris, to start their new life in Cincinnati. It was going to be a huge adjustment for Ellen. She had been born and raised on the east coast and traveled extensively in Europe. She came from a significantly connected family in New Jersey society and had only lived outside of the New York City metropolitan area on an interim basis in Pittsburgh during the summers, when Hoyt played there. The move to the outskirts of the midwest was indeed going to be cultural shock for Ellen. Then, on Sunday, December 7, 1941, the Japanese attacked the U.S. Pacific fleet at Pearl Harbor and suddenly the country was at war. Here was the chance of a lifetime job waiting for Hoyt in Cincinnati and at that moment it was unclear as to whether or not there would even be any baseball played in the coming season.

Also during 1941, Hoyt's career almost took a different turn. On June 6, 1941, his former teammate Lou Gehrig, just a few weeks shy of his 36th birthday, finally succumbed to his long arduous bout with amyotrophic lateral sclerosis, which commonly became known as Lou Gehrig's disease. Immediately, the Hollywood film mogul Sam Goldwyn saw box-office potential in Gehrig's life story. Goldwyn began to cast various actors for the part of Gehrig in the forthcoming film and one of the persons being seriously considered for the part was none other than Waite Hoyt. However, as the script was being written and planning for the filming progressed, it was decided that the film should be elevated into a major release and Gary Cooper was cast in the part of Gehrig with Teresa Wright in the role of his wife, Eleanor.

Babe Ruth traveled to California and played himself in the film. Naturally, when the daily filming schedule ended, Ruth headed out on the town for the night. However, not being so young anymore, the strain of heavy work and heavy partying caused Ruth to break down physically and he contracted pneumonia. Nonetheless, he did a fine job of acting and fully recovered. The film, *Pride of the Yankees*, opened in late July 1942, 13 months after Gehrig's death, and was a huge success. So much for Hoyt's potential film career.

With the future uncertain, on January 1, 1942, the Hoyts left New York for Cincinnati. In 1942 Cincinnati was somewhat of an insular community, detached in its outlook and experience with accepting relocating professionals. Other than the large numbers of poor southern whites and blacks who annually migrated to the city seeking employment opportunities in its industrial base, the city had not really experienced any significant wave of immigration since large numbers of Germans arrived in the mid-to-late 19th century. So it was not without foundation that the arrival of Waite Hoyt in Cincinnati to broadcast the Reds games was viewed as no big deal. In fact, most Cincinnatians felt that Hoyt's tenure in the city would be short. The opinion most often expressed was that Hoyt would gain some experience at the microphone and when the first broadcasting job became available in Boston, New York or Philadelphia, he and the family would dash to Union Terminal and catch the first thing smokin' its way east. However, the 42-year old Waite Hoyt would spend the last 43 years of his life in the Queen City and in his own words, "I found a level of happiness I'd never known anywhere else, young or old."[21]

As for the future of baseball in 1942, on January 14 Commissioner Landis wrote to President Roosevelt and asked for direction: "Baseball is about to adopt schedules, sign players, make vast commitments, go to training camps. What do you want us to do? If you believe we ought to close down for the duration of the war, we are ready to do so immediately. If you feel we ought to continue, we would be delighted to do so. We await your order."[22] Controversy was already brewing in the country about young able-bodied men playing a game for money, while other young able-bodied men marched off to fight in the war. It took Roosevelt only a day to reply to Landis, informing him that it would be in the best interest of the country to keep baseball going. In what became commonly known as Roosevelt's "green light letter," he stated that people were going to be working long, hard hours and needed a recreational outlet to keep their morale up. Roosevelt acknowledged that a lot of younger players would be drafted into the armed services, but the use of older players he felt should not dampen the popularity of the game. The season was on and Waite Hoyt had a job.

In March of 1942 Hoyt appeared at the Reds spring training camp at Plant Field in Tampa, Florida, ready to begin his job as the team's radio broadcaster on WKRC and spokesman for Burger Beer. Everyone at the Reds spring training camp — manager Bill McKechnie, the players and the fans who had come down from Cincinnati — were impressed with Hoyt. J. G. Taylor Spink, who had spoken on Hoyt's behalf with the Reds and Burger Beer, wrote in the *Sporting News* "Folks who watched Waite Hoyt in the press box at Plant Field, Tampa Fla., when he was building up a background for his job of broadcasting Cincinnati games this summer, were impressed, first of all, by his seeming youthfulness. Hoyt doesn't look the part of a man with 22 years of professional ball behind him. Poised, alert and well groomed. Hoyt looks exactly like a movie casting director's idea of a radio announcer, despite the fact he still has to broadcast his first game."[23]

In order to get to know the players better, Hoyt obtained permission from Bill McKechnie to put on a Cincinnati uniform and work out with the team. Although he was careful to not undermine the Reds coaches, the players respected Hoyt and sought him out for advice. Therefore, before spring training had wrapped up pitcher Whitey Moore had added a slider to his pitching repertoire courtesy of Hoyt. (Unfortunately the new pitch came to late to save Moore's career; 1942 would be his last season in the major leagues.)

Hoyt's inaugural season in the Reds broadcast booth was one of many challenges. First of all, he had to develop a style that kept listeners' attention to a team that was only mildly competitive. The 1942 edition of the Cincinnati Reds was a team with fairly good pitching, but one that lacked run production. The Reds had a solid starting pitching rotation with Johnny Vander Meer, who led the staff with a record of 18–12 and led the league in strikeouts (186), along with Bucky Walters (15–14, 2.66 ERA), Paul Derringer (10–11, 3.06 ERA) and Ray Starr (15–13, 2.67 ERA). However, the Reds scored only 527 runs in the season — third lowest in the league. They finished the season with a record of 76–76 in fourth place in the National League, 29 games behind the pennant-winning St. Louis Cardinals. The 1942 Reds were a lackluster team, but Hoyt refused to hype the club for sake of hype. His style of reporting was one of honesty and he felt no need to insult the intelligence of his listening audience. He had an excellent speaking voice, fine diction and a superb knowledge of the game. The players respected him and he began to build a modest following with the fans.

Hoyt also quickly discovered that broadcasting in the ballpark was a vastly different experience than broadcasting in a studio. At Crosley Field the press box was situated atop the upper grandstand and open to the elements — cool in April, hot and muggy in August. Describing the environment of the rooftop press box to author Curt Smith, Hoyt remarked, "Jesus, we could have been killed. It was always jammed 'cause it was so goddamned small — you could hardly crowd three people in it. You had these steel chairs with pads on the seats, and when rain came in the booth, the floor got flooded and you were scared to death some thunder was going to hit your microphone. When I think back, when the wind started to blow, the booth would sway back and forth. It's a miracle it didn't collapse."[24] Also, Hoyt had to share the broadcast booth space with Dick Nesbitt and Dick Bray, two competing broadcasters from other Cincinnati radio stations who were seated nearby, chirping away at their own play-by-play accounts within his hearing range.

Hal McCoy — veteran baseball reporter for the *Dayton Daily News* and recipent of the 2002 J. G. Taylor Spink Award, presented by the National Baseball Hall of Fame for meritotius contributions to baseball writing—confirms Hoyt's description of the conditions in the Crosley Field press booth: "It was, indeed dangerous, especially in the rain. Soggy copy was one result. Getting down the steep dangerous stairs to and from the clubhouse was a chore and you had to go through the crowd. It was very dangerous in that it was high and narrow and you had to climb over other writers to get in and out of your work place. But the ice cream and burgers were great ... and FREE!!!"[25]

Road games were yet another problem, but one that Hoyt was uniquely prepared to handle as a result of his remarkable penchant for showmanship. For the first 10 years that he broadcast the Reds games he did not travel with the team. He sat in a studio and recreated the action of road games being transmitted over a Western Union ticker tape, which sent coded messages of plays from Wrigley Field, the Polo Grounds or Ebbets Field, etc. While broadcasting ballgames from a table in a radio studio from a ticker tape could hardly generate the excitement equal to the spontaneous action that took place in the ball park, Hoyt kept his game accounts lively and accurate. The listening audience was well aware of the fact that the game was canned and there was no attempt to deceive them. Nonetheless, they accepted Hoyt's forced style of reporting these events as the best that could be done under the conditions.

In 1943 Hoyt was joined by Lee Allen to broadcast the Reds games on WKRC. However, Allen was terminated after about six weeks when he attempted to increase his salary and threatened the station with union intervention. Following that brief period of having a sidekick in the booth with him, Hoyt did a solo broadcast of Reds games for the next 11 years until being teamed with Jack Moran on station WSAI beginning in the 1955 season.

However, it was Hoyt's experience as a player that soon began to separate him from the crowded pack in the Cincinnati broadcasting competition. When inclement weather came and Hoyt was forced to fill airtime during the delays he was at his best, suddenly reliving his rich experiences in baseball to the delight of his listening audience. Even in his very first year behind the Reds microphone he shared with his audience what he considered to be his personal all-star team, based on players he had seen or played with or against: First base, Lou Gehrig; second base, Eddie Collins; shortstop, Everett Scott; third base, Pie Traynor, Buck Weaver and Joe Dugan; right field, Babe Ruth; center field, Tris Speaker; left field, Ty Cobb; catchers, Mickey Cochran, Gabby Hartnett and Bill Dickey; pitchers, Walter Johnson, Carl Hubbell, Herb Pennock and Lefty Grove. Using the skills that he had fine-tuned at WOR, in his crisp dialogue Hoyt gave a brief description of why he thought each player deserved to be on his all-star team and then added personal remembrances of each. It was unlike anything that the Cincinnati listening audience had ever heard before and they craved more of the same. By the end of the 1940s Waite Hoyt's rain-delay broadcasts would become legendary.

During the 1944 season Hoyt was at the microphone on June 19 when 15-year old Joe Nuxhall made his wartime debut for the Reds, becoming the youngest player to ever pitch in a major league game. Nuxhall was brought into pitch by manager Bill McKechnie with the Reds trailing defending National League champion St. Louis Cardinals 13–1. When he left the game the score was 18–1. Nuxhall lasted for ⅔ of an inning, giving up two hits and five walks, and finishing with an ERA of 67.50. However, Nuxhall would return to the majors in 1952 and pitch for 15 years before retiring following the 1966 season and then moving into Hoyt's old job in the Reds radio broadcasting booth, where he remains even today.

Following the 1944 World Series, Billy Jurges, Don Gutteridge and Lefty Gomez had to cancel a planned trip to entertain troops in Europe as part of a USO Camp Shows tour. Waite Hoyt joined Paul Waner along with Paul Derringer and went in their place as a replacement group. The USO tour was just one of the many things outside of broadcasting responsibilities that Hoyt was doing on a regular basis. By now Hoyt and Ellen had purchased a home in the Cincinnati neighborhood of Linwood and settled in with son Chris. Although Hoyt had doubts, he had truly gained wide acceptance in the Queen City.

Perhaps some of his mild paranoia was a result of his dark side. He was, as Red Barber had said, a hard drinker. Regardless of his youthful frolicking while drinking himself half blind with Babe Ruth and Joe Dugan during the Roaring Twenties, as he matured he had never really slowed down except for occasional periods of self imposed abstinence. Now he was in his middle 40s, and although he would remain sober for weeks at a time, he seemed to be a functional alcoholic, as his occasional binges, which were only known to Ellen and few close associates, didn't seem to interfere with his broadcasting duties. It was a typical pattern of alcoholics, whom studies have shown develop well-planned work routines and tend to be overcautious in order to avoid accidents and detection. Then suddenly in late June 1945, he hit bottom.

Beginning in 1945 the Reds switched their radio broadcasts of games to station WCPO in Cincinnati. On Tuesday evening, June 19, Hoyt completed broadcasting his sports program at 6:15 P.M. over WCPO. He then would not be heard on the airwaves again for over two months. The next morning on June 20 he left his home at 1297 Crestwood Avenue in Linwood and went to meet Lee Allen at the now defunct Hotel Sinton in downtown Cincinnati at 4th and Vines Streets. He and Allen had been invited by a local jeweler to lunch at the Sinton. The lunch included martinis, but following lunch Allen and Hoyt took a seat at the hotel bar and began drinking double martinis. Suddenly Hoyt was totally helpless and on a bender as his addiction overwhelmed him. With the alcohol in his system in tight control of his thought process, he missed the broadcast of the Reds game that day. The press and public were curious. Where in the world was Waite Hoyt?

On Thursday morning, June 21, Hoyt's mysterious absence made front-page news as *The Cincinnati Enquirer* reported, "WAITE HOYT MISSING; AMNESIA SUFFERER, WIFE SAYS." Ellen Hoyt knew what was going on; this was not the first time that Waite had gone on a prolonged binge. Nonetheless, Ellen did what she could to protect Hoyt's reputation and concocted a cover story. Ellen told the press that Waite suffered from occasional bouts of amnesia. She stated that this was the third time he had disappeared since being struck on the head with a baseball while playing in Detroit in 1930. She then went through the usual formalities of filing a missing persons report with the Cincinnati Police Department, giving a description of Hoyt, the clothes he was wearing and his automobile (a two-tone green sedan bearing the Ohio license plate number 647-BU).

As *The Cincinnati Post* and national papers picked up the story off the wire, reports of people spotting Hoyt began to roll in to the press and police alike. One report had Hoyt being seen on June 21 in Richmond, Kentucky. Hoyt's former Yankees teammate Earle Combs lived in Richmond and operated a cold storage business there. Richmond police chief Ray Maupin even confirmed the story. However this report proved to be erroneous when at 5:00 A.M. on June 21, the Cincinnati Police found Hoyt's car locked and undisturbed at Curtis Street and Gilbert Avenue in the Walnut Hills section of Cincinnati. Another report on Hoyt came from a Clifton Heights resident who said that she saw Hoyt on Wednesday night standing in front of grocery store at Peeble's Corner. Other reports had sightings of Hoyt in Chicago and Lexington, Kentucky. What no one knew at that time was that Hoyt had never left downtown Cincinnati. After leaving the Sinton Hotel bar on Wednesday afternoon he had checked into a suite at the Netherland Plaza Hotel only two blocks away and continued to drink in isolation for two more days and nights.

On Friday morning, June 22, Hoyt checked out of the Netherland Plaza Hotel and began to wander uptown. Sick, weakened and poisoned by the huge amount of alcohol in his system, he began to walk north on Broadway, very slowly. When he reached the corner of Broadway and Reading Road, he went into a cafe. The establishment by Hoyt's later account, was a sleazy place. Shaking and sweating profusely, he ordered a shot of whiskey. The bartender, aware of Hoyt's condition, asked him if he was alright. Yes, he replied, although he was shaking so badly he had to hold the shot glass with both hands to get the whiskey to his lips. He was finally able to get the whiskey down and then went outside and stood on the curb. At that moment the realization of how helpless he was began to descend upon him. He began to cry. His day of reckoning had arrived. He went to a public telephone and called Good Samaritan Hospital. He was connected with a nun from the Sisters of Charity by the name of Sister Andrew. She told Hoyt to take a cab to the hospital and they would be waiting for him.

Ellen Hoyt, now aware of Waite's condition and location, told *The Cincinnati Post* that Hoyt had returned to his home in Linwood late Thursday evening very ill and was now under a doctor's care and resting. Once again she used the amnesia excuse to protect Hoyt. She even stated that it was possible that he would be back at the microphone doing Reds games radio broadcasts by Monday. Of course it was all subterfuge. Hoyt was being detoxified in the hospital and his recovery would be a lengthily process. Meanwhile, Lee Allen took over Hoyt's duties at the WCPO microphone at Crosley Field.

As Hoyt struggled with his circumstances at Good Samaritan Hospital, he began to sink further, feeling powerless against the demon rum and so distraught on how he had let everyone down, that he considered suicide. Then, according to Hoyt speaking on the Donn Burrows video production of *The Life & Times of Waite Hoyt — Waite's World*, he woke up one day in the hospital and there was a man standing at the foot of his bed. The man told Hoyt that he knew how helpless he felt, but there was hope. The man then asked a favor of Hoyt. He wanted to visit him often and talk about his problem. Hoyt consented and his recovery began. The man was from the local chapter of Alcoholics Anonymous (AA).

AA had been founded in 1935 by two alcoholics and by the mid–1940s its acceptance as a self-help group was becoming a widely used modality of therapy. The spirit of AA is that it is a fellowship of men and women who have admitted that they are powerless when confronted with alcohol. By sharing their experiences with each other, they gain strength and continue on a perpetual course of recovery one day at a time.

Sister Andrew was aware of the healing potential of AA and had contacted them on Hoyt's behalf. According to Hoyt, Sister Andrew was a small lady who gave him enormous hope. During Hoyt's hospitalization, the two spent many quiet afternoons during the summer of 1945 discussing their philosophies of life. Hoyt told Sister Andrew he had wanted to quit drinking for years, but couldn't. As the two continued their dialogue, Hoyt slowly began to feel renewed; as he talked his problems through he became stronger. Also during his hospitalization, he received a telegram from Babe Ruth. The Babe had read about Hoyt's illness in the New York papers and sent him the following message: "Read about your case of Amnesia. Must be a new brand."[26] Finally, on August 28, 1945, 68 days since sitting down at the bar at the Hotel Sinton, Waite Hoyt returned to Crosley Field to broadcast the Cincinnati Reds games once again. As the news of the real reason for Hoyt's absence became common knowledge around the Cincinnati area, there was of course some concern about the reaction of his sponsor on the Reds radio broadcasts, Burger Beer. Could an admitted alcoholic be a pitchman for a brewery? Hoyt decided to confront the problem head on; he admitted to his listening audience that the rumors were true, he was an alcoholic. To his surprise his listening audience showed compassion, stood by him and letters of support arrived in large numbers. Down at the Burger Brewery on Central Parkway, brewmasters and executives alike huddled behind closed doors wrestling with the Hoyt question. However, it became a moot point as the public support for Hoyt continued to gain momentum. In the end Burger Beer knew they had someone special doing the Reds broadcasts and selling their product. Burger salesman liked the association with Hoyt and since he had become the pitchman for the suds, sales had increased significantly. In fact, since Hoyt began broadcasting Reds games even the right-field bleachers at Crosley Field had become synonymous with Burger Beer, as he referred to home runs into the bleachers as having been hit into "Burgerville."

The following year Hoyt diligently continued his recovery with attendance at AA meetings and attempted to put his marriage and professional life back on track. His marriage was shaky at best. Ellen paid little attention to Hoyt's professional career, ordered a ban on his business associates in their home and seemed to have developed a taste for alcohol herself. However, still somewhat distraught over the failure of his first marriage, Hoyt was determined to see that his second marriage succeeded.

The hallmark of Hoyt's early recovery process came during that same year when he boldly stood up in front of a jam-packed room of individuals at an AA meeting and admitted his powerlessness over alcohol. In the speech he said in part, "Better than all else — the truth is refreshing. For some fortunate reason —fortunate for us— people are willing to help someone who is making a comeback. You see before you an alcoholic who has attained some measure of recovery. You've heard admissions by him about his drinking days, and I imagine you tacitly admit there has been some improvement in him. Therefore you borrow from him some of his confidence and I hope, desire."[27]

In fact, Waite Hoyt was well on the way to recovery. Hoyt possessed that unique personal quality of being able to learn from his mistakes. In his words, "When it came to alcohol. I was able to put myself on trial and determine my own guilt and my own weakness. I'm just that far away from being a drunk again. I cannot handle alcohol."[28] Years later Red Barber was to remark on Hoyt's triumph over the bottle. "He's No. 1 in my book. I admire a man who did what he did. He turned himself around. We don't like to change ourselves, but that's what he did when he went to AA. It's easier to beat someone else than ourselves. That was a far better win than any ball game he ever won."[29]

8

A Broadcasting Legend

The pre–World War II Cincinnati Reds had been World Champions in 1940 and the war-time Reds were at least to some degree competitive. However, the post-war Reds were the pits, perpetually finishing in the second division. While Waite Hoyt was stuck with the job of making these mediocre Reds team seem interesting in the late 1940s, other baseball broadcasters were gaining national notoriety and even becoming legendary for their calls on famous plays. Millions of baseball fans even today can still recite word-for-word Red Barber's call of Al Gionfriddo's game-saving catch of Joe DiMaggio's drive to the left-field bullpen in the 1947 World Series ("Swung on, and belted. It's a long one, deep to left field. Back goes Gionfriddo. Back ... back ... back. It may be out of here. No! Gionfriddo makes a one-handed catch against the bullpen fence!"). The same for Russ Hodges' call of Bobby Thompson's "Shot Heard Round the World" in the final game of the 1951 National League playoffs between the Giants and Dodgers.

Hoyt said " [Mel] Allen and [Red] Barber always had great material to work with — they were good news broadcasters. I was a bad news broadcaster. Mostly, anyway."[1] In 1946 the Reds finished in sixth place. Hoyt states that during the 1946 season Reds president Warren Giles called him into his office and said, "Waite, why aren't you more enthusiastic about the Reds? Why are you always low-keying it?"[2] As an example Giles mentioned the style of Cubs broadcaster Bert Wilson and a couple of others.

"I got mad as hell," said Hoyt.[3] "I told him, 'Why in the shit shouldn't Bert Wilson cheer? They won the pennant last year, didn't they? They've got a great park to play in and they've got some stars and they win some games. But us, your top hitter's a lousy .267 or whatever the hell it is. Your

155

top pitcher's won eight games. What is there to cheer about? Christ, if I cheered like Bert Wilson with the bums we've got, people would think I was blind or the village idiot. Or maybe both."[4]

To compensate, Hoyt told baseball stories, including those from his own major league experience, and attempted to build up a few of the Reds players. He did have a little help in the 1947 season when pitcher Ewell Blackwell had a fine year posting a record of 22–8. Along the way Blackwell won 16 straight games, including throwing a no-hitter when he beat the Boston Braves 6–0 on June 18. In his next start against Brooklyn, Blackwell just missed duplicating Johnny Vander Meer's 1938 feat of pitching two consecutive no-hitters when Eddie Stanky hit a single up the middle with one out in the ninth inning. In all, Blackwell led the National League in 1947 in wins (22), strikeouts (193), complete games (23) and most strikeouts per nine innings (6.36). Hoyt had a very high opinion of Blackwell: "Ewell Blackwell, had he not hurt his arm and been sick, could have been the greatest pitcher — or one of the greatest ever."[5]

But in 1947, other than "Blackie," there wasn't much to cheer about as the Reds finished in fifth place. Nonetheless, Hoyt's reputation had already been established with his Cincinnati audience. Russ Hodges, who did the New York Giants radio broadcasts, stated, "Waite Hoyt is authoritative. When he makes a statement there is no doubt as to its accuracy. When Hoyt says it's so, the Cincinnati public goes by what he says."[6]

Political commentator and life-long Cubs fan George F. Will once advanced the opinion that, "Radio is a medium of the imagination, which is to say a medium that engages the mind. And baseball is the sport that most engages the mind. It has a pace, a one-step-at-a-time orderliness (working through a lineup, a batting order) that demands quick and constant thinking about what has just happened and what will, or at any rate should, happen next."[7] Similarly, Waite Hoyt had an orderly way about broadcasting a game; he spoke in the past tense to ensure accuracy. Author Curt Smith stated, "Unlike any broadcaster in the totality of baseball, Waite Hoyt aired play-by-play in the past, not present tense. He was a chronicler, not sportscaster; he narrated action after the fact; on radio, his accents, like his life, bridged, not disengaged, the years."[8] Also, like Red Barber before him, Hoyt learned the various tricks of trade to ensure accuracy, following the movement of the outfielder, not the flight of the ball when a fly ball was hit to the outfield. In 1948 the Cincinnati Reds began televising some of their games over WCPO-TV and Hoyt became the first sportscaster to simultaneously broadcast over radio and television. When WLW-T took over the televising of games in the late 1950s the station hired its own broadcasting team of George Bryson and former Reds first baseman Frank McCormick. However, Hoyt's large and extremely loyal listening audience didn't take well to the cornpone announcing style of Bryson and sleepy commentary of McCormick. They were use to listening to Hoyt's accurate, sophisticated, well-informed and most of all familiar voice on the air waves. Consequently, in a considerable number of homes, bars and clubs in Cincinnati, the volume on the television was turned off and the radio turned on to the station where Hoyt and Jack Moran were broadcasting to provide the game commentary over the television broadcast.

In early 1948 Babe Ruth, although dying from his throat cancer, began touring for the Ford Motor Company to promote American Legion Baseball. During a stop in Cincinnati, Waite and Ellen dropped by to see the Babe at his hotel. What they found was a Babe worn out by the pain of his affliction and drowsy from the sedatives he was taking. On the coffee table in front of the couch where Babe sat was a bottle of beer that he was he was drinking for the food content. Seeing the pitiful sight that Ruth had become and how tired the struggle was making him, Waite and Ellen decided to make an early exit. Nonetheless, according to author Robert Creamer, Ruth asked the couple to wait a minute while he went to the refrigerator and retrieved a small vase with an orchid it. He then presented it to Ellen, telling her that he had never given her anything.

On the evening of August 16, 1948, Hoyt was in the studio and about to recreate the Reds vs. Pirates game from Pittsburgh using the coded messages coming over the wire. At 7:01 P.M. an assistant Ed Kennedy heard a bulletin alarm on the Associated Press tele-type machine, pulled it off, looked at it and without saying a word, handed it to Hoyt. Babe Ruth was dead. Hoyt was of course stunned. According to Hoyt, "It was just as much of a sickening jolt as if I hadn't known. It was as if someone had chipped part of my life away."[9] At 7:30 P.M. Hoyt went on the air and informed his listening audience of the demise of the Bambino. "This is one time I'm not going to enjoy broadcasting a ball game," he told his listeners sadly.[10] Hoyt also said that after the game, if the listeners would stay with him, he would have a few words to say about the Babe. Two hours and 18 minutes later the game was over. The Reds, behind the five-hit pitching of Johnny Vander Meer, had beaten the Pirates 5–3 and since the Dodgers had beaten the Braves, the Reds were now in seventh place in the National League, trailing first-place Boston by 15 games.

As Hoyt began his eulogy of Ruth, he stated that he had broadcast that evening with his mind half on Ruth and half on the ball game. Hoyt called Ruth his hero. He would speak for 50 minutes, working without a script in what is regarded as his finest hour in broadcasting. It was an off-

Waite Hoyt (National Baseball of Fame Library, Cooperstown, N.Y.).

the-cuff and sincere tribute. He spoke of Ruth's foibles and unique personality: "The world was a big night club to Ruth — and he was both the star performer and the audience as well. If ever a guy loved life — and lived it — that fellow was Babe. Yet strangely — he never got into public rows. He was wisely conscious, there was a certain cautious conduct to be maintained in public — and he did just that."[11] Hoyt stated that Babe would go to church on Sundays and put a $50 bill in the collection plate and then stand outside on the steps and sign autographs for half an hour.

As Hoyt continued to speak that evening the word spread around Cincinnati that Waite Hoyt was on the air talking about Babe Ruth, and a lot of additional listeners turned the dial on their radios to WCPO. Hoyt said that the Babe tutored Lou Gehrig in hitting and that he learned a lot from him. Hoyt told the infamous story of the day at the Polo Grounds when Ruth, having been selected by his teammates to represent the Yankees, was to welcome the Allied commander and French hero of World War I, Marshall Foch. Prior to the game Ruth went over to Foch's box and was about to commence with his appointed duty when he forgot the visiting dignitary's name. To compensate, Ruth approached Foch and stated, "Hey

Gen., they tell me you were in the war."[12] A similar faux pas, according to Hoyt, occurred when Ruth was to greet President Calvin Coolidge and forgot his name. Nonetheless, "The Babe sauntered over to the box, wiping his face with a large red bandanna. He leaned close to the somewhat startled president and after a moment exclaimed: "Hot as hell, ain't it, Prez!"[13]

Hoyt also spoke about how Babe should have had a chance at managing a big league team. "That was his ambition. Babe felt like an outcast because nobody would let him try it."[14] Concluding his tribute that evening, Hoyt said that Babe had led one hectic life, from the time it began until one minute past seven this evening. He said that there would never be another Babe Ruth ever. There would be someone who might break his home run records, but they would never equal the other side of him.

Hoyt's listening audience was deeply moved by his heartfelt tribute to Ruth and following the broadcast the station was flooded with telephone calls and telegrams from fans. It was that evening that Waite Hoyt became a broadcasting legend. Hoyt later told others that he regretted not having made a tape of the broadcast. However, according to an article published in *The Cincinnati Enquirer* in 1984, Hoyt's assistant at the time, Ed Kennedy, was said to be in possession of an aluminum disc recording of the Hoyt's eulogy to Ruth. Apparently a recording was made and copies are now turning up for sale on eBay. Interestingly, the day after Hoyt's tribute, Mel Allen — the voice of the New York Yankees — broadcast his short scripted five-minute tribute to the Babe and recorded it for posterity.

Waite Hoyt was invited to serve as an honorary pallbearer at Ruth's funeral services at St. Patrick's Cathedral in New York City. Nearly 6,000 persons were on hand in the Cathedral to witness Ruth receiving last rites. As Ruth's casket was being removed from St. Patrick's, former teammate Jumpin' Joe Dugan whispered to Hoyt, "Lord, I'd give my right arm for an ice-cold beer."[15] Hoyt nodded at Dugan and replied, "So would the Babe."[16] Then, as 75,000 persons lined the streets around St. Patrick's, Ruth's remains were taken to Yankee Stadium where for two days an estimated 82,000 fans waited in the rain to file past his bier and pay final tribute to The Sultan of Swat.

As a lasting tribute to his friend, Hoyt wrote the text to *Babe Ruth As I Knew Him*, a 50-page magazine on the life of Ruth (published by Dell Publishing Co., Inc., in 1948). In a letter to author Robert W. Creamer that Hoyt wrote in 1969, he states, "Branch Rickey said my book, pamphlet, on Ruth was the best he'd ever read on the Babe and it had 19 mistakes in it. I wrote it in two nights and all I received was 1500 dollars.

That was a labor of love."[17] Many copies of the magazine still exist and are often listed for sale or auction on such outlets as eBay on the Internet.

Regardless of the fact that the 1948 Reds finished in seventh place they drew a total attendance of 899,975. Likewise the 1949 Reds came within one game of finishing in the National League cellar but remained a big draw, finishing with a season attendance of 823,386. Hoyt developed a strategy to energize the dullness of the Reds teams: "When you're broadcasting, build the other guy up. Praise him. Otherwise, when you beat him, you haven't beaten anyone. Stay young in heart. Live in the present and don't bore modern fans to death with silly dribble about how superior everything was years ago. It's just not true."[18] Regardless of Hoyt's attempts to keep the games interesting during his broadcasts, the Reds continued their long occupancy of the second division into the early 1950s.

By 1952 the Reds had not finished in the first division since 1944 and attendance now sunk to among the lowest in the major leagues. Consequently the Reds executive management owner, Powell Crosley Jr., and general manager, Gabe Paul, felt that something radical needed to be done. For the past few years the Reds had been managed by Luke Sewell. In July, with the Reds well on their way to another losing season, pressure was being put on Sewell by the press and fans alike to resign. Sewell eventually quit, offering as his parting shot his belief that the second-guessing press brought the fans down on his head, adding that Cincinnati had, "the worst fan clientele in the country."[19]

On July 28, 1952, Gabe Paul hired Rogers Hornsby as Sewell's replacement. "I picked Hornsby because I wanted a hard-nosed baseball man," said Paul.[20] Hornsby's tenure as Reds manager would be a stormy affair. *Cincinnati Post* sportswriter Earl Lawson stated in his book *Cincinnati Seasons: My 34 Years with the Reds*, "As a person Hornsby was one of the most prejudiced, uncouth, thoughtless individuals I've ever met. He also was the worst manager the Reds had during the 34 years I covered the club."[21] Hornsby finished with 27–24 record as manager in 1952 as overall the Reds finished in sixth place with a record of 69–85.

The following season the Reds put the 57-year-old Hornsby's still considerable batting skills on display as part of a pre-game exhibition for the Main Street Businessmen's Association night at Crosley Field. With Waite Hoyt pitching to Hornsby, he drove a couple of balls to the base of the scoreboard in left center. Hoyt remembered the first time he ever saw Rogers Hornsby hit. In 1922 the Yankees had their spring training camp in New Orleans. The previous season Hornsby had led the National League in hitting with a .397 average. So when the St. Louis Cardinals arrived in

New Orleans to play the Yankees in an exhibition game, everyone was interested in seeing what Hornsby could do at the plate.

Miller Huggins had selected Harry Harper to pitch the first four innings and then would send in Waite Hoyt to pitch the final five innings. In his first two times at bat against Harper, Hornsby had two hits—a triple and a single. Now it was Hoyt's turn to take over mound duty and face Hornsby. Hoyt's recollection of the event was, "I had studied him. I thought I had him figured out. In those days I was fast. I believed I could tease him with one or two bad and low outside, then pitch him a high hard one under his chin—across his chest. It worked fine until I got the ball across—or nearly across his chest. Hornsby belted that one over the wall. And—it was a long homer at that."[22] In his next two turns at bat against Hoyt, Hornsby got two more hits,—a double and single. Now with five hits in five times at bat, he faced Hoyt again in his sixth at bat. "On his sixth appearance, I was pretty well convinced I was facing the greatest right-handed batter I had ever seen. I turned to the outfield to wave Elmer Miller back fifty feet. Miller played a hunch and didn't move. I pitched— Hornsby swung—and the tying and winning runs scored on the blow that Rajah parked over Miller's head. Six hits in a row. I had seen enough. I had seen [Nap] Lajoie hit a single into left field off me with one hand—but Hornsby was even greater as a batter."[23]

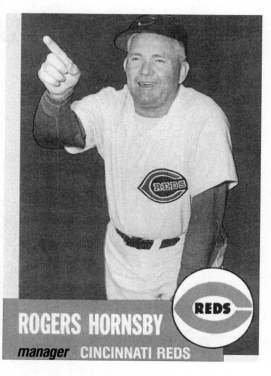

Rogers Hornsby remains the greatest right-handed hitter in major league history. He won seven National League batting titles, six consecutive between 1920–1925. Three times he hit over .400 in a season and won two triple crowns. His lifetime batting average of .358 is second only to Ty Cobb's .367.

It was a little ironic that two of the participants in one

Rogers Hornsby, the Ultimate 1953 series (Topps Archives, the Topps Co., Inc.)

of the greatest World Series (1926) ever played were winding up their respective careers in baseball in Cincinnati, but both Hornsby and Hoyt took their respective roles with the Reds extremely serious—in different ways. While they shared a common fate in the National League standings in Cincinnati, the real difference between the two was that Waite Hoyt had an immensely popular public persona in the community where as Rogers Hornsby had been a public relations nightmare. But that was Hornsby's managerial style. His tenure as manager with the Cardinals, Braves, Cubs and Browns had been no less controversial. In all Hornsby managed for 13 years in the major leagues, winning 680 games and loosing 798.

During the 1953 season the All-Star game was played in Cincinnati and Hoyt had his first opportunity to do a radio broadcast of a major league event nationwide. Hornsby was the antithesis of what we refer to today as "politically correct" and fell into disfavor with general manager Gabe Paul following some anti–Semitic remarks (Paul was himself Jewish). Likewise, a lot of the Reds players did not care for Hornsby either. Hornsby was sarcastic with the press and humiliated his pitchers. At one point Hornsby even publicly stated, "I'd rather have old Grover Cleveland Alexander all looped up than my entire pitching staff."[24] One of his players, infielder Grady Hatton even went so far as to go to Gabe Paul with complaints that Hornsby was urinating in the clubhouse shower.

Still, Hornsby had set in motion what several seasons later would become one of the Reds' most exciting teams in the past 15 years. Hornsby liked heavy-hitting teams. He converted Big Ted Kluszewski from being a line-drive hitter into a home run hitter by working with him in spring training to level his swing. He also engineered the deals that brought the Reds Jim Greengrass and Gus Bell. As a result, in the 1953 season the Reds hit 166 home runs with Ted Kluszewski hitting 40 (a franchise record), Gus Bell 30, Jim Greengrass 20, Andy Seminick 19 and Willard Marshall 17. Also Klu-

Ted Kluszewski, the Ulitmate 1953 Series (Topps Archive, the Topps Co., Inc.)

szewski (108), Bell (105) and Greengrass (100) each hit the 100 RBI mark for the season. Defensively, the Reds were in fielding percentage (.978) second only to the pennant-winning Brooklyn Dodgers (.980). But this was of little concern to Hornsby. He had always maintained that you can shake good fielders out of trees. However, the Reds' downfall was their pitching. Lefthander Harry Perkowski led the team with 12 wins and the Reds staff compiled a 4.64 ERA, third highest in the league.

Regardless of his critics, in Hornsby's short tenure in Cincinnati he had made an indelible mark on the Reds' style of play. The power-hitting, slick-fielding, poor-pitching Reds style of play that Hornsby had fashioned on the 1953 Reds team would become the franchise's signature for the next 30 years, beginning with the Reds almost slugging their way to the 1956 National League pennant, then pussy-footing their way to the 1961 National League pennant and climaxing with The Big Red Machine teams of the 1970s that won six division titles, four National League pennants and two World Championships. Waite Hoyt later remarked, in regard to the 1956 team, "The funny thing is that the '56 club was a hell of an outfit. We had Frank Robinson — he was Rookie of the Year — Gus Bell, Wally Post, and Big Klu [Kluszewski], [Johnny] Temple, Roy McMillan. But no pitching."[25]

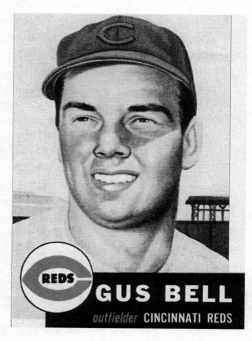

The 1956 National League pennant race was hand-to-hand combat between the Brooklyn Dodgers, Milwaukee Braves and Cincinnati Reds. Along the way first place was occupied for 126 days by the Braves, 17 days by the Dodgers and 16 days by the Reds. The pennant race was not settled until the final weekend of the season with the Dodgers winning the pennant by one game over the Braves and two games over the Reds. The Reds hit 221 home runs, tying the major league record that was set by the 1947 New York Giants. Rookie of the Year Frank Robinson led the team with 38 home runs, followed by Wally Post

Gus Bell, the Ultimate 1953 series (Topps Archives, the Topps, Co., Inc.)

with 36, Ted Kluszewski withx 35, Gus Bell with 29 and Ed Bailey with 28. Even part-time catcher and pinch hitter Smoky Burgess hit 12 home runs in 229 at-bats and pitcher Joe Nuxhall also hit 2. As for pitching, the Reds did have a little; Brooks Lawrence won 19 games and at one time had won 14 games in a row. Also, relief pitcher Hershell Freeman posted a mark of 14–5.

The surprising 1956 season that the Reds experienced came at the time in which radio broadcasting of ball games in Cincinnati by Waite Hoyt was in its golden era. In 1956 the Reds drew over a million (1,125,928) fans through the Crosley Field turnstiles for the first time in franchise history and Waite Hoyt had as much to do with drawing those fans as any of the players. The economic boom of the 1950s had made consumer goods more than readily available. It seemed that every household in Cincinnati not only owned a radio or television, but also at least one portable radio. It was the battery-powered portable radio, and its cousin the transistor radio that came on the market the following year, that built Hoyt's popularity to such an enormous status, unequaled in Queen City broadcasting history, and drew people to Crosley Field.

During the summer of 1956, with air conditioning still in very few homes, it was commonplace all over the hardworking city of Cincinnati for men and women to seek relief from the stifling heat and sit outside on their porches in the evening listening to the Reds radio broadcasts of Waite Hoyt and Jack Moran on WSAI. It was possible on any evening in July or August to walk down nearly any neighborhood street in Price Hill, Clifton Heights or Oakley and not miss a play being described by Hoyt or Moran on the radio as you passed each house. Furthermore, on many of these porches the occupants were also sipping a cold Burger Beer, as suggested by Hoyt. When the ball game ended, the neighborhoods would suddenly become silent as another work day beckoned and Cincinnati went to bed. Waite Hoyt had just not cultivated a listening audience in Cincinnati; he had created a listening culture.

By now Waite Hoyt was broadcasting for Burger Beer on an extensive radio network of about 20 stations in Ohio, Indiana, Kentucky and West Virginia. Also included were television stations WCPO-TV in Cincinnati, WHIO-TV in Dayton, Ohio, WLW-C in Columbus, Ohio and WJAZ in Huntington, West Virginia. Hoyt's rain-delay broadcasts were now famous along his network and Burger Beer was ecstatic over the success of them. Here was the only man in the United States who could hold his audience and continue to sell their product for the entire duration of a period of non-action. It was pure gold to the coffers of the Burger Brewing Company. Actually, Hoyt's rain-delay monologues were re-runs of his 1939 program on WOR in New York. He had written a huge amount of scripts for the program that was broadcast at the end of Brooklyn Dodgers games. Now in Cincinnati, during the rain delays he simply tapped his memory of those scripts and began speaking casually with his audience. Waite Hoyt had show-business blood in his veins and using his WOR format during Cincinnati rain delays worked — big time.

The downside of the popularity of the radio and television broadcasts of major league games by Waite Hoyt — as well as Ernie Harwell, Red Barber, Mel Allen, Harry Caray and others — was that it was taking a toll on the status of minor league baseball. In fact, radio and television broadcasting, along with the franchise-hopping of the Braves from Boston to Milwaukee, the Athletics from Philadelphia to Kansas City, the Dodgers from Brooklyn to Los Angeles, etc., had caused a decline in the number of minor leagues from 59 in 1949 to 28 by 1956. During the same period, minor league attendance had decreased from 41 million to 17 million. Nonetheless, radio and television broadcasting of major leagues games would continue to grow with the advent of such programming as *NBC's Game of the Week*.

Although by the late 1950s Hoyt and his family had been thoroughly ensconced in Cincinnati for a considerable time now, on occasion Waite still traveled back east to revisit his glorious past. "My visits to Yankee Stadium occur very seldom," he later said of that time. Once every few years. But I am always overcome by the magnitude of the Stadium itself. The hundreds of employees in and under the stands; the added press rooms; the Stadium Club. The players' dressing room — with lounge rooms. I look back to recall what a magnificent structure we thought the Stadium was when we moved from the Polo Grounds in 1923.

Just a handful of officials ran the business in those days. I can imagine any rookie player just joining the Yanks, and on entering the Stadium, being indelibly impressed — marked for life. The whole Yankee project is self-inspiring. If it has its weaknesses, and doubtlessly it has, they are not, however, immediately apparent to the young player or the casual observer. The tradition is not only a personal possession of the Yankee player — it has its tentacles in the front office. They like to win."[26]

During the summer of 1959, Hoyt went back to Yankee Stadium for the annual Old-Timers Day. Later he remarked to his friend Lee Allen, who was now working for the Hall of Fame in Cooperstown, that former pitcher Tom Zachary was there and not a happy camper. "Tom Zachary was peeved, [and with good cause] because in introducing him, Mel Allen — with true Jewish-Eddie Cantor comic style-made more of Zachary's prominence as the guy off whom Ruth hit his 60th homer than a fellow who won 11 straight for us one year."[27]

By 1959 Waite Hoyt and Jack Moran were doing their radio broadcast back on WKRC. Major league baseball had become bi-coastal with the Brooklyn Dodgers and New York Giants finding greener pastures in California. Meanwhile the power-hitting, pitching-poor Reds were back to their old ways, finishing in a tie with the Chicago Cubs for fifth place in the National League. Impressed with the way the 1956 Reds kept pace with the pack through power hitting, prior to the 1959 season Gabe Paul had made a trade with the Pittsburgh Pirates that he felt somewhat certain was going to bring Cincinnati it first pennant since 1940. But it proved to be one of the acknowledged worst trades in the history of major league baseball and paved the way for Paul's eventual exit from the Reds front office a year later.

On January 30, 1959, Paul traded Smoky Burgess, Harvey Haddix and Don Hoak to Pittsburgh for Frank Thomas, Whammy Douglas, Jim Pendleton and Johnny Powers. The trade immediately helped plug the holes in the Pirates lineup, with Hoak playing third and hitting .294 and Burgess catching and hitting .297. Harvey Haddix would win 12 games, and on May 26, 1959, pitch the best game in major league history. (After pitching 12 perfect innings, he would lose the game in the 13th). These same players would play major roles in the 1960 season as the Pirates won their first National League pennant since 1927.

However, the trade was a complete bust for the Reds. Frank Thomas, who had hit 161 home runs in the past six seasons for mostly dismal Pirates teams, was the keystone in the deal. Thomas had been converted by the Pirates from an outfielder to a third baseman.

Gabe Paul thought that by adding Thomas to the Reds lineup he was going to solve his third-base problem and also add additional power to a Reds lineup that had sunk from first in the league in home runs in 1956 to last in 1958. However, Frank Thomas never lived up to his billing in the 1959 season. Veteran Willie Jones took over the hot corner spot and Thomas wound up in a utility role, appearing in just 108 games. He split his playing time between third base, the outfield and first base, with a paltry 12 home runs and .225 batting average. Consequently, the notorious Crosley Field boo-birds were relentless in the abuse they heaped upon Thomas, forcing Gabe Paul to unload him expediently.

On December 6, 1959, less than a year since he had been acquired by the Reds, Frank Thomas was traded to the Chicago Cubs for left-handed relief pitcher Bill Henry, along with Lou Jackson and Lee Walls. Waite Hoyt was critical of the trade from the standpoint that Gabe Paul did not attempt to get more for Thomas in the deal. Hoyt stated in a letter to Lee Allen, "Guess by now you have digested all the 'ramifications' of the Henry deal. Although I cannot say we suffered too much — as Thomas is a negative Character who isn't generally liked, and who must do it all in a big way to be of value. Of course, we didn't get a pennant in return, but we couldn't expect that. The sad note is that I hear we could have had Dick Donovan from the White Sox for Thomas—but as always I guess numbers appeal to Gabe more than specific quality."[28] Dick Donovan had been the fourth starter on the 1959 pennant-winning White Sox, posting a record of 9–10. He would pitch for 15 years in the American League, finishing with a life-time record of 122–99. His best year was 1962 when he went 20–10 for the Cleveland Indians.

As the Christmas season approached in 1959, Hoyt (now 60 sixty years old) was contented with life. He was about to begin his third decade living in Cincinnati and was looking forward to the coming holiday season. His son, Chris, had been away at college attending Princeton University in New Jersey. Hoyt was of high hopes that Chris would graduate Phi Beta Kappa and then pursue his Masters degree. By now Chris Hoyt had married. He and his wife, Judy, were expecting a child the following summer. Waite Hoyt had a genuine devotion for his son and daughter-in-law and was giddy with excitement about the coming Christmas holiday as he anticipated the couple's visit.

Although Chris Hoyt had the privilege and comfort of growing up in a country club atmosphere, he found a personal discomfort living in shadow of his famous father and struggled with that identity crises for a long time. He disliked being introduced as the son of Waite Hoyt and at times was even estranged from him. In the video production of Hoyt's life (*The Life & Times of Waite Hoyt— Waite's World*) by Donn Burrows, released in 1997, Chris Hoyt demonstrated some very open and deep unresolved conflict, not only with his father but also his mother, Ellen. In the production, Chris Hoyt describes his parent's marriage as a mismatch. He stated that his father "put up with a lot of crap" from his mother and he could not understand why Waite was so determined to see the marriage continue. Also in the Burrows' production, Chris Hoyt stated that as his father's popularity snowballed in Cincinnati, there was even talk of Waite running for the office of mayor. However, he said that his father declined the opportunity to seek public office because he was concerned that Ellen, whom he described as a "loose cannon," would be a liability to his efforts.

If indeed there was more than a tongue-in-cheek notion that Waite Hoyt was considering seeking public office in the Queen City in the early 1960s, there would have been another, more fundamental, obstacle to overcome. At the suggested time period that Chris Hoyt stated his father was considering a possible candidacy, Cincinnati did not have an election process for direct election of mayor. In the Cincinnati of the early 1960s municipal elections were held with nine at-large seats on the city council up for election every two years. So there would be anywhere from nine to 15 candidates running for city council every two years. Subsequently, the candidate receiving the most votes in the election was recognized as the mayor through an ongoing informal tradition. Nonetheless, if Hoyt had been a candidate for Cincinnati's city council in the late 1950s or early 1960s, there is sufficient reason to believe that he may indeed have had enough voter appeal to run a very strong race — possibly ending up as the top vote-getter and the people's choice for mayor.

Still, whether or not the story of Hoyt's considering a run for public office is valid or not, it remains questionable if Hoyt — a hands-on guy who liked to take charge of all the endeavors he participated in — would have ever attempted to enter a process that was so totally foreign to him and one in which he had absolutely no control over the outcome. The reality in the circumstance — Ellen being a deterrent to Waite seeking public office — seems to suggest that she may have been more of an excuse than a reason not to run for public office.

Donn Burrows, who not only produced the aforementioned video, but also was a close friend of Waite Hoyt's in his declining years, feels a certain amount of empathy for son Chris. Burrows stated, "I think that growing up with a father who was on the road, talking to an audience more than to his own son, he was devoted to his wife to such an extent his son felt whipped. I think that Chris wanted to see more of his father, like any son would. Chris did not want to share his father as much as he was forced to with Waite's fame."[29] Burrows went on to say that perhaps from Chris Hoyt's point of view, Waite just let Ellen have her own way a little too much. There was perhaps a certain degree of dysfunction in the Hoyt household and according to Donn Burrows, "it decimated Chris for many years and while he has learned to live with it, he still feels the pain of it."[30] Nonetheless, after experiencing some debilitating personal problems in the 1970s Chris Hoyt rebounded and went on in the 1990s to become the founder of a successful consumer-based growth strategy called "Co-marketing." The concept joins manufactures and retailers together in constructive ways to enable both of them to build volume and profits. The concept has been embraced by many giant consumer products companies including Procter & Gamble.

Regardless of the topsy-turvy domestic scene in the Hoyt household, as the decade of the 1960s approached Waite found himself in larger personal demand than ever before. Everyone in the Reds broadcasting area wanted Waite Hoyt to be part of their event and by December 1959 he was making speeches four to five times a week. In many cases, notwithstanding functions supported by Alcoholics Anonymous, he was serving as master of ceremonies for banquets around the Cincinnati area totally unrelated to sports. While privately he described these duties as a huge headache, he participated out of the civic responsibility he felt for the community at large. One night might find him addressing the Dayton Rotary Club, the next night a banquet for General Electric, and so on. In addition, he was in the process of filming 40 shows for local television in Cincinnati in which he would discuss various persons he had met, including New York mayor Jimmie Walker, George M. Cohan and George Marshall. Then there was spring training on the horizon and it was time to leave for Florida.

In 1960 the Cincinnati Reds would again have a dismal season, finishing in sixth place (67–87), 28 games behind the pennant-winning Pittsburgh Pirates. Once again Waite Hoyt did a credible job behind the microphone, attempting to generate fan interest for a lackluster ball club. But the Reds attendance dropped off to 663,486, their lowest figure since 1953. With all the happiness and good fortune that Waite Hoyt had experienced in Cincinnati there was one thing lacking: he wanted badly to be the broadcaster on a National League pennant winner. That would finally come the following year.

At the end of the 1960 season general manager Gabe Paul resigned and joined the front office of the expansion team Houston Colt 45's, who would be starting up play in the National League in the 1962 season. Hired to replace Paul was the former assistant general manager of the New York Yankees, and most recently president of the Detroit Tigers, William O. DeWitt Sr. No one expected big things from the Cincinnati Reds in the 1961 season. While DeWitt thought he had a very competent manager in Fred Hutchinson and the team had a solid core of a few players such as Frank Robinson, Vada Pinson, Jim O'Toole and the recently re-acquired Wally Post, he recognized that he was going to have to shake things up and provide some help for Hutch.

Immediately DeWitt went right about the task at hand. On December 3, 1960, he sold out-of-control second baseman Billy Martin to the Milwaukee Braves. Then on December 15, 1960, DeWitt sent All-Star shortstop Roy McMillan to Milwaukee for pitchers Joey Jay and Juan Pizzaro. The same day he sent along pitcher Cal McLish to the Chicago White Sox for third baseman Gene Freese. Now, all this wheeling and dealing was somewhat confusing to the Cincinnati fans, and the trade of the perennial Crosley Field favorite Roy McMillan to the Braves was roundly unpopular in the Queen City. In fact, popular local television variety show hostess Ruth Lyons invited DeWitt on her noontime show (*The 50-50 Club*) on WLW-T and gave him a verbal thrashing, remaining strongly forthright in stating her negative feelings over the McMillan trade while the studio audience cheered her on.

In March, as the Reds were in Florida preparing for the coming season, long-time owner Powell Crosley Jr. died. This event was unsettling to the team, the City of Cincinnati and fans alike as it raised some serious questions of vulnerability for the team, with its sinking attendance, being sold and relocated. In memory of Crosley the Reds sewed black armbands on their uniforms and proceeded to open the season by losing 18 of out their first 24 games. Then on April 27, 1961, DeWitt made one more trade, sending popular catcher Ed Bailey to San Francisco for second baseman Don Blasingame and pitcher Sherman "Roadblock" Jones. The trade seemed to energize the Reds and in May they were hot, finishing the month with a record of 20–6. Suddenly this team of mostly veterans referred to in the press as The Ragamuffins were challenging the Giants for the league lead. Then in June, the Reds went 19–12 and moved into first place. According to Waite Hoyt this Reds team was described by one Dodgers official as "A conglomeration of castoffs who have banded together for one last stand."[31] In Hoyt's words the 1961 Cincinnati Reds were "Just the shabbiest bunch you ever saw, and then somehow, for some reason, they put it together, and they just took off."[32]

In the middle of the season, on July 17, 1961, Ty Cobb died. In his remembrance of Cobb, Hoyt stated that when former Detroit Tigers great Harry Heilmann died at the age of 56 on July 9, 1951, he had gone to Detroit for the funeral and then appeared on a television program with Ty Cobb. Following the broadcast, Hoyt and Cobb got together and discussed baseball. "When the show was over we went down to a room ... and Cobb talked about batting ... talked for an hour and a half. I learned more about batting listening to Cobb talk, in those ninety minutes ... than I ever knew before in all my career."[33] Unfortunately, old wounds were still open with Cobb's adversaries; his funeral was avoided by baseball and only seven people were in attendance.

Meanwhile The Ragamuffin Reds rolled on toward the 1961 National League Pennant, posting a 18–12 record in July. Then it was nip and tuck with the Los Angeles Dodgers, the pre-season favorites. By August the Reds had slipped back into second place. Then came an historic series with the Dodgers at the Los Angeles Coliseum. In mid–August the Dodgers went cold, and on the evening of August 16 they were shut out in both games of a twi-night doubleheader by the Reds Jim O'Toole and Bob Purkey. At the time the Dodgers were in the middle of a ten-game losing streak and their season was collapsing around them. The Reds were now running in open field and no one was able to catch up with them. Frank Robinson would lead the Reds, winning the National League MVP award while hitting .323, with 37 home runs and 124 RBIs. Also, Joey Jay would post a (21–10) record, giving the Reds their first 20-game winner since 1947, while Jim O'Toole would finish 19–9.

On September 26, 1961, the New York Yankees Roger Maris hit his 60th home run of the season off Baltimore Orioles pitcher Jack Fisher, thereby tying Babe Ruth's single-season record. As the news of Maris' epic feat circulated around the world it was hardly even noticed in Cincinnati. The Reds had just beaten the Chicago Cubs that afternoon at Wrigley Field 6–3 before a sparse crowd of 3,327 and were now assured of at least a tie for the pennant. All Cincinnati was poised to explode in a victory celebration as it waited for the results of a doubleheader that evening in Pittsburgh between the Pirates and Dodgers to see if the Reds would clinch the pennant. Unfortunately there are no known tapes of Waite Hoyt broadcasting the pennant-clinching game that day in Chicago.

As the Reds team, along with Waite Hoyt, left Chicago for the trip home, a huge crowd began to build in downtown Cincinnati at Fountain Square. As news circulated that the Dodgers had won the first game of the twin bill 5–3, it did little to dampen the spirits of the huge crowd. By 9:00 P.M. had swelled to over 30,000 and was still growing. Radio speakers were set up on the square and the second game was broadcast over the assembled hoard of humanity that was cheering wildly for the Pirates. By now the Reds had arrived at Greater Cincinnati Airport and their caravan of buses was heading down the Dixie Highway for Fountain Square. Mayor Walton Bachrach had gone to the airport to meet the team, but was unable to get out of his car due to the huge crowd that had gathered there. The Reds caravan arrived at Fountain Square at 9:22 P.M. and at 9:56 P.M. it was official — the Pirates had taken the second game 8–0. The 1961 National League pennant belonged to the Reds. Immediately Cincinnati exploded!

According to Waite Hoyt, the spontaneous celebration "was like V-J Day and V-E Day, and all other big days Cincinnati has known — all rolled into one."[34] As the celebration continued toward midnight, players made statements over a rigged-up PA system and Hoyt took a place atop one of the buses and sang a few songs from his vaudeville days. This was what he had hoped to experience since coming to Cincinnati and now it was all real. However, the best was yet to come as the following morning it was announced by baseball commissioner Ford Frick that Waite Hoyt of Cincinnati and Bob Wolff of Minnesota would be doing the radio play-by-play of the 1961 World Series.

In the end, the powerful New York Yankees won the series in five games. Nonetheless, it was a historic World Series. Entering the series, Yankees pitcher Whitey Ford had previously pitched 18 scoreless innings against the Pittsburgh Pirates in the 1960 series. In the opening game of the 1961 series at Yankee Stadium Ford proceeded to shut out the Reds 2–0. Now he had pitched 27 straight scoreless innings in World Series competition. In game four of the series, played at Crosley Field, he came back to pitch another five innings of scoreless ball before leaving with an ankle injury, and in the process broke Babe Ruth's record of 29.2 innings of scoreless ball in World Series competition.

For Waite Hoyt, going back to Yankee Stadium as radio broadcaster of the Reds in the 1961 World Series was one of the most prestigious moments for him in his broadcasting career. By 1961 Hoyt had broadcast approximately 2,900 games for Burger Beer. Never at a loss for words, Hoyt amused his listening audience with a blooper in the 1961 World Series. Heading into a station break, he announced "This is the Burger Beer Broadcasting Network."[35] However, the World Series was sponsored by the Gillette Safety Razor Company. When Hoyt realized his blunder, he amused his audience as he stated, "We owe Gillette one in next year's series."[36]

1961 seemed like open season on the records of Babe Ruth, with Whitey Ford breaking the Babe's World Series scoreless-inning record and Roger Maris breaking his single-season record for home runs with 61 (despite the asterisk attached to the statistic by baseball commissioner Ford Frick due to the fact that Maris had hit his home runs in a 162-game season as opposed to the 154-game season that Ruth played in). Nonetheless, Maris was paraded around the country during the winter from one rubber chicken dinner to another. In early January 1962, Waite Hoyt reported seeing Maris at a banquet in Columbus, Ohio, looking glum. "He [Maris] sat with his chin resting on a chair in front of him looking completely bored."[37]

As usual, the off-season was a time of considerable activity with Hoyt. In the first three weeks of January he had given nine speeches and made nine television appearances. Also, he was making weekly television appearances with Paul Dixon, a highly popular local television personality in Cincinnati in the 1950s and 1960s. The demand for his services seemed to be endless. Now Hoyt was also tackling a new project. Persuaded by William Exam, an executive with the William Morrow Publishing Company in New York, to write his life story, Hoyt set about diligently knocking out about 300 pages chronicling his career in baseball and beyond. However, as Hoyt perused the pages of his nearly completed manuscript he became intensely dissatisfied and mentioned in a letter to Lee Allen that most of it was froth. In the end the work never satisfied Hoyt's expectations of his life story and the book was never published. On the family front, by now Chris Hoyt had graduated from Princeton and was working for General Electric in New York. Also Chris and his wife, Judy, were expecting their second child that coming June. These circumstances delighted Waite Hoyt to no small end and the role of grandfather seemed to fit him just right.

In early January 1962, Jack Moran resigned from the Reds broadcasting team to take the position of sports director on WCPO-TV. Moran had been working with Hoyt as his broadcasting partner since 1955 on WSAI 1955–1958 and then (WKRC 1959–1961. Although the Reds were still the biggest sports attraction in town, both college and professional basketball had been gaining huge market shares in the Queen City. Oscar "The Big O" Robertson had just completed his brilliant collegiate basketball career at the University of Cincinnati in 1960, and the following year the Bearcats won the NCAA tournament, making them the 1961 national champions. Also, both the Xavier Musketeers basketball team and professional Cincinnati Royals of the NBA had large followings, so WCPO felt that wintertime sports in the city needed extended coverage.

So with Moran off to greener pastures in TV land and spring training on the horizon, Hoyt was going to have a new radio broadcasting partner in the booth with him for the 1962 season. The Hoyt-Moran act was going to be a hard one to follow, as the personalities of the two seemed to fit very well. According to Moran's widow, Barbara, "Jack really thought a lot of Waite and from what I know he was a very good man."[38] Moran had no problem playing the straight man for Hoyt and always knew when to let him take center stage. According to Hoyt, there were 200 applications for Moran's job, including former Reds outfielder Ival Goodman. Eventually the job went to Gene Kell, who would hold down the position until the end of the 1963 season, when Claude Sullivan would come on board to join Hoyt for his final seasons behind the microphone in 1964 and 1965.

In the 1962 season the National League had two new expansion teams beginning play — the New York Mets and the Houston Colt 45's. To stock these team each of the existing eight National League teams made a certain number of players from their rosters available for an expansion draft. In the draft the Reds lost several players, including outfielder Gus Bell and infielder Elio Chacon to the Mets, and three pitchers — Ken Johnson to the Colt 45's and Sherman "Roadblock" Jones and Jay Hook to the Mets. Waite Hoyt's assessment of the damage to the Reds was minimal: "I hated to see Ken Johnson go. He had some good stuff. Roadblock Jones won some good games; I don't know how he would have been over the long haul. Jay Hook won't be missed. He has to reorganize his pitching philosophy. Hook seemed to pitch on the same level. He didn't raise or lower his sights. I once said to him, 'You must make up your mind whether you're going to be a baseball player or an engineer.'[39] Hook had recently completed a Masters degree in engineering at Northwestern University and was now working on a doctorate. As it turned out none of the players lost by the Reds in the expansion draft had any effect on the outcome of the team's play in the 1962 season. The fact of the matter was that all the players lost in the draft had miserable seasons and the Reds— despite winning 98 games, with a monster season by Frank Robinson (39 home runs, 136 RBIs, .342 batting average) and 20-game seasons by Bob Purkey (23–5) and Joey Jay (21–14)—could not overcome the San Francisco Giants and finished in third place in the National League.

In 1963, by popular demand Burger Beer released a recording produced by Personality Records of some of the existing rain-delay broadcasts of Waite Hoyt from the 1950s and 1960s. The recording was extremely popular and was followed by the release of a second volume the following year. The cover of volume one, titled *The Best of WAITE HOYT in the Rain*, featured Hoyt wearing a rain coat with in his left hand both an umbrella and microphone, while holding a case of Burger Beer under his right arm. Today both recordings regularly appear for sale on eBay and can also be found in many used record shops around the country. The recordings are in a sense the only real mother lode of material remaining that memorialize Hoyt's thousands of Reds radio broadcasts. Other than that, WKRC in Cincinnati still has a few tapes, primarily from the 1963 season. Also, Hoyt's final radio broadcast on October 3, 1965, of the Reds vs. Giants game from Candlestick Park was preserved by the National Baseball Hall of Fame and Museum. The broadcast was recorded on two reels of tape, contain the entire game and can be listened to by visitors at the museum in Cooperstown, New York.

The Reds never won another pennant during Waite Hoyt's tenure doing the radio broadcast play-by-play of the games. They finished fifth in 1963, second in 1964 and fourth in 1965. During the 1965 season it was announced that after 25 years of sponsoring Reds radio broadcasts, Burger Beer was out and that another Greater Cincinnati area brewery, Wiedemann Beer, would become the new sponsor for the 1966 season. Even until this very day there continues to exist a conflict of opinion on whether or not Waite Hoyt was offered the opportunity to continue as Reds radio broadcaster with the new sponsor. One version of the story states that Wiedemann Beer reasoned that after Waite Hoyt had been so closely associated with Burger Beer for 25 years, he became too highly identified with that product to be effective as a salesperson for their product. Waite Hoyt himself seemed to support this version.

Now this wasn't the first time that the issue was raised in regard to a baseball broadcaster being too closely identified with one brand of beer to be able to pitch another. In 1945 Harry Caray began broadcasting games for the St. Louis Cardinals sponsored by Griesedieck Beer. In 1953, after beer baron August Busch bought the ball club, Budweiser Beer took over as sponsor. Immediately, the question was raised if Harry Caray had become too closely associated with Griesedieck Beer to sell Budweiser. So August Busch polled 100 of his distributors and they all agreed that Harry Caray should stay on as broadcaster. At that time in 1953 Budweiser was number two in beer sales nationally. However, by 1957 Budweiser was the number one-selling beer in the USA and Harry Caray continued to hype the sales of Bud until 1969.

On the other hand, Hoyt's friends in the media have over the years offered a more simplistic, romantic reason why Waite Hoyt was not offered the opportunity to continue broadcasting the Reds games when the Wiedemann Beer sponsorship began — that Hoyt, out of a sense of undying loyalty to Burger Beer, who stood by him during his darkest days of alcohol dependency, felt it was almost sacrilegious to broadcast the games for Wiedemann Beer. Whatever the reason for Hoyt's decision (perhaps it was a little of both), in the end it was academic; he was 66 years old at the end of the 1965 season and decided to retire. So be it.

Throughout his broadcasting years Waite Hoyt was always fair in his reporting of the games and criticism of the players. According to Reds relief pitcher Jim Brosnan who authored a book on the 1961 Reds titled *Pennant Race*, following a game during that season, Hoyt stated in his post-game wrap-up on the radio from Crosley Field that, "If Hutchinson had a little pitching today, the Reds would still be in the game. Those four runs that Maloney gave up look mighty big."[40] The pitcher that Hoyt was making reference to was a young 21-year-old Jim Maloney, then in his second season with the Reds. Maloney was listening to the radio in the clubhouse. Subsequently, Maloney yelled out, "That-second guessing old s.o.b.! I guess he could do any better."[41] Well, fast-forward and by 1965 fireballing Jim Maloney had become the ace of the Reds pitching staff. In 1965 Maloney would post a season record of 20–9 with an ERA of 2.54, striking out 244 batters in 255 innings. Also, during the season Maloney pitched two no-hitters. He would eventually pitch three no-hitters in his career and if it had not been for a bad break in 1967 he might have pitched four.

No-Hitter — Johnny Bench celebrates the final pitch of Jim Maloney's third no-hitter, Crosley Field, April 30, 1969 (the Cincinnati Reds).

On the evening of August 16, 1967, Maloney was well on his way to pitching the first-ever no-hitter at Forbes Field in Pittsburgh. After retiring 19 consecutive Pirates he walked Matty Alou. In the top of the seventh Maloney tripled into right-center off Pirates pitcher Woody Fryman. As he rounded second base heading for third, he aggravated a previous injury to his right ankle. "I felt the pain when I touched second base and again when I made a sudden stop after rounding third,"[42] said Maloney. He ended up having to leave the game. For the record, the Reds went on to win that game 4–0 as Bill McCool came on in relief of Maloney and allowed two hits over the final 2 ⅔ innings.

However, the first of Maloney's three career no-hitters came on June 14, 1965, at Crosley Field. In the game he pitched 10 innings of no-hit ball against the New York Mets before being beaten 1–0 in the 11th inning on a home run by Johnny Lewis. That evening the game was being broadcast on television back to New York. There exists in baseball a very old tradition that no one mentions anything about a no-hitter in progress. Every 10-year-old kid that plays baseball in Little League and Knot Hole, every high school player and major league player alike, knows that it is considered bad luck to talk about a no-hitter in progress. In essence, it is a great, time-honored taboo in the game. Well, not that hot June evening in Cincinnati as Maloney was overwhelming the Mets batters with his blazing speed and control.

The word reached Waite Hoyt in the Reds radio broadcasting booth that the Mets television broadcasting team of Bob Murphy, Lindsey Nelson and Ralph Kiner were talking over the air about Maloney's no-hitter in progress. Hoyt, who called five no-hitters in his broadcasting career, handed the microphone over to Claude Sullivan, then stormed down to the Mets broadcasting booth and admonished the trio of Mets broadcasters for their indiscretion. Ralph Kiner attempted to rationalize their collective action by saying that if they didn't talk about the no-hitter in progress, it would not be fair to their sponsors.

It was that evening that Hoyt realized that the game was changing in ways he never thought possible. However, Kiner is far from being alone in his indiscretion of blowing the whistle over the air waves about a no-hitter in progress. Joe Garagiola believes it is now a standard modus operandi for a broadcaster. "I believe in telling the people,"[43] says Garagiola. "In fact, I'll try to build up the audience by saying, 'If you've got any friends not listening, call them up. We might have a no-hitter here tonight.'[44]

A sad footnote to this scenario is that Ralph Kiner, who at 81 years old is still hanging on broadcasting New York Mets games part time, is often compared to Waite Hoyt in his broadcast style in bringing a strong knowledge of baseball strategy and history into the booth. However, unlike the eloquence of Hoyt, Kiner is also known for having committed gross mispronunciations at the microphone over the years that became known as "Kinerisms." One such famous instance is Kiner's faux pas, "We'll be back after this word from Manufacturers Hangover."[45]

On September 5, 1965, Waite Hoyt Day was celebrated at Crosley Field prior to the Reds vs. Phillies game. The event was sponsored by the Chamber of Commerce and Cincinnati Mayor Walton Bachrach started the festivities by reading a proclamation making it Waite Hoyt Day in the city. With a microphone set up just to the left of home plate and Crosley Field announcer Paul Sommerkamp acting as master of ceremonies, various dignitaries, along with friends and associates of Hoyt's, approached to make short comments. One by one they filed by the microphone: Bill DeWitt Sr., president of the Reds; Pat Harrington, president of Burger Beer; catcher Johnny Edwards representing the Reds players; Pat Harmon of the *Cincinnati Post* representing the Cincinnati sports writers, and so on. Ed Kennedy, who had worked with Hoyt behind the scenes in the broadcasting booth in the 1940s, described Hoyt as the man that "made the rainy day famous."[46] Then, with his dear wife, Ellen, at his side, a bounty of gifts was showered upon them, including an European vacation.

Hoyt then approached the microphone and thanked the thousands of fans who had come to share the day with him, even turning away from the grandstand to face the right-field bleachers and thank those fans as well. In his emotion-charged speech Hoyt stated, "I wish I could shake hands with everyone here. Words can never express the depths of my affection and gratitude. I remember walking out of Ebbets Field after the Dodgers released me in 1938 and wondering what was going to happen and wishing there were someway I could still be a part of the game. And today, here I stand thanking all of you for what has happened. This day had to come some time. Good-bye and good luck and thank you."[47] A few moments later Waite Hoyt walked off the field to a rousing standing ovation from the crowd.

On September 23, Hoyt broadcast his last home game at Crosley Field as the Reds beat the Giants 7–1. Then, on October 3, 1965, after 24 years, he broadcast his last game for the Reds from San Francisco's Candlestick Park. All through the broadcast Hoyt was swamped with telegrams of thanks and well wishes. After the final out he unceremoniously thanked his listening audience and stated that his 50-year association with major league baseball was over. It was the end of the golden era in Cincinnati baseball broadcasting. In all, Waite Hoyt had broadcast nearly 4,000 games for the Reds.

9

The Hall of Fame Calls

In the fall of 1965, with Waite retired from broadcasting, the Hoyts continued living in the cozy community of Hyde Park at 2374 Madison Road, but they were considering a full-time move to Florida. Meanwhile, Hoyt occupied his time by continuing to paint and work at his public relations job with Burger Beer. As a matter of fact, his ability at painting landscapes had become quite sophisticated. In November Hoyt addressed the annual banquet of the Cincinnati chapter of Alcoholics Anonymous, held at the Sheraton Gibson Hotel Roof Garden in downtown Cincinnati. As usual, whenever he spoke huge crowds were in attendance. That evening the rooftop ballroom of the Sheraton Gibson Hotel was no exception, with more than 500 people in attendance, both alcoholics and non-alcoholics alike. The assembled mass of friends, curiosity seekers and the press had come to pay tribute to Hoyt just as much as the continuing sobriety of the assembled membership. Hoyt began his speech that evening by stating, "I suppose that most of you seated at these tables are wondering just who are the alcoholics and who are not? Well, I'm Waite Hoyt, I was an alcoholic and a good one too!"[1] The crowd roared its approval.

Hoyt had now enjoyed 20 years of sobriety and had been an ardent supporter of the philosophy set forth by Alcoholics Anonymous, which included not only abstinence from alcohol, but participating in the 12th Step. The 12th Step is a sort of volunteerism whereby AA members help others afflicted with the disease of alcoholism by answering calls for help in the middle of the night. These summons of desperation can come from practicing alcoholics who are at the end of the rope and facing the moment of the truth in their lives (such as Hoyt did down on lower Broadway in June 1945), or from recovering alcoholics facing a crisis that could result in them suspending their sobriety and suddenly beginning to drink again. Through it all Waite Hoyt was there for everyone who needed him and more than once answered the cry for help in the dead of night. When Hoyt had started to attend AA meetings in 1945 there were perhaps 25 members participating in the local organization. Often non-profit charitable organizations such as The Salvation Army would send drunks up to the organization's headquarters, seeking a way out of their seemingly hopeless battle with the bottle. But by 1965 AA had taken on a much more diverse community of persons seeking self-help that now included many professionals, both men and women.

Following the 1966 season, Hoyt's old friend from his days at WOR in New York, Red Barber, was fired by the New York Yankees. Barber had left the Brooklyn Dodgers broadcasts following the 1953 season in a salary dispute. He was then hired by the Yankees and joined Mel Allen. Soon after Jim Woods was hired to provide a trio of broadcasters on the Yankees airwaves. During the 1956 season Woods was replaced with Phil Rizzuto, who was released by the Yankees as an active player on Old Timer's Day. While the enormous egos of both Barber and Allen had forced them to be indifferent towards one another in the booth, nothing had changed with their collective elitism towards former ballplayers attempting to become broadcasters. Consequently, both Barber and Allen showed a total disdain for Rizzuto in the broadcasting booth, at times tantamount to overt hostility. After the 1964 season the Yankees canned Allen.

In 1966 the New York Yankees had a horrible season, finishing in last place in the American League for the first time since 1912. As the season was concluding an anemic crowd of only 413 fans showed up for one of the games at Yankee Stadium. Red Barber, against the direct orders of the ball club executives, told the cameramen to pan their lens across the stands. Outraged by the perceived insolence and insubordination of Barber, the Yankees fired him. The broadcasting career of Red Barber had come to an end. He then took up writing and had several books published. Now the Yankees broadcasts were for the first time the primary domain of a former ballplayer as Phil Rizzuto became the lead man. Rizzuto would go on to broadcast Yankees games well into the 1990s, having at various times such former ballplayers as sidekicks in the booth as Joe Garagiola, Jerry Coleman, Bill White, Bobby Mercer and Tom Seaver.

By 1968 Waite Hoyt was back in broadcasting, doing a five-minute television program five days a week on channel 16 (a UHF station out of Dayton, Ohio). In addition, he continued to write various newspaper columns and was participating in volunteer work around Cincinnati. For several years now there had been a charity in Cincinnati known as The

Kid Glove Game Committee. The group annually sold tickets to an exhibition game played by the Cincinnati Reds with another major league club such as the Detroit Tigers. A certain percentage of the proceeds from the game would go to benefit the Knothole baseball teams around Cincinnati in purchasing equipment for their season. When Hoyt joined the committee they were averaging around $35,000 in annual sales. Hoyt suggested the kids playing Knothole baseball should be the ones selling the tickets, rather than the committee. With the kids out on the street hawking the tickets, sales tripled in a very short time.

The 1968 major league season had been dominated by pitching. In fact in the annals of baseball history 1968 has become known as The Year of the Pitcher. Low-scoring games were commonplace and by the end of the season 335 shutouts had been pitched. Denny McLain would become the major league's first 30-game winner since Dizzy Dean in 1934, finishing the 1968 season with a record of 31–6. Don Drysdale would pitch six consecutive shutouts while throwing 58 ⅔ straight scoreless innings, breaking a record held by Walter Johnson since 1913. Bob Gibson won 22 games and finished with an ERA of 1.12. Three no hitters were thrown in the National League and two in the American League, with Jim "Catfish" Hunter of the Oakland Athletics tossing a perfect game against the Minnesota Twins. Even the All Star game lacked hitting as the National League won 1–0 when Willie Mays scored a run on a double-play ball in the first inning. Tom Seaver struck out five batters in the two innings he pitched.

All the hype in the press about the dominance of the pitchers in 1968 amused Waite Hoyt. In the summer of that year Hoyt wrote with characteristic, tongue-in-cheek humor on the matter in a letter to his former broadcasting partner and long-time friend, Lee Allen, who was by now historian at the Hall of Fame in Cooperstown: "I am reading constantly about the superiority of today's pitchers and I cannot help but think how blanched and nervous Ruth and Gehrig and Foxx and Simmons and Hornsby and Frisch would be hitting against [Jerry] Arrigo, [George] Culver, [Sonny] Siebert, [Bob] Lee, [Billy] McCool, [Jim] Maloney and the rest. I doubt whether Cobb and Jackson or Terry or O'Doul or the Waners would want to go to the plate—certainly not after the fourth inning when the pitching gets tougher. And against Marichal, Drysdale, Gibson (real good pitchers, by the way) the Yanks and A's and Cards and Giants wouldn't even show up."[2] In any event, in a perceived remedy for the 1969 season, major league baseball lowered the height of the pitching mound from 15 inches to 10 inches.

In the same letter Hoyt mentioned that someone he didn't identify "had made a crack" that 14 players who were on the American and National

League rosters in the first All-Star game in 1933 were in the Hall of Fame. He went on to say that the same person was in serious doubt if 14 players on the 1968 All-Star roster would make it. Whoever that person might have been, they were wrong. In fact 16 players on the 1968 All-Star roster were eventually voted into the Hall of Fame. The list includes from the National League: Steve Carlton, Tom Seaver, Juan Marichal, Willie Mays, Don Drysdale, Hank Aaron, Johnny Bench, Bob Gibson, Willie McCovey, Tony Perez and Billy Williams. From the American League: Rod Carew, Harmon Killebrew, Mickey Mantle, Brooks Robinson and Carl Yastremski. In addition, three other players on the 1968 All-Star roster could eventually wind up in Cooperstown: Ron Santo, Tony Oliva and Pete Rose, who is currently ineligible due to his lifetime ban from major league baseball. (However, Rose has applied for reinstatement and the matter is under consideration by the commissioner.)

Also during the summer of 1968, Hoyt was planning to attend the annual Old Timer's Day at New York's Yankees Stadium and was forced to pre-record 30 shows for his five-minute television program in Dayton. Now nearly 69 years old, he was becoming increasingly conscious of his place in baseball history. The Hall of Fame had eluded him and suddenly he was having serious doubts as to whether or not he would ever get the call from Cooperstown. He was aware of the upside and downside of his career — although he had won 237 games he had never pitched a no-hitter. Although he had pitched in seven World Series and won six games, he had never pitched in an All-Star game. There was even a sense of skepticism developing in him about the process for entering the Hall. In the class of 1968 Joe "Ducky" Medwick was being inducted and Hoyt felt that, although Medwick deserved the honor based on his .324 lifetime average for 17 years in the big leagues, he had achieved entry to the Hall only after a vigorous campaign of self-promotion and help from a sportswriter.

It also bothered Hoyt immensely that his former Yankee teammate Bob Meusel had never gotten the call from Cooperstown. "Meusel should be in the Hall of Fame without question," said Hoyt.[3] "He was a much better ball player than Ralph Kiner [inducted in 1975]. He had possibly the most powerful throwing arm of our day or any day. He was compelled to play the sun field always as the club didn't want to injure Babe Ruth's eyes. Meusel was a great outfielder — who appeared lazy in running because, being six three in height, he took long loping strides. He never appeared in a hurry — and wasn't. I suppose that was mistaken for indifference — and possibly he was to a degree — but he wanted to win, and he certainly contributed to the Yankee cause. He was fast too — never stole many bases — but then the Yanks of those days didn't steal bases as they depended mostly on Ruth, Gehrig, Meusel and Lazzeri for the long ball. Being thrown out attempting to steal only broke up rallies. He batted .309 lifetime average — and although he played in practically the identical number of games as Kiner, and in the almost same number of bats, drove in more runs than Kiner, who in the days immediately following W.W. 2 and against subnormal pitching hit 360 Hrs. as against Meusel's 156 — in days when Ruth and Gehrig were the only bona fide H.R. hitters."[4]

Regardless of the passion with which Hoyt advocated for Meusel's place in Cooperstown, there are two sides to the story. Another view of Meusel was presented by author Bert Randolph Sugar: "Bob Meusel put up numbers that would qualify him to join his two teammates [outfielders Babe Ruth and Earle Combs], in the Hall of Fame but, according to those who watched him play with a cold, almost indifferent detachment, they could have been better — much better. Bob Meusel was an immensely unpopular Yankee, his manner surly, his face a clenched fist, his personality that of a dead fish. During his last year with Yankees, when he had apparently mellowed and affected a friendlier manner, sportswriter Frank Graham wrote: "He's learning to say "hello" when it's time to say 'goodbye.'"[5]

Hoyt simply saw all these indifferences inherent in Meusel's personality as being that of a loner who was well dressed, lived well, didn't drink anymore than the rest of his teammates and had a great family. Bob Meusel did of course play in the shadow of his more famous teammates Ruth, Gehrig and Lazzeri. Yet he is one of one of just two major league players to have hit for the cycle three times in his career, and he won the American League home run and RBI titles in 1925. Despite the fact he had a lifetime batting average of .309 and that he stole 140 bases in his career, he was often referred to by the press as Languid Bob. Apparently he never projected himself. Bob Meusel died in 1977 and remains one of those mysterious candidates not in the Hall of Fame. For Meusel to ever achieve enshrinement in Cooperstown will require an intensive lobbying campaign from the New York media not unlike those that elevated marginal players such as Brooklyn Dodgers shortstop Pee Wee Reese and New York Yankees shortstop Phil Rizzuto into the Hall of Fame.

As for Hoyt's comparison of Meusel to Kiner, he fails to point out that first of all, Kiner's entry into the major leagues was delayed by military service in World War II. Then, when he entered the majors in 1946 he proceeded to lead the National League in home runs the first seven of the 10 years he played in the major leagues and when he finished his career in 1955 his home run percentage (7.1) at that time was second on the all-time list only to Babe Ruth (8.5). Of course, there has always been some controversy in the home run totals of Kiner due to the fact that in 1947, his second season in Pittsburgh, the Pirates management had shortened the distance to the left-field fence to accommodate Hank Greenberg, whom had they had acquired from the Detroit Tigers. The shortened dimensions in left-field became commonly known as Greenberg's Garden and later evolved into Kiner's Korner. However, when it came to power hitting Ralph Kiner was the real thing. Twice in his career he hit over 50 home runs in a season, hit 13 grand slams, hit two or more home runs in game 34 times and batted over .300 three times.

As for the quality-of-pitching argument that Waite Hoyt makes in the Bob Meusel vs. Ralph Kiner comparison, Kiner probably did face weaker pitching in the post-World War II National League than Meusel faced in the American League of the Roaring Twenties." It is understandable that typical National League pitchers of the era such as Rex Barney, Ken Raffensberger and Ralph Branca are hardly the likes of Lefty Grove, Walter Johnson and Stan Coveleski that Meusel had to face. Nonetheless, Kiner still had to face some pretty tough pitchers in the 1940s in the presence of Harry Brecheen, Johnny Sain, Warren Spahn and others, which would in any generation not constitute a day at the beach. The fact of the matter is that arguments about the quality of pitching exist in every generation of major league play. Most recently, the quality of pitching came into question whenever expansion teams were added in 1961, 1962, 1969, 1977 and 1994. And in fact, in every year of expansion, major league home run totals did exceed those of the previous season. Nonetheless, when Ralph Kiner was elected to the Hall of Fame in 1975 he was in his last year of eligibility on the regular ballot and, as it turned out just barely squeaked by receiving 273 of the 272 votes needed for election.

RALPH KINER
outfielder PITTSBURGH PIRATES

Ralph Kiner, the Ultimate 1953 Series (Topps Archives, the Topps Co., Inc.)

Career Statistics
Bob Meusel vs. Ralph Kiner

Player	Yrs.	G	AB	Hits	HR	RBI	BA	SB	BB	SO
Bob Meusel	11	1407	5475	1693	156	1067	.309	140	375	619
Ralph Kiner	10	1472	5205	1451	369	1015	.279	22	1011	749

On February 3, 1969, Hoyt was staying at the Belleview Hotel in Clearwater, Florida, and just coming off the golf course at Bellean when he received a telephone call that he (along with Stan Coveleski, had been elected to the Hall of Fame by the veteran's committee. As Hoyt held the phone, he began to shake and cry. His thoughts immediately flashed back over the past half a century. He thought of his father, Addison, and all the encouragement that he had given him, the years he spent struggling in the minors and that winter morning receiving the news that he had been traded to the Yankees. His career was now complete. After regaining his composure, Hoyt then made a mad dash to the cottage where he and his wife, Ellen, were staying to share the news with her. Unable to locate her, Hoyt left word with someone in an adjacent cottage to tell her about the call from the Hall of Fame. Later, Hoyt was to learn that the message had reached Ellen and she immediately began to phone her friends, telling them, "What do you think, what do you think, Waite's in the House of Fame."[6]

It was baseball's centennial year and the induction ceremonies at Cooperstown for the class of 1969 included Roy Campanella, Stan Coveleski, Stan Musial and Waite Hoyt. The ceremonies took place on July 28 and as the program got underway, Commissioner Bowie Kuhn introduced the assembled Hall of Fame members who were on hand for the occasion, including Lefty Grove, Pie Traynor, Charlie Gehringer, Dizzy Dean, Bill Terry, Ted Lyons, Ray Schalk, Joe Cronin, Zack Wheat, Edd Roush, Sam Rice, Luke Appling, Heinie Manush, Casey Stengel, Redd Ruffing, Lloyd Waner and Joe Medwick.

In 1969 the Hall of Fame ceremonies had not yet become as politicized as they seem to be today. There was no controversy on who was being inducted and who was not. The records of the ballplayers enshrined at that time were accepted without apathy. Each inductee was considered on the merit of their accomplishments on the ball field and the statistical reasoning for their selection was crystal clear. The inductions at that time did not include the emotional second-guessing that is so ever present in the inductees of today. Furthermore, there were no petitions being circulated and signed along Main Street in Cooperstown or in gift shops for players on baseball's ineligible list, such as Shoeless Joe Jackson or Pete Rose. The criteria for induction was apparent in the selection; it was a rather sterile process and no one questioned it.

A ancient Greek philosopher once stated, "You never know how glorious the day has been until evening comes." For Waite Hoyt, like the other Hall of Fame inductees, it was a day of introspection. A day to reflect on how you had arrived at such a glorious moment in your life. A time to realize how the collective efforts of your work had pushed you to excel in your chosen profession of baseball just a little bit more than the average player. Of course, breaks were and still are part of the game, but in baseball the pathos of the old Protestant work ethic forever rings true: nothing begets success like motivation and hard work. Waite Hoyt had simply never let himself down. When he was climbing he grabbed a handle before slipping, when he was on top he kept his balance. On July 28, 1969, he truly had a right to feel proud of all he had done in his remarkable career.

The overwhelming feeling of accomplishment at Cooperstown is often felt by all present at the induction ceremonies, regardless if they are enshrined or not. Steve Blass, former Pittsburgh pitcher and current Pirates radio broadcaster on KDA, put it best: "I went to Maz's [Bill Mazeroski] induction at Cooperstown last summer [2001] and it occurred to me that all those guys that were there, I played with. I'm very proud of my career and what I accomplished."[7]

Roy Campanella spoke first that day. In a wheelchair and paralyzed as a result of an automobile accident in early 1958, Campanella expressed his love of the game in glowing terms: "When you love a game like this, you're not worrying about your paychecks on the 1st and 15th. When your playing money is no object. I know, I played nine years for nothing. But God knows it was the silver lining at the end of it, too. But I loved it as much in the major leagues as I did the first nine that I played for practically nothing."[8]

Then it was Stan Coveleski's turn to address the assembled baseball dignitaries, fans, press and former players. Coveleski reminisced in his acceptance speech about his experience as a youth working in the coal mines of Pennsylvania, pitching semi-pro ball and how he was eventually signed by Connie Mack to pitch for the Philadelphia Athletics.

Now it was Hoyt's turn. Baseball Commissioner Bowie Kuhn did the introduction and while he had the dates in Hoyt's career somewhat skewed in his remarks, he did capture the spirit of Hoyt's remarkable achievements in baseball. With his wife, Ellen, son, Chris, and his family standing nearby, Hoyt then stepped up to the microphone and spoke in the most elegant of terms, saying in part, "Standing before you here this morn-

Waite Hoyt (left) and Bowie Kuhn at the Hall of Fame Induction Ceremony, July 28, 1969 (National Baseball Hall of Fame Library, Cooperstown, N.Y.).

ing, I think that every day since February the second when I was notified that I was in the Hall of Fame has been one of excitement, trepidation, pulsation, almost in a quivering which makes one very anxious about the day. But this arrival at the Hall of Fame is not arrived at through one man's talent or one man's ability. There are contributions made by everyone that I've ever come in contact with. These fellows sitting on the platform here with me that I played against have made contributions to my life. All the fans have made contributions, the sports writers, the people who sympathized when you lost and encouraged you when you were frustrated. The people who wrote kindly of you when you needed help. The teammates who bolstered your own spirits. Everyone that ever came in contact with me in my history in baseball, has made some contribution to my life for which I am eternally grateful. And then after your career is over you look back and you wonder if your work has been good enough, has it satisfied your ambitions, have you accomplished what you started out to do. And you always think you were never good enough."[9]

Hoyt's remarks had touched the very hearts of all that were present that day and as he concluded they rose from their seats in tribute. Later, in a good-natured way, Hoyt was to state that to become a member of Hall of Fame a player had to have three things going for him: natural ability, a long career without injuries and being a New York Yankee. However, Hoyt was also honest with himself and later would remark that if he had never quit drinking it is doubtful that he would have made the Hall of Fame. At that point in time Hoyt joined former Yankees teammates Babe Ruth (1936), Lou Gehrig (1939), Bill Dickey (1954), Herb Pennock (1948) as well as manager Miller Huggins (1964) in the Hall of Fame. Eventually following him into the Hall would be Earle Coombs (1970) and Lefty Gomez (1972). Over a year later writer Bob Considine probably summarized the induction of Waite Hoyt into the Baseball Hall of Fame better than anyone when he wrote, "Waite Hoyt classed up Baseball's Hall of Fame the moment he entered it."[10]

Stan Musial was the final speaker at the ceremonies that day and actually gave the longest speech of the morning, taking time in his words to acknowledge all three of the other new inductees who spoke before him. Musial stated that "Campanella was a joy on the ball field. He was a happy guy and a hard hitter and a good catcher and he always tried to distract me with a lot of conversation at the plate."[11] On Hoyt, Musial stated, "I never saw Waite Hoyt pitch, but I remember him as a fine competitor and of course a fine baseball announcer all those years in Cincinnati. Of course, I've always admired Waite's ability to speak, an ability that I frankly don't have."[12] Musial then spoke from the heart about Stan Coveleski: "When I think of Stanley Coveleski, I think of my father. He was a Polish immigrant from Poland and he was a great baseball fan. And when I was young I always remember him talking about Babe Ruth. I know how thrilled he would be here today, not only with me but also with Stan Coveleski."[13]

10

Protecting the Ruth Legacy

On January 5, 1970, Waite Hoyt spoke at a testimonial dinner in Cincinnati for Pete Rose. Rose, a Cincinnati native, had grown up listening to Hoyt broadcast the Reds games on radio. So when Pete came up to the big leagues in 1963 he and Hoyt became fast friends. In fact, Hoyt would often sit next to Rose and converse with him during flights on Reds road games. Rose told author Roger Kahn, "Waite liked to sit in the dugout and tell us about the old times and the big stars he played with. The stories about Babe Ruth were always funny. And the ones about Cobb were mean. Mean stories."[1] Later that year Hoyt was again seriously considering living out his retirement in Florida. However, still very much in demand for public speaking and community work, in December 1970, with the Vietnam War still in progress, Hoyt led a group of major league players on a USO goodwill trip to Japan, Guam and the Philippines. The small group included Ron Taylor of the New York Mets, Richie Hebner of the Pittsburgh Pirates and Ed Kirkpatrick of the Kansas City Royals. The group visited military hospitals and showed films of the recent season and talked with troops in an attempt to boost morale. It also provided a time for Hoyt to reminisce about his ground-breaking 1922 trip to the Far East and allowed him to reflect on how much that area of the world had changed, how industrialized and modern it had become over the ensuing 48 years.

In late 1969 Hoyt had resigned from his public relations job with Burger Beer. In the early 1970s there were still four independent breweries operating in Cincinnati including Hoyt's former employer of many years. However, the local brewing industry was beginning to face declining sales due to the expanded marketing of large regional breweries into the Cincinnati area, such as Stroh's of Detroit. In 1972, in an effort to compete with Stroh's "Bohemian Beer," Burger remarketed its Tap brand as "Bohemian Tap" and also made a decision to reprise its sponsorship of Cincinnati Reds games by bringing back Waite Hoyt to broadcast televised games. Hoyt was signed by Avco Broadcasting and contracted to join announcer Tom Hendrick as the "color man." They would do the telecast of Reds games throughout a wide network that included Cincinnati, Dayton, Columbus, Lima and Zanesville in Ohio and Indianapolis over in Indiana. Burger Beer was confident that having Hoyt once again on the air as the pitch man for their product would give their salesmen a huge opportunity to tie in their personal promotions with the Reds telecast.

Although it was a pennant-winning year for The Big Red Machine, Hoyt's encore lasted for only that season. His return to broadcasting did little to help Burger Beer regain its market share in the Cincinnati brewing business, and in reality Hoyt viewed his return to the broadcast booth as more of a community-service effort than a revival of his broadcasting career. Today even the most informed of Cincinnati Reds fans has but a faint recollection of Hoyt ever being behind the microphone during the 1972 Reds telecasts. Waite Hoyt had been synonymous with radio broadcasting and the brief transition into television had not worked.

Following the 1970 season, Reds executive vice president and general manager Bob Howsam and his assistant, Dick Wagner, made a decision to not rehire radio broadcaster Jim McIntyre. McIntyre had been teamed with Joe Nuxhall doing the Reds radio play-by-play since the 1967 season. The first choice of Howsam and Wagner for a replacement was ex-Houston Astros radio broadcaster Harry Kalas. However, when Kalas opted to accept a Philadelphia Phillies offer instead, Nuxhall was joined by a young, unknown announcer in his late 20s by the name of Al Michaels. Nuxhall and Michaels were almost an overnight sensation and quickly became established as a powerful team in the new era of Reds radio broadcasters in the Cincinnati area.

With Nuxhall and Michaels firmly established as the legitimate Reds broadcasting team, the ghostly return of Waite Hoyt on television during the 1972 season was regarded by most fans as little more than a novelty. While there was still the same old familiarity of Hoyt's voice over the air waves, it seemed as if it was something coming out the past and no longer seemed to fit. Hoyt was the voice of the old Cincinnati Reds teams of Ewell Blackwell and Grady Hatton, Ted Klusezwski and Gus Bell, Frank Robinson and Joey Jay. The intimacy of Crosley Field was gone and the Reds now played in a huge new 52,000-seat stadium on the Cincinnati riverfront. Furthermore, the team carried the moniker of The Big Red Machine and was packed with MVPs and All-Star players such as Johnny Bench, Pete Rose, Joe Morgan and Tony Perez. It was an exciting team that was winning pennants. Although it still rained in Cincinnati, with local heroes in abundance now, Hoyt's old stories about Babe Ruth and the '27 Yankees just no longer held fan interest in the Queen City like they once did.

However, it was all moot now. The following year the Burger Brewing Company went out of business. The big brewery on Central Parkway that had for decades perpetually buzzed with activity and emitted the distinctive, intangible aroma of bubbling suds night and day was suddenly silent and non-aromatic. Now Waite Hoyt was unemployed once again, without any prospects for the first time since being cut loose by the Brooklyn Dodgers in 1938. Throughout his life Waite Hoyt had been a person who exhibited fierce loyalty and he felt a personal loss with the demise of Burger Beer, as he had never forgotten that during the darkest moments of his own personal battle with the bottle the brewery had been there, steadfast behind him. His years with Burger had been a symbiotic relationship. It had been a great run and perhaps no other personality in the Cincinnati broadcasting history had ever been so closely associated with a single product than Waite Hoyt with Burger Beer. The only possible exception may have been another person also associated with a Queen City brewery; for nearly two decades local comedian Bob Schreve pitched Schoenling Beer and its popular product "Little Kings Cream Ale" during all-night weekend movies televised on WCPO-TV. Schreve was also widely popular with fraternities on the University of Cincinnati campus and his crazy antics pitching the suds on the tube became so outrageous and controversial that Schoenling Beer eventually dropped its sponsorship of the all-night movie program.

But in the early 1970s baseball in Cincinnati had entered into a new era — a glorious one and one that no longer seemed to have room for Hoyt. The television broadcasting venture had been a risk worth taking. But over the years Hoyt had simply become indelibly etched in people's minds as a radio broadcaster from another era and by 1972 the Reds air waves belonged to Joe and Al. Waite Hoyt was a broadcasting pioneer and Riverfront Stadium was a massive, modern structure. Hoyt missed the friendly confines of cozy little Crosley Field. Hoyt told author Curt Smith, "You were close to the fans, you knew them. Crosley Field bred intimacy. You were on top of the place, you recognized a lot of people there, and they'd be calling right up to you. I mean, you could hear them on the air. The moment you enter Riverfront Stadium or Three Rivers Stadium or any of those places, you feel like you're witnessing an exhibition, a spectacle. It's like a giant coliseum. You feel alone. There's not the companionship — it's cold, sterile."[3] Author Ellen Frell stated, "In broadcasting Hoyt found a way to mix baseball and brains, the physical and the mental sides of his being that had conflicted in earlier years. And perhaps the microphone connecting him, the speaker, with the never-ending stories from a distant time was the most effective way he could find to be part of the public and the fans, yet retain some of the solitude he loved."[2]

When Al Michaels left Cincinnati after the 1973 season to become the voice of the San Francisco Giants, Joe Nuxhall was joined by Marty Brennaman. Brennaman's tenure in the Reds broadcasting booth over the next 27 years would result with him receiving the 2000 Ford C. Frick Award for broadcasting excellence by the National Baseball Hall of Fame. Through the 2003 season the long run of Nuxhall and Brennaman continued broadcasting the Reds games on WLW.

Following the television debacle in 1973 Hoyt went to work for the World Wide Travel Agency and the American Automobile Association (AAA) of Cincinnati. But soon boredom set in and he told close friends that he was going to surrender — i.e., resign. Domestic life in the early 1970s was a little darker for Hoyt. His dear wife, Ellen, began to develop Alzheimer's disease. As her condition degenerated Hoyt, was forced to eventually place Ellen in a long-term care center in order to provide for round-the-clock care.

In the Donn Burrows video production of Hoyt's life (*The Life & Times of Waite Hoyt — Waite's World*), Chris Hoyt stated that there was no known history of Alzheimer's in the family and alleges that more than likely his mother's condition was a result of frying her brain with alcohol and pills. Regardless, the loss of Ellen's companionship was devastating to Waite. Years before, while on the road in St.

Joe Nuxhall and Marty Brennaman, 700 WLW.

Louis and broadcasting Reds games, Hoyt had demonstrated his devotion to Ellen when he wrote a poem entitled "The Immortal" that closes with the line "She's my darling — she's my wife — who's outstanding in my life and decorates my personal Hall of Fame. The committee of one, your husband, Waite."[4] It seems that whatever the shallow conflict that son Chris was experiencing in his relationship with his mother, he failed to understand one fundamental aspect of his father's marital relationship — that Waite loved Ellen very sincerely and very deeply.

Despite the ever-changing world of Waite Hoyt in the early 1970s, one thing remained constant — with his massive repertoire of Babe Ruth stories, he was still considered by all the greatest living authority on The Sultan of Swat. Branch Rickey once told Red Barber that Hoyt probably knew the Babe more intimately than anyone else. So it was not coincidental that when Red Barber was writing a newspaper column on Ruth for *The Miami Herald* in the centennial year of 1969, he called his old friend Waite Hoyt. As part of the baseball centennial year festivities, the sportswriters had just voted Babe Ruth as the greatest player of all time. Hoyt told Barber, "To me, no question, Ruth was the greatest figure baseball ever saw ... and possibly the greatest player. Ruth and Cobb were so far and away that there is no way of convincing a modern ball player of their all-around abilities and greatness. There is no way today to convey the destructive potential of Ruth. His very presence in the lineup intimidated the other team, even if he was hitting a hundred and a quarter. When you consider his magnetism ... his accurate throwing.... His fine fielding ... his uncanny baseball savvy.... I don't see how anybody could be any better."[5]

Babe Ruth was both a fierce and smart competitor on the ball field. Although he possessed awesome power, if he found the opposing team's infield sleeping he would lay down a bunt. He stole bases, took the extra base when running out hits and slid with reckless abandonment. He also played his position in the outfield with skill and finished his 22-year big league career with a lifetime fielding average of .968, making 4,787 putouts in 2,503 games. Despite what the record shows, Hollywood still has a fixation on portraying Ruth as a big slow, lumbering buffoon. The epitome of such portrayals occurred in the 1992 celluloid bomb *The Babe*, directed by Arthur Hiller and starring John Goodman and Kelly McGillis. At least while Waite Hoyt was alive there was someone around to set the record straight on Ruth.

However, with each passing year, as the number of people that had close encounters with Ruth in their lives began to dwindle Hoyt became more and more proprietary in the way he parceled out his remembrances of the Babe. At times Hoyt took on a posture that led one to assume that he was the sole protector of the Babe's legacy. On the other hand, he also had become quite tired of not being paid for all the writing that he had done on Ruth in his career. For more than 20-odd years now Hoyt had written on a variety of topics, sometimes as much as five to six pages a day — radio scripts, news articles, letters, and even scripts for others.

In the late 1960s and early 1970s Robert W. Creamer, a senior writer for *Sports Illustrated*, was compiling research for a book he planned to write on the life of Babe Ruth. Creamer was hopeful that Waite Hoyt would collaborate with him on providing information about Ruth for his book and wrote to him. Now, Hoyt had some issues with *Sports Illustrated* and vented them to Creamer, telling him in a letter, "I have read pieces time and time again in that periodical with which I disagreed — written in positive sense by Johnny-come-latelies, who never have thought to consult one of us, or pay us for a piece or viewpoint. I have been in this business since 1915 — I have written with Frank Graham, written for Ruark [Robert Ruark, novelist and essayist], written for weekly papers, radio, some short mag pieces. I have never received a real decent figure for any of it but radio. Stanley Frank distorted a piece we wrote together, even after I edited my portion. In short, I have knowledge, fact, information — why should I give it away."[6]

Creamer, well aware of Hoyt's feelings about being ripped off in providing information without compensation, still felt that he was a veritable font of information on Ruth. So he decided to take his chances and dropped in on him while he was staying in Palm Beach, Florida. For three days Creamer then twisted Hoyt's arm in an attempt to get him to participate in a dialogue on the Babe. Hoyt was reticent at first. He explained to Creamer that Babe Ruth had evolved as a large part of his livelihood in speaking engagements and personal appearances, and as such he did not like to give information away. Also, Hoyt was of the mind-set that Babe Ruth was just too enormous of a topic to cover in any reasonable sized chronicle of his life and times, and he told that to Robert Creamer as well. In some respects Hoyt was now rapidly approaching a point of exaggeration in his knowledge of the Babe's journey through life. He felt to cover the Babe's story in a truly comprehensive manner would require a work of over 1,000 pages. Furthermore, Hoyt insisted that if the story was going to be told, it would have to be written his way. It was quite apparent that Hoyt had become overly protective of the Babe — not just from a concern for his own personal economic welfare, but more as a self-appointed custodian of Ruth's legacy. The reality was that from Waite Hoyt's perspective, if Babe Ruth's story had now become a commodity, then he felt he had superficial copyrights to it.

Making a living off a close association with a famous person is certainly not anything new or illegal. In fact, it is a common practice. Heavyweight boxing great Muhammad Ali once stated that he had made Howard Cosell too famous. There is indeed a lot of truth in that statement as Cosell's notoriety as a sports broadcaster seems to have risen concurrently with the enormous popularity of Ali in the 1960s as undisputed heavyweight champion. With Ali sending one challenger after another to the canvas in what became known as The Bum of the Month Club, Cosell positioned himself to horn in on the action with strategic ring-side interviews and commentary. Suddenly, Cosell was acting as if his friendship with the champ had deep roots. Making a buck from having close encounters with notable persons has also provided a living for scores of others from professions outside of sports too. Special Assistant to the President Arthur M. Schlesinger and Press Secretary Pierre Salinger made a tidy living for decades with book sales and talk show appearances from their employment by President John F. Kennedy.

However, with Waite Hoyt waffling on cooperating on the Ruth book, Creamer sought out others, including Joe Dugan and Bob Shawkey. When he had completed his research on Ruth, Creamer then went back to Hoyt for verification of the facts. Creamer said, "Of all the people I talked to he [Hoyt] gave the best picture of Ruth, the most rounded picture. He certainly didn't make him into a plaster saint or anything like that. He told me the things that Ruth did wrong. Waite Hoyt liked to be appreciated. And maybe that's why he talked so much about Babe Ruth — just to be associated with him."[7] After all was said and done, Creamer was gracious enough to acknowledge Hoyt's reticent efforts. In the acknowledgements in his book, Creamer cites Hoyt as being the most helpful of all the former teammates of Ruth's who shared their knowledge and remembrances with him.

In 1974, after several years of work, Robert W. Creamer's book *Babe — The Legend Comes to Life* was published. The book was well received by the critics and is reasonably accurate. Creamer does, however, embellish a few incidents surrounding the Babe and offers a new version of a few others that seem to sidestep Waite Hoyt's involvement. Nonetheless, today, as a sort of testimonial to Creamer's book on Ruth, it is the only the book on the Bambino that is sold at the Maryland Baseball Museum & Babe Ruth Birth Place in Baltimore. As a matter of fact, staff at the museum routinely use Creamer's book as a reference guide to look up answers to questions about the Babe from tourists. Meanwhile, 30 years after first being published, Creamer's book on Ruth continues to be sold alongside current works in bookstores nationwide.

However, it seems that Creamer did not forget the snub that he received from Hoyt during the pursuit of his research for the book. In a sense he repaid him tit-for-tat too, in the fact that Waite Hoyt is only mentioned in a cursory way on 20 of the 424 pages of text in the work, while his contemporaries such as Carl Mays and Herb Pennock receive a great more detail form the author in their playing and social experiences with both Ruth and the Yankees.

Waite Hoyt read Creamer's book but did not really care for it. He felt it was not necessary for the author to exaggerate about Ruth in order to make him colorful; there was no need to attempt to make him what he already was. What is rather satirical, though, is that while Waite Hoyt spent a lifetime writing and telling stories about Ruth and received very little monetary reward, when he passed away in the early 1980s, by default and by virtue of writing one book, Robert W. Creamer suddenly assumed the self-appointed role of the world's greatest living authority on Babe Ruth and has continued to relish and prosper in the association without any embarrassment.

In 1972 Professor Marshall Smelser of the University of Notre Dame was also attempting to write a book on Babe Ruth. He too, like Creamer, sought Hoyt out as a resource, but was turned away. Hoyt even offered as an excuse to Smelser, "I am under contract to do a book for World Publishing which would have much of my material on Ruth included. They might consider any contribution of mine to another book an infringement."[8] However, Hoyt's book on Ruth, like his autobiography, would not materialize as once again his nearly obsessive-compulsive penchant for perfection would raise its ugly head.

In the early 1970s, as Henry Aaron of the Atlanta Braves was making steady progress on breaking the Babe's all-time career home run mark of 714, the over-protective custody of the Ruth legacy assumed by Hoyt gradually became a daily obsession. Hoyt went to great lengths to point out to all interested parties the statistical differences between the route of Babe Ruth's home run record as opposed to the assault on that record being waged by Henry Aaron. Now, such statistical comparisons are a pretty normal occurrence among baseball fans, sportswriters and historians alike. In fact, some notable baseball authors such as Bill James have made a good portion of their livelihood in developing statistical models and calculating arguments using players' career records as a basis for comparison. Furthermore, it is widely known that some of the arguments that James raises in his classic work *The Baseball Abstract* are so respected that they are often used by agents representing major league players in salary negotiations with team owners.

It is an unfortunate statement on our American society today that the race card often surfaces when the home runs records of Babe Ruth and Henry Aaron are discussed and compared. But in fairness to Waite Hoyt, it should be pointed out that there was not one iota of racism in his comparisons of Ruth to Aaron. Throughout his life Hoyt was a model of a fair-minded man and led a life that was void of racial intolerance at all times. Waite Hoyt had too much dignity to ever waste his time in such ugly matters as bigotry. His comparisons of Ruth and Aaron were statistical arguments of the career achievements of these two remarkable ballplayers based on milestones at different points in their individual careers. In fact, it would be fallacious to suggest that there was any underlying racism in Hoyt's comparisons between Ruth and Aaron, as one has to also take into account that he often made similar hard statistical comparisons between ball players of the same race, such as those arguments he raised in his comparisons between Bob Meusel and Ralph Kiner.

Furthermore, long before Henry Aaron came into the picture as a possible candidate to eclipse Ruth's career home run record, Hoyt, in his zeal to protect Ruth's legacy, even advanced strong opinions on Roger Maris' challenge to Ruth's single-season home run record of 60 in the 1961 season. A few years after that memorable occurrence, Hoyt was to write in a letter to Arthur Daly of the *New York Times*, "It was also amusing to me when those squads of writers and photographers invaded the Yankee Stadium, then followed Maris to Baltimore — and the daily reports were so magnified, the feat assumed the proportions of Lindbergh's flight across the Atlantic. No one pulled for the Babe — nor gave a damn except Ruth. There was no record to break except his own — no inspiration from newspapers and crowds of fans— no excitement at all."[9]

Waite Hoyt was no longer alive by the time Mark McGwire and Sammy Sosa launched an assault on the single-season home run record of Roger Maris in the 1998 season. Hoyt would have been 99 years old. However, if he had been living, it is certain that he would have taken exception with Robert W. Creamer, who stated, "Unlike Maris and McGwire, Ruth played baseball in a world that had no television sets and few radios, no nightly sports highlight show, no TV cameras and tape recorders catching his every word and action. The Babe wasn't afraid to pop off, didn't have to be careful of what he said to reporters. In short, it was easier for the Babe. He had comparatively little pressure. In 1920 when he shattered the old home run record of 29 by hitting 54, and in 1921 when he topped that with 59, no one else was in the same ballpark with him as far as hitting home runs was concerned. There was no Ruth and Maris ahead, no Griffey and Sosa close behind."[10]

Before Henry Aaron emerged as a legitimate challenger to Babe Ruth's all-time home run record, Waite Hoyt had been focusing on the plights of Mickey Mantle, Ted Williams and Willie Mays. Early in the 1967 season Mickey Mantle hit the 500th home run of his career. Mantle wound up hitting 536 career home runs but missed a significant numbers of games because of injuries and hangovers during his 18 years in the major leagues. Ted Williams, with 521 career home runs in 19 years lost five complete seasons due to military service in World War II and Korea. Likewise Willie Mays with 660 career home runs in 22 years, lost an entire season due to military service during the Korean War. However, Hoyt reasoned that if Babe Ruth during his career had not spent three years as a full-time pitcher and half of another as a part-time pitcher, then he possibly would have far exceeded his career total of 714 home runs. It's a fair argument, but those seasons would have been played during the dead ball era, so the difference in Ruth's home run totals might have been minimal.

Shortly after Mickey Mantle clouted his 500th home run, Hoyt stated in the same letter to Arthur Daly mentioned above that, "Now comes the great ado about 500 home runs and the possibility of Willie Mays hitting 715, or at least breaking Ruth's record of 714, and if no one does it, who would have had the best chance, had they not gone to war, been ailing or whatever. I do not deny, Mantle (if well) and Williams without military service and also Mays (and Feller in a different category) would have improved their records no end. But I can also believe, Ruth hitting the lively ball all his career, and never having been a pitcher with a transition to make, and with some other guys records to achieve and break—forced to step up production, might have hit 800 home runs—who can tell how many in 2500 more at bats."[11]

In the late 1960s Hoyt was already charting the statistical differences between Babe Ruth and Willie Mays, noting that through May 26, 1967, Mays had hit 547 home runs in 8,216 at bats, while pointing out that at that pace Willie would need approximately 2,500 more times at bat to catch Ruth. Hoyt wrote in his notes comparing Mays and Ruth, "I assume, one man blessed with stamina and physique and ability might play 25 years—and by longevity alone will break Ruth's record. But let's not talk of Willie Mays as in the same class as a home run hitter, or even a hitter. He needs but 183 more times at bat to equal Babe's lifetime at bats, and he still will be some 150 homers short."[12]

Comparisons of great ball players and debates on their career statistics will go on throughout eternity; it fuels the hot stove and it's what makes the game fun. As a famous newspaper journalist in the 1920s stated, "It's the stuff that dreams are made of." Even at this point in time, a dialogue on comparing players from different eras continues on a grand scale. Willie Mays is currently third on the all-time career home run list with a total of 660. However, by the end of the 2003 season Barry Bonds had hit 658 home runs and should pass Mays early in the 2004 season. Furthermore, Bonds, who will turn 40 during the 2004 season, shows no signs of slowing down and is only 56 home runs shy of catching Babe Ruth and 97 behind Henry Aaron.

San Francisco Giants manager Felipe Alou, who played with Willie Mays (1958–1963) and now manages Bonds, was asked to compare the two players. "Willie is the best player I ever played with or against, and Barry is the best player I've ever managed or managed against," said Alou.[13] "It's very difficult to compare Barry and Willie. One guy plays left field; the other guy played center. One guy bats left-handed; the other batted right-handed. Willie is the best ball player I ever saw. He was instinctive, but he also always knew what to do. He had a charisma and he was spectacular. I regard him as a special player and I thought of Hank Aaron as a machine. Willie was the best of his era, better than Hank, Roberto Clemente and Frank Robinson. Those other guys could do a lot of things, too, but it was the way Willie did it."[14]

On June 10, 1972, Henry Aaron hit home run number 649, passing Willie Mays (who was still active at the time) to become number two on the all-time home run list. Now only the Babe loomed before him and the all-time home run record. Suddenly, his name, his life, his achievements on the ball field were cast into every comparison possible with Ruth. Author Lonnie Wheeler stated, "The man [Ruth] was so distinct that he became an adjective: He was Ruthian. There would never be such a thing as an Aaronian clout. There would never be another baseball player who could foster the language and legacy that Ruth did, because there cannot be. It was his lot to be the symbol and savior of the game, its slugger, its prototypical Yankee, its beloved Bambino. Babe Ruth is the most romantic, colorful, conspicuous, influential, historic, epic and legendary figure in baseball. It's just what he is. In the History of Baseball, he is lesson number one. This was the message that was shoved into Henry Aaron's face as his home run total approached 700. It was all too true ... and all too irrelevant, because Hank Aaron never desired to be Babe Ruth or to take his place. He had no interest in bringing down anybody's hero."[15] Aaron was himself distraught with all the comparisons between himself and Ruth and told Braves catcher Paul Casanova, "I'm not trying to break any record of Babe Ruth. I'm just trying to make one of my own."[16]

Nonetheless, as Henry Aaron drew ever closer to the Babe's home run record, Waite Hoyt, like the rest of the baseball world, began to compare the records of two in every category possible. Hoyt began to take notice that there was a great disparity between the numbers the two players had in at bats and the number of home runs they hit. In fact, Aaron hit home run number 714 in his 11,289 major league at bats, whereas Ruth needed only 8,339 at bats to reach the 714 plateau. At one point Hoyt wrote to C. C. Johnson Spink of *The Sporting News*, requesting statistical comparisons between Ruth and Aaron on how many home runs each had hit on the road and at home, how many bases on balls did Aaron have through 1973 and how many intentional passes did he receive, etc.

At his Hyde Park home in Cincinnati with no radio or television audience to address on the matter, Waite Hoyt began a methodical, solitary calculation of detailed statistical analysis on 8½ x 11 white ruled pads. He compared every aspect of Aaron's batting record with Ruth's—games played, at bats, runs, hits, doubles, triples, home runs, RBIs, base on balls and batting average. Through some determined research Hoyt arrived at the conclusion that to really get a close comparison of the efforts of Aaron vs. Ruth, the key year to analyze was 1967. According to notes of Hoyt housed in the archives of the Cincinnati Historical Society, he wrote, "Closest in proximity in times at bat etc., were Aaron and Ruth after the season of 1967. Aaron had been to bat 8,283 in his lifetime. Ruth 8,399. So there was a difference of Ruth being to bat 116 more times. In his slim margin of 116 more times at bat, Ruth had hit 233 more home runs, and 668 more runs batted in, 52 more triples; 55 more doubles; and 1,254 more bases on balls. Ruth's slugging average was .690 — Aaron's .560. Who's kidding who?"[17]

Hoyt finally got around to summarizing his analysis of Ruth vs. Aaron and Mays, stating the following: "Ruth is vastly superior in most all departments or so close in all totals (considering at bats) the results are only embarrassing to the Mays—Aaron supporters. It should be kept in mind the fact that in either category, Mays' and Aarons' excessive times at bat reduce the basic ratios to such illogical conclusions as to make comparisons ridiculous."[18]

On July 13, 1973, Aaron's home run total stood at 673. In the second to the last game of the 1973 season, with only 1,362 fans in attendance in Atlanta, Aaron hit home run number 713. Now he was just one home run away from tying Ruth's record. When the 1974 season began the Braves were scheduled to play their first games in Cincinnati. The Atlanta front office wanted Aaron to sit the three-game series out and wait until the team played in the Braves home park, Atlanta Stadium. However, baseball commissioner Bowie Kuhn intervened and ordered that Aaron should play in the opening game at Riverfront Stadium on April 4. So, on Aaron's first trip to the plate against the Reds Jack Billingham he hit number 714. Aaron then sat out the next game in the series, but once again under pressure from the commissioner's office was forced to play in the last game of the series on Sunday. Facing Clay Kirby, he struck out twice and grounded out, then was replaced in the lineup.

The next time Aaron played was on April 8. With 53,000 fans on hand in Atlanta and a national television audience watching — including Waite Hoyt — he hit home run number 715 off Los Angeles Dodgers left-hander Al Downing. It

Hank Aaron's 715th home run, Atlanta Stadium, April 8, 1974 (National Baseball Hall of Fame Library. Cooperstown, N.Y.).

was all over; there was a new record. Before Aaron retired in 1976 he had established the new, all-time career record for home runs at 755. Hoyt's obsession with Aaron's home run quest had been in part out of loyalty to his friendship with Ruth and part statistical, being the baseball purist that he was. His statistical endeavor in the Aaron home run record challenge was not unlike the national debate in 1961 when Roger Maris hit 61 home runs, eclipsing Babe Ruth's single season record. It seems that almost as soon as Maris' 61st home run landed in the right-field stands at Yankee Stadium, Commissioner Ford C. Frick moved to make a distinction between the achievements of the two with the placement of an asterisk next to the new record home run total set by Maris.

Another factor in Waite Hoyt's interest in Henry Aaron's quest of the Babe Ruth home run record was also economics. By Hoyt's own admission, Babe Ruth and his legacy were providing a large part of his income. With Aaron now the new all-time home run king, the nation's marketing machine was focused on him rather than Ruth. All at once Aaron was being offered scores of endorsements—he was appearing on all sorts of television programs, was offered movie roles, and had his picture on all the major magazines. Magnavox was even offering him $1 million for the ball he hit for home run 715. For the moment at least, Babe Ruth was relegated to the wings of baseball's big historical stage show. No doubt it was a bitter pill for Waite Hoyt to swallow after decades of his aggrandizement of the Babe, but the spotlight was on Henry Aaron.

Regardless of who becomes that all-time leader in home runs, there will always be room for Babe Ruth in baseball folklore. Lonnie Wheeler is correct; Ruth is lesson number one. Yet Ruth the man was complex and was probably only understood, if at all, by those who were close to him during his life. The rest of us will have draw our own historical conclusions. In a letter to Robert W. Creamer in 1969, Waite Hoyt perhaps summarizes the legacy of Babe Ruth best: "I am almost convinced, you will never learn the truth on Ruth. I roomed with [Joe] Dugan. He was a good friend of Babe's. But, he will see Ruth in a different light than I did. Dugan's own opinion will be one in which Dugan revels in Ruth's crudities and so on. While I can easily recognize all of this and admit it freely—yet there was buried in Ruth humanitarianism beyond belief—an intelligence he was never given credit for, a childish desire to be over-virile—living up to credits given his home run power—and yet a need for intimate affection and respect—and a feverish desire to play baseball, perform and live a life he didn't and couldn't understand."[19] In short, the life of Babe Ruth just seemed to be larger than the actual man, and it was Waite Hoyt who seemed to comprehend that fact the best.

The Top Ten Leading Home Run Hitters of All-Time
(through the 2003 season)

Rank/Name	Years	Games	AB	Hits	HR	%	RBI	BB	SO	BA
1. H. Aaron	23	3298	13364	3771	755	6.1	2297	1402	1383	.305
2. B. Ruth	22	2503	8399	2873	714	8.5	2213	2056	1330	.342
3. W. Mays	22	2992	10881	3283	660	6.1	1903	1463	1526	.302
4. B. Bonds*	17	2569	8725	2595	658	7.5	1742	2070	1387	.297
5. F. Robinson	21	2808	10006	2943	586	5.8	1812	1420	1532	.294
6. M. McGwire	15	1874	6187	1626	583	9.4	1414	1317	1596	.263
7. H. Killebrew	22	2435	8147	2086	573	7.0	1584	1559	1699	.256
8. R. Jackson	21	2820	9864	2584	563	5.7	1702	1375	2597	.262
9. M. Schmidt	18	2404	8352	2234	548	6.6	1595	1507	1883	.267
10. S. Sosa*	14	2012	7543	2099	539	7.1	1450	800	1977	.278

*Still active

Ranking of Selected Other Notable Players
(through the 2003 season)

Rank/Name	Years	Games	AB	Hits	HR	%	RBI	BB	SO	BA
11. M. Mantle	18	2401	8102	2415	536	6.6	1509	1754	1710	.298
12. J. Foxx	20	2317	8134	2646	534	6.6	1921	1452	1311	.325
13. R. Palmeiro*	17	2567	9553	2654	528	5.5	1687	1224	1244	.291
15. T. Williams	19	2292	7706	2654	521	6.8	1839	2019	709	.344
16. E. Banks	19	2528	9421	2583	512	5.4	1636	763	1236	.274
21. F. McGriff*	17	2483	8685	2477	491	5.6	1543	1296	1863	.285
22. K. Griffey*	14	1914	7079	2080	481	6.8	1384	940	1256	.294
57. R. Kiner	10	1472	5205	1451	369	7.1	1015	1011	749	.279
80. H. Greenberg	13	1394	5193	1628	331	6.4	1276	852	844	.313
97. R. Hornsby	23	2259	8173	2930	301	3.7	1584	1038	679	.358
125. R. Maris	12	1463	5101	1325	275	5.4	851	652	733	.260

*Still active

11

Eventide for Hoyt

By the fall of 1976 Waite Hoyt was 77 years old. Healthwise he was beginning to experience a slow decline. His eyesight was troublesome to him and since the early 1960s he had been wearing tri-focals. Now he was beginning to experience periodic episodes of chest pain. Nonetheless, retired and comfortable, he was still in demand as a speaker and kept busy with community affairs around Cincinnati. The mediocre Cincinnati Reds teams of Hoyt's 24 years in the broadcasting booth were now a thing of the past. Over the 11 years since he had retired as the Reds radio broadcaster the Cincinnati franchise — now referred to as The Big Red Machine — had evolved into the most powerful team in major league baseball.

In 1975 the Reds ran away with the National League West division race, winning 108 games and outdistancing the second-place Los Angeles Dodgers by 20 games. The Reds then defeated the Pittsburgh Pirates in the NLCS and won the World Series, defeating the Boston Red Sox in a thrilling seven-games series. In the fall of 1976 the Reds completed a four-game sweep of the New York Yankees in the World Series and thereby became the first team in the National League to win back-to-back World Championships since the New York Giants defeated Waite Hoyt's New York Yankees in the 1921 and 1922 World Series. By now the press and fans alike around the country were beginning to make comparisons between the 1976 Big Red Machine team and the 1927 New York Yankees Murderers' Row team that had long been considered baseball's best team ever.

The Washington Star was curious about this comparison and contacted Waite Hoyt, a member of the 1927 Yankees team. The *Star* asked Hoyt to compare the '27 Yankees with The Big Red Machine team of 1976.

In particular the *Star* wanted to know Hoyt's opinion of how many of the Reds players could have cracked the Yankees' starting lineup in 1927. Hoyt responded by saying, "Only two: catcher Johnny Bench and shortstop Dave Concepcion."[1] However, he had some doubts about Concepcion. In regard to Bench, Hoyt pointed out that the 1927 Yankees used three catchers: Pat Collins, Benny Bengough and John Grabowski. "That position was considered a weak link in the otherwise awesome New York lineup," said Hoyt.[2] As for shortstop, "I give a slight edge to Concepcion over Mark Koenig. But Koenig rose to the occasion in 1927."[3] Going around the infield, Hoyt took Tony Lazzeri over Joe Morgan at second base, Joe Dugan over Pete Rose at third base and Lou Gehrig over Tony Perez at first base. "The New York outfield of Meusel, Ruth and Combs compared to [Foster, Griffey and Geronimo] is no contest."[4] As for the pitching, Hoyt — ever the statistician — simply pointed out that the 1927 Yankees staff had 82 complete games as opposed to the 1976 Reds pitching staff, which had 33 compete games.

That Waite Hoyt found his 1927 Yankees vastly superior to the 1976 Reds should really not come as a surprise to anyone. In essence he had been asked to compare his own team with another, thereby throwing objectivity out the door. This exercise suddenly put Hoyt in a position of competition once again and he suddenly was in his old uniform and on the mound. Nonetheless, comparing a team from one era against one from another continues to fascinate fans. During the 1981 strike-shortened season a computer program was developed to simulate a game between The Big Red Machine and the Murderers' Row team. The game was played out and broadcast over a Cincinnati radio station. The results were that the Reds beat the Yankees in the bottom of the ninth inning on a home run by Johnny Bench off Waite Hoyt. When Hoyt was told about this scenario he was livid.

What is surprising in Hoyt's comparison of the 1927 Yankees to the 1976 Reds is that he selected Joe Dugan over Pete Rose at third base. While Hoyt never elaborated on that selection, it certainly does not mean that he was snubbing Rose. To the contrary, Hoyt thought very highly of Pete Rose. On June 22, 1982, playing for the Philadelphia Phillies, Pete Rose got hit number 3,772 of his career, thereby passing Henry Aaron to become number two on the all-time hit list behind Ty Cobb. The next day, *Philadelphia Inquirer* staff writer Peter Pascarelli contacted Waite Hoyt in Cincinnati to get his assessment of how Rose compared to Cobb.

Hoyt had played against Cobb and later became friends with Rose when he first came up to the majors with the Reds in 1963 while Hoyt was still doing the Reds radio broadcasts. "I'm very close to Pete," Hoyt said.[5]

"When he first broke into the majors, his dad once asked me to look out for him. Pete would sit with me on the Red's team flights and he'd ask me to talk about Cobb and the others. I played with and against him. And I remember telling him way back then that the modern world is based on power. And 15 years ago, I said to him that now is the time for some guy with the similar kind of makeup and ability as Cobb to project himself out front. Home runs had become common. Pete has always been a very good student of everything in his profession. He is one shrewd fellow. If he had decided to get an education instead of being a ballplayer, he would have been brilliant, because I'd say Pete probably has an IQ that must be 140. There's no doubt in my mind that Pete would have done well against the great pitchers of my day.... Most of the hitters were Rose-type hitters, so Pete would have done well at any time."[6]

Hoyt stated that the basic difference between Cobb and Rose was that Ty played angry, whereas Pete played with joy. Hoyt then stated, "What makes Rose's presence in the company of baseball's immortals so remarkable is that his actual skills are not that remarkable. He doesn't have great speed. He doesn't sparkle in fielding or throwing or running. But you take the whole cloth, and Pete gets the job done. Your have to admire what he's been able to do with the abilities he was given. To me, there isn't a question that if Pete avoids a serious injury, he'll equal Cobb's total. And I'll be rooting for him along with everybody else."[7] Waite Hoyt never lived to see Pete Rose pass Ty Cobb and become the all-time leader in hits. When Hoyt died Rose was still about one year and 100 hits away from breaking Cobb's record.

In early 1977 public television station WCET in Cincinnati approached Hoyt about producing one more extravaganza where he would expound on his lifetime experiences. As Hoyt carefully considered the format for the show he was acutely aware of the fact that his old rain-delay stories were by now old hat in Cincinnati. Furthermore, he

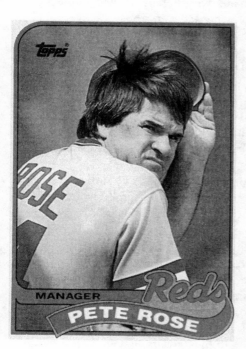

Pete Rose, 1989 (the Topps, Co., Inc.).

knew that the Reds radio broadcasting audience was now firmly in the grasp of Joe Nuxhall and Marty Brennaman. People in Cincinnati were no longer repeating his ancient shtick with balls being hit into Burgerville, they were now mimicking Joe Nuxhall's familiar "Get out of here" and Marty Brennaman's "And this one belongs to the Reds." The format was going to have to be different. But Hoyt was a showman; he had been down this road before.

What Hoyt decided to do was develop a program structure that was more in depth in terms of his relationships and the meaning behind some of their activities. Now, because he was Waite Hoyt, he knew that he was going to have to draw in some of his reminiscences about his life and Hall of Fame baseball career and do programs on Miller Huggins, Ed Barrow, Herb Pennock and even his final act at Ebbets Field. But in this endeavor he also wanted to go outside of the game and include some of the prominent people that he had known such as the Marx Brothers and Jimmy Durante. In Hoyt's words, "As this is to be my bow out, and such a wide horizon of latitude is granted, try to make it the best you've ever done."[8]

The program was titled *Waite Hoyt ... Through The Years* and was co-hosted by Laurie Durbrow. The program had its debut at 7:30 P.M. on Thursday, June 9, 1977, and the series ran for 21 weeks into November. On opening night the National Baseball Hall of Fame sent a congratulatory telegram to Hoyt. The program attracted a modest following and did well it its time slot ratings for being broadcast on a PBS station. What is more important, though, is that all 21 programs were preserved for posterity on videotape and not lost in the electronic abyss like most of Hoyt's memorable rain-delay broadcasts (or not recorded at all, such as his 1948 tribute to Babe Ruth). However, with the conclusion of the WCET series, for Waite Hoyt, the fat lady finally sang.

By the following summer, nearing 79 years, Hoyt was traveling in England and other destinations in Europe. The following year he went to Atlanta to address a reunion of Chi Psi fraternity alumni from Middlebury College. During his brief attendance at the school in 1918 Hoyt had become a Chi Psi. Since he was speaking in the south he decided to tell a story with a southern flavor. Hoyt stated that in 1929, as the Yankees were leaving Mobile, Alabama, where they had played an exhibition game in spring training, catcher Bill Dickey a (native of Louisiana) ran into an former female acquaintance at the railway depot. "Bill Dickey, Bill Dickey!"[9] the young woman exclaimed in what Hoyt described as a "voice full of syrup and crinoline."[10] "What ah you doing heah?"[11] "I'm playing with the Yankees," Dickey said.[12] "Why, Bill, couldn't you find some nice Southern boys to play with?"[13]

As Hoyt stood at the dais he broke into his familiar loud and robust laughter — ha, ha, ha — ha, ha, ha — so well known to the tens of thousands of people of who had their lives touched in such in a positive way during his long and magnificent career. For a brief moment it was almost as if he and Jack Moran were once again sitting in the broadcasting booth, perched high above old Crosley Field. Those who knew Hoyt and loved him wanted it go on forever. Nearly three generations of Reds fans from central and southern Ohio, southern Indiana, Kentucky and West Virginia had gotten their first taste of the thrill of major league baseball by listening to Hoyt on the radio in the 1940s, 1950s and 1960s.

But now it was eventide for Hoyt. In late February and early March 1981 he had two cataract operations and in general was not feeling well. On November 23, 1982, his dear wife, Ellen, passed away. However, soon he was to marry again. Hoyt's third marriage — to Betty A. Derie — took place on Saturday, March 5, 1983, at the home of Mr. and Mrs. Richard Levy in Chicago. The couple set up their household in Hoyt's Mt. Adams apartment in the Highland Towers on Celestial Street.

Waite's first contact with Betty had been in 1948 through a fan letter she had sent him. "I sent him a fan letter in 1948,"[14] said Betty. "It was the night after his big broadcast, the night Babe Ruth died. He sent me an eloquent response — Waite answered every fan letter he ever received. After that, we had a pen-pal relationship, although I wasn't the only one. There were people he exchanged letters with for 30 years and more."[15]

In the 1950s Warren Giles was president of the National League and the league offices were located in Cincinnati in the Carew Tower. Betty came into face-to-face contact with Hoyt in 1959 when she was hired as a secretary in the National League office. Two years after she had started the job, Waite inquired through a contact at the National League office if Betty would like to work for him. She immediately accepted. Betty idolized Waite and the two shared a companionship that was genuine and loving. While they were married for only a brief period of a year and half before Hoyt died, they used every moment they had together to strengthen their mutual bond. Often, following dinner, they would spend time conversing with each other late into the evening. They had even acquired two copies of the *Baseball Encyclopedia*.

Throughout late 1983 Hoyt's condition continued to deteriorate and his chest pain became more frequent. On August 7, 1984, he suffered a heart attack and was admitted to Jewish Hospital in Cincinnati. During the hospitalization he was to suffer two more heart attacks. The last one, which came on Saturday morning, August 25, was fatal. At the age of 84, only a few weeks from his 85th birthday, The Schoolboy Wonder passed

away. Author Truman Capote had died that same day, however, in what
seemed to be one last attempt at an encore; Capote was forced to take his
final curtain call alongside Hoyt.

Newspapers around the country, including the *New York Times, Sporting News*, etc., carried Hoyt's obituary and of course the Cincinnati newspapers printed special chronicles of his life. Then, as baseball and
Cincinnati said their good-byes, visitation was held at the Mack-Johnson
Funeral Home on E. McMillan Street in the Queen City neighborhood of
Walnut Hills. Finally, on August 29 at 10:00 A.M., funeral services were
held at Christ Church in downtown Cincinnati. Outside, a long line of
mourners stretched down 4th Street waiting to enter and pay their final
respects. Hoyt was laid to rest in Spring Grove Cemetery, not far from the
grave of his beloved Yankees manager Miller Huggins. Everyone in Cincinnati and beyond had felt like they knew Waite Hoyt, so when he passed
on everyone felt a loss. The late Nix Denton, who was a part-owner and
writer for the *Clermont Sun* (Batavia, Ohio), once stated, "You aint nothin'
until you've been introduced to Waite Hoyt."[16]

Waite Hoyt's gravesite at Spring Grove Cemetery, Cincinnati, Ohio (photograph
by John H. Ruschulte).

Even today, 20 years after his demise, when the name of Waite Hoyt is mentioned to those who knew him, he is remembered with a deep reverence. In the words of Hal McCoy, "Waite Hoyt was special. We all know that. I know it because he took a young, no-nothing beat writer like me just starting out and treated me like a veteran. Never talked down to me. I was enthralled sitting in the media dinning room, listening to his great stories about baseball and life. Nobody else ever said a word. They listened because what Waite said meant something. He was a great man and a great friend and one hell of a baseball guy."[17]

Waite Hoyt's true legacy is found in his 1969 Hall of Fame induction speech, where he expressed self-doubt about the quality of his life's work. In a retrospective analysis of his career he questioned that work after starting out in life to accomplish his goals and then seeing all his work in life completed: "And you always think that you were never good enough."[18] True, Waite Hoyt was a perfectionist and spent a lifetime battling insecurity, never being satisfied with his work. But let there remain no doubt that what he did not recognize was indeed good work. To his several hundred thousand loyal fans, listeners and friends, he was without equal among his peers. When Hoyt was behind the microphone he just didn't go through a fundamental exercise of broadcasting a game. Each new day was a challenge for Hoyt and he wanted his audience to feel that they were listening to the best that there was in the game. When all was said and done, he made everyone believe that he was.

12

Hoyt and His Contemporaries

Regardless of his dual role in baseball history, when Waite Hoyt was elected to the National Baseball Hall of Fame in 1969, it was on the merit that he had been a major league pitcher for 21 years and won 237 games, most of which were with the New York Yankees Murderers' Row teams during the Roaring Twenties, not because he had been a legendary radio broadcaster of the Reds games in Cincinnati for 24 years. With the success of The Big Red Machine teams of the 1970s and the rapid rise of popularity in his successors—Joe Nuxhall, Al Michaels and then Marty Brennaman—in the Reds broadcasting booth, Hoyt quietly faded into the background.

But because he was out of sight did not mean that he was out of mind in Cincinnati. By the early 1980s Waite Hoyt had been retired from broadcasting the Reds games for nearly 20 years. Donn Burrows stated that he would often have lunch with Hoyt during the early eighties. "I would sit with him at a table and a flood of people would come up to him, tell him how much they enjoyed listening to him, especially his rain delays. I had grown up in Detroit and knew him from the baseball history books as the ace of the great '27 Yankees, and yet in Cincinnati not one person asked him about his playing days, it was all about his broadcasting career. It's when I realized I was talking with a Hall of Fame broadcaster too. Not just a Hall of Fame pitcher."[1]

Nonetheless, it appears that others had forgotten about Hoyt. In 1987 the Cincinnati Reds, under licensing by major league baseball, released for sale a 75-minute video presentation titled "The Official History of the Cincinnati Reds." It's a little ironic, perhaps even a little sad, that in the entire production not one mention of Waite Hoyt and his role as Reds broadcaster is made. There is not even an utterance of his famous rain-delay chatter that so endeared him to his audience for over two decades.

But the snub of Waite Hoyt extends far beyond the borders of Cincinnati. It is an unfortunate fact that when the national media of today makes references to the great radio baseball broadcasters of the past, the name of Waite Hoyt is usually excluded from that lofty level of recognition. It seems that being recognized as one of the great baseball broadcasters is the domain of Mel Allen, Red Barber, Vin Scully, Russ Hodges and a few privileged others. That Waite Hoyt is never mentioned in that regard is probably due to the fact that he labored his entire broadcasting career for what is referred to in today's terms as a small market team. Likewise, Hoyt's sparse recognition as a pioneering baseball broadcaster is also a factor of the limited national exposure he had broadcasting baseball events such as the All-Star game and World Series. In fact, his only broadcasting experience in a World Series came in 1961 when he did the radio broadcast of the Cincinnati Reds ragamuffins team and the New York Yankees.

In the late 1930s and early 1940s radio executives held the belief that former big league ballplayers lacked the basic intelligence and vocabulary necessary for broadcasting, and that they would require extensive work with a voice coach to have any chance at all to succeed. For the most part those entering baseball broadcasting at that point in time were college educated. Red Barber, who had broadcast the Reds games in the middle 1930s and then moved on to the Brooklyn Dodgers in 1939, was a University of Florida dropout. By Saam, who was doing the Philadelphia Athletics games in 1938, was a graduate of Texas Christian University. Jimmy Dudley, who broadcast the Cleveland Indians from 1948 — 1967 and the Seattle Pilots in their only season in 1969, was a graduate of the University of Virginia. Russ Hodges, who was doing the Cubs and White Sox in the late 1930s and early 1940s, had a law degree from the University of Kentucky. Mel Allen, hired in 1940 to broadcast the Yankees games, was a graduate of the University of Alabama and a lawyer. And so on. The trend in hiring college graduates in baseball broadcasting continued for quite a long time. Milo Hamilton and Harry Kalas were both graduates of the University of Iowa. Jack Buck was a graduate of Ohio State and Lindsey Nelson a graduate of the University of Tennessee.

Nonetheless, Waite Hoyt, with one semester of college education under his belt, has his place in baseball broadcasting history assured — he was one of the first former big league players, along with former catcher and manager Charles "Gabby" Street, to make the transition from the playing field into the broadcasting booth. It is also a fact that the intelligent, flamboyant and eloquent style that Waite Hoyt exhibited on his radio work in New York City in the early 1940s had a lot to do with breaking down the hiring barriers faced by former major league players in broadcasting.

However, when Hoyt began broadcasting games for the Cincinnati Reds in 1942, he was actually preceded by another former big leaguer — Jay Hanna "Dizzy" Dean in St. Louis. In 1941 Falstaff Beer hired Dizzy Dean to broadcast for both the St. Louis Cardinals and St. Louis Browns games. Dean proceeded to immediately reinforce every bit of doubt that network executives had about former ballplayers' oratory capabilities. His speech was so illiterate that the St. Louis Board of Education demanded that he be taken off the air. He referred to statistics as "statics." As someone once said about him, "When a critic asked if he knew the King's English, he replied, 'Yes sir, I do and I know the Queen's English too.'² Dean stated on the air that he had received a letter from a lady who taught English in a grade school somewhere in the Midwest, who strongly objected to his frequent use of the condemned contraction of "am not," — "ain't." The teacher felt that Dean's constant use of the word was setting a bad example for his youthful listeners. Dean's response was to send a letter back to the teacher stating that a lot of those people who are objecting to his use of the word "ain't" — "ain't eatin' as good as ole Diz." Falstaff Beer, determined to cash in on Dean's massacre of the English language, published and distributed a 32-page booklet titled *Dizzy Dean Baseball Dictionary* by Jay Hanna Dean that offered definitions of various words of his whimsical on-air vocabulary.

On the other hand, Dean was a storyteller and his down-to-earth style was popular with rural listeners and by the middle 1940s he was considered a rising star in baseball broadcasting. In 1953 the first televised *Game of the Week* made its debut on ABC with Dizzy Dean at the microphone. While the broadcasts were banned from all major league cities, Dean carried the show and racked up enormous ratings of 11.4 percent of all households with sets and 51 percent of all sets in use — which interpreted meant that 75 percent of all sets in use outside of big league cities were tuned in to the ramblings of Dizzy Dean. In 1955 the *Game of the Week* moved to CBS, and Dean along with it, as opportunities for former major league ballplayers in broadcasting were now becoming abundant. However, by 1966 major league baseball had changed networks, going to NBC, and Dean was out.

Curt Gowdy took over as the new primary announcer on NBC, doing a huge volume of work from 1966–1975 that included every All-Star game, every World Series and the *Game of the Week*. Joining Gowdy in the broadcast booth in 1967 for the *Game of the Week* broadcasts was former Brooklyn Dodgers shortstop Pee Wee Reese, who had been doing the games with

Dizzy Dean for several seasons. Reese, like Dean, was too equally lacking in the oratory arts to permit him to do eloquent play-by-play. Reese was to remark on his broadcasting venture, "How do like that? They're paying me to talk into a microphone and I still pronounce the damn word 'th'owed.'"[3]

Following the 1967 season, NBC dropped Pee Wee Reese from its *Game of the Week* broadcasts and replaced him with former New York Yankees shortstop Tony Kubek. Reese was then hired by Hudephol Brewing Company in Cincinnati to broadcast the Reds games on television for the 1968 season. When Reese arrived in Cincinnati he was chauffeured around town and presented by the brewery and media as if he were a major broadcasting star. In short, both the Reds and Hudephol Beer were hoping that Reese would be the second coming of Waite Hoyt to Cincinnati baseball broadcasting. But he didn't last; after one season Reese was history.

As for Gowdy's work, with a little help from history he wound up being at the microphone on NBC during the sixth game of the 1975 World Series, between the Cincinnati Reds and the Boston Red Sox, when at 12:34 A.M. Carlton Fisk hit a solo home run that hit the left-field foul pole to give the Red Sox a 7–6 win, tie the series at three games each and send it into a seventh game. Sixty-two million viewers were watching that night. The next night, as the Reds overcame an early 3–0 Red Sox lead to defeat them 4–3 on a single by Joe Morgan with two out in the ninth inning for the World Championship, 75,890,000 fans watched the game on NBC. The huge audience of nearly 76 million was quite a jump from the 5 million fans who had listened to the first World Series radio broadcast of Waite Hoyt's New York Yankees playing against the New York Giants in 1922 and the 38 million who in 1950 viewed the World Series on television that was broadcast as far west as Omaha.

Pee Wee Reese (1952) 1995, Dodgers Archive Commemorative set (the Topps Co., Inc.)

Throughout the 1940s former major league ballplayers other than Waite Hoyt, Gabby Street and Dizzy Dean were a rarity in the baseball broadcasting business. As the 1950s arrived, Waite Hoyt continued to labor and love it in Cincinnati. He, like a lot of the broadcasters in major league baseball, had become entrenched with fan loyalty in the cities where he worked. In Pittsburgh, Bob Prince began broadcasting the Pirates games in 1948 and continued for five decades. In Washington, Arch McDonald — who had been the voice of the Senators from 1934–1938, then spent 1939 doing the Yankees games—came back to the nation's capital in 1940 and continued to broadcasting Senators games there through the 1957 season. In 1948, Jimmy Dudley began his career broadcasting games for the Cleveland Indians through the 1967 season. Russ Hodges, who had previously broadcast games in Chicago (1938–1945), then with Mel Allen did the Yankees (1946–1947), moved over to the New York Giants in 1948 and eventually went west with the team to San Francisco in 1958. Vin Scully had started to do Brooklyn Dodgers games in 1950 with Red Barber; he took over as the primary broadcaster when Barber was terminated in 1953 and eventually went west to Los Angeles with the team, continuing to broadcast Dodger games throughout the 1960s, 1970s and 1980s. Jack Brickhouse did the Cubs and White Sox broadcasts in 1940 and New York Giants in 1946. In 1948, Brickhouse came to WGN in Chicago and broadcast 5,060 Cubs game before retiring at the end of the 1981 season. Ernie Harwell had broadcast for the Dodgers in 1950 and the Giants from 1951–1953 before becoming the voice of the Baltimore Orioles from 1954–1959. In 1960 Harwell moved to Detroit and then broadcast the Tigers games until the end of the 1991 season. Bob Elson broadcast games for 40 years for the Cubs, White Sox and Oakland Athletics. And of course, by the 1950s Mel Allen was already a legend in broadcasting with the Yankees, where he was in the booth nearly every year from 1939–1964, calling plays for the Bronx Bombers.

All of these broadcasters, like Waite Hoyt, were endeared by the city in which they labored and by the team for which they broadcast. Furthermore, everyone of them was as widely popular and respected in Pittsburgh, Cleveland, Detroit, Chicago, etc., as Hoyt was in Cincinnati and they all made a ballgame seem exciting to their fans. In fact, Ernie Harwell did his broadcasts with an incredible passion for the game. Harwell also authored the book *The Game for All America*, which is considered some of the most eloquent prose ever written on baseball. The book has been translated into six languages. However, unlike Hoyt, not one of these laymen broadcasters had any major league experience as a ballplayer and that is what set Hoyt apart from his contemporaries behind the microphone.

The basic difference between listening to a ballgame broadcast by

Waite Hoyt in the 1950s and 1960s and other legendary broadcasters such as Bob Prince, Jack Brickhouse, Bob Elson, Mel Allen and even Ernie Harwell, was that when folks were listening to Hoyt on the radio they were not just part of a current major league moment, they were suddenly electronically linked and enraptured with the entire history of baseball. It wasn't just a ballgame they were listening to, it was a delightful experience of connecting the memories of past summers with the present via the magnificence of Waite Hoyt acting as the medium. There was a genuine sense of nostalgia that was evident in Hoyt's broadcasts that is lost today on the air waves with the silly antics of Bob Uecker and Tom Paciorek, the painful dullness of Tom Seaver, John Sterling and Tim McCarver, and the unconvincing attempts of Bob Costas to make his listening audience believe he has a rich, personal, historical link with baseball that goes far beyond his actual years.

While Waite Hoyt is rightfully entitled to share in the credit for opening the door in the broadcasting booth for former big leaguers, it was Joe Garagiola who burst through and knocked the door of its hinges. After serving in World War II, Joe Garagiola came back to St. Louis and played for his hometown Cardinals in 1946. The Cards won the National League pennant and World Series that year, defeating the Boston Red Sox 4–3 in the series. In 1951 Garagiola was traded to the hapless Pittsburgh Pirates, which would provide him with a future bonanza of humorous stories in his broadcasting career. Then on June 4, 1953, along with Ralph Kiner, Howie Pollet and Catfish Metkovich, Garagiola was traded to the Chicago Cubs for six players and $150,000 in cash. He finished up his nine-year playing career in 1954 after being sent to the New York Giants late in the season on waivers.

Harry Caray had been broadcasting St. Louis Cardinals games on KMOX since 1945. At first Caray was teamed with Gabby Street. However, following the death of Street in 1951, Caray was joined in the booth by Milo Hamilton. In 1955 the St. Louis Cardinals fired Hamilton from their broadcasting team and hired Joe Garagiola to do the games with Caray. Subsequently, Joe and Harry, both St. Louis natives, worked together for the next seven years, during which time Garagiola slowly gained national attention.

By 1961 Garagiola was broadcasting the All-Star game and two years later the World Series. During the next two decades he would become the second most recognizable baseball broadcaster in America behind Mel Allen. Now he was making frequent appearances on NBC's *The Tonight Show with Johnny Carson*. By 1965 he even replaced Mel Allen as the announcer for the New York Yankees and by the late 1960s was a co-host

on NBC's *Today Show* with Bar-
bara Walters and Hugh Downs.
Still later along with Tony Kubek,
Garagiola broadcast the NBC
Game of the Week from 1975–
1983.

It certainly was not intentional, but what Garagiola had
done to catapult himself into
national media limelight was to
take Waite Hoyt's broadcasting
style and turn it inside out. Joe
Garagiola, like Waite Hoyt, was
a great story teller. However, he
added a new twist to the mix —
large doses of humor. As the per-
sonable Garagiola reminisced on
the air about his boyhood St.
Louis friendship with Yogi Berra
and memories of teammate Stan
Musial, he amused his listeners
while at the same time doing

Joe Garagiola

excellent play-by-play work. What his on-air stories lacked in historical
significance of the game, he made up for by substituting the element of
human frailty. He spoke of outlandish experiences while playing on
entrenched second-division teams such as the Chicago Cubs and Pittsburgh Pirates of the early 1950s. Only Garagiola could make an experience of playing on a team that lost 112 games seem entertaining. In short,
while Waite Hoyt was telling classic baseball stories about Ty Cobb, the
mighty Babe Ruth and the World Champion 1927 New York Yankees during rain delays in Cincinnati to 30,000–40,000 listeners, Garagiola was on
late-night national television with a couple of million viewers tuned in
doing a stand-up comedy routine with his stories about Ralph Kiner and
Hank Sauer sharing the same outfield in Chicago. It got everyone's attention and it worked.

One can only speculate about what impact on Waite Hoyt's broadcasting career an appearance on late night television with Jack Paar or
Johnny Carson may have had. But is certain that had the curtain gone up
on Hoyt as he belted out one of his songs from his old vaudeville act and
then sat down to reminisce about the Bambino with Jack or Johnny on
The Tonight Show, his tenure as a pitchman for Burger Beer might have

suddenly been over and he may have found himself on NBC's *Game of Week* and reaching dizzying heights in his broadcasting career.

Yet, in the opinion of sports broadcaster and producer Donn Burrows, Waite Hoyt was right where he wanted to be: "I think he loved Cincinnati and did not aspire to be on the air any place else. He had a legion of Reds fans from West Virginia, Indiana, Kentucky and beyond because the Reds were the King and he was the best known of the Reds. Families looked at him as someone to have in their home on a Saturday or Sunday afternoon. They might not be baseball fans, but they were Waite fans and they loved having him in their home. He might have gotten more national appeal in New York City, but he would never have been as intimately intertwined with his fan base as he was as the voice of the Reds."[4]

While Waite Hoyt confined his comedy routines to the stage of the Palace Theatre, former major league catcher Bob Uecker would eventually follow in Garagiola's footsteps, using humor as a method to attract an audience with huge success. However, unlike Garagilola, Uecker was unable to integrate historical baseball stories into his routine. In short, Uecker did slap-stick in the broadcast booth. In 2003, Uecker, the longtime radio broadcaster of the Milwaukee Brewers, was presented with the Ford C. Frick Award by the National Baseball Hall of Fame's board of directors. In Uecker's six-year major league career with four teams he played in 297 games and had a lifetime batting average of .200. Off the playing field he had over 100 appearances on *The Tonight Show with Johnny Carson*, where he would make light of major league baseball and his own playing experience. (His number of appearances on *The Tonight Show* were nearly equal to the number of hits he had in his major league career.) Uecker also did ABC's *Monday Night Baseball* in 1970s and 1980s and by the 1990s had even stared in a popular movie that lampooned baseball, *Major League*.

Current ESPN baseball broadcaster Joe Morgan, the former second baseman for the Big Red Machine teams of the 1970s and a member of the Baseball Hall of Fame, sees Bob Uecker in a positive light. Morgan, who did television broadcasts with Uecker on NBC, feels that he helped him become a better broadcaster: "I think that Bob Uecker helped make me a better announcer. I've always taken the game too seriously, because it was my livelihood. Bob doesn't take anything too seriously, and from working with him I think I can laugh about things, where before, I'd get mad when I saw something dumb."[5]

With Waite Hoyt, Dizzy Dean, Gabby Street and then Joe Garagiola leading the way, by the late 1950s former major league ballplayers were becoming more common in the broadcasting booth. In 1956, Phil Rizzuto, after being released as an active player by the Yankees, joined Mel Allen and Red Barber in the Yankees broadcasting booth. Former Cleveland Indians shortstop Lou Boudreau joined the Chicago Cubs broadcasting team for the 1958 and 1959 seasons. When Charlie Grimm, who had played 20 years in the major leagues, was fired as manager of the Cubs after the 1959 season, he and Boudreau did a flip-flop; Boudreau became manager and Grimm replaced him in the broadcasting booth. Meanwhile, down on the southside of Chicago, Ralph Kiner had joined Bob Elson at Comiskey Park to broadcast the White Sox games.

Still, the hazing of former big league ballplayers in the broadcasting booth persisted. In New York, Mel Allen and Red Barber resented Phil Rizzuto, a former ballplayer, coming into the Yankees broadcasting booth and often demonstrated open hostility toward him on the air. In reality, the hazing goes on until this very day. In 1974, Marty Brennaman, a graduate of the University of North Carolina, was picked from a list of 20 applicants to succeed Al Michaels as the radio play-by-play announcer for the Cincinnati Reds, thus being teamed with former big league pitcher Joe Nuxhall. Regardless of the success that Brennaman has enjoyed over the past 29 years collaborating with Nuxhall while behind the microphone on the Reds broadcasts, including being named the recipient of the 2000 Ford C. Frick award, he still seems to carry a bias against jocks in the booth. In an interview with *Cincinnati Enquirer* reporter Paul Daughety, published on November 9, 2003, Brennaman stated that he wouldn't want Pete Rose in the radio booth because he doesn't feel that Rose could do play-by-play.

Still another continuing bias against former major leaguers in the broadcast booth is exhibited in the lack of former major leaguers turned broadcasters who have been recipients of the Ford C. Frick award presented by the National Baseball Hall of Fame each year since 1978 for major contributions to baseball. In the 26-year history of the award, to date only two former major league players have been honored: Joe Garagiola in 1991 and Bob Uecker in 2003. Perhaps that could change, as currently two of the six members appointed by the Hall of Fame to vote on announcers for the award are former ballplayers: Joe Garagiola and Joe Morgan (The others are Bob Costas, Ernie Harwell, Vin Scully and Chuck Thompson.)

Style is what baseball broadcasting is all about. Mel Allen had style. However, Allen's style of broadcasting was one of being a cheerleader, one that over-emphasized the accomplishments of the players and embellished the flow of the game. To some degree Harry Caray did much of the same, but with a tinge of humor and sarcasm thrown in that was unique. Yet through his enormous exposure on the air waves by the 1960s Mel Allen had become one of the most recognizable voices in America. So recognizable was Allen's voice that it was considered on the same level of familiarity as that of John F. Kennedy and Winston Churchill. While Allen's voice may have been recognizable to the masses across America, the resonate effects of his chatter were no less identifiable on the regional scale as broadcasters such Hoyt in Cincinnati, Prince in Pittsburgh and Brickhouse in Chicago. In the early 1960s any baseball fan within any direction of 100 miles of Cincinnati would have been able to distinguish the voice of Waite Hoyt from that of any other notable personality in a heart beat. Furthermore, Caray and Garagiola's broadcasts on powerful KMOX in St. Louis often carried far and wide on clear Midwest evenings from St. Louis to Memphis, Tennessee, in the south and Lincoln, Nebraska, in the north.

As for today's broadcasters, Joe Morgan states that his style of broadcasting is to control the flow of information and not get wrapped up in the technicalities of the game: "I try to act like I'm sitting in your house with you, your wife, your son, maybe your daughter. Part of the game, I'm going to talk to you; you know a lot about the game. Another part, I'm talking to your wife, who knows a little bit. Another part, I'm talking to your son, being more instructional. Another part, I'm talking to the little girl, trying to tell her why this game is fun to watch. It's my job to make sure that I connect with all those viewers."[6]

Joe Morgan, 1976 (the Topps Co., Inc.).

Waite Hoyt's style was of course to blend reminiscence with the present and he did a magnificent job of it. Author Curt Smith stated in his book *Voices of The Game*, "Unlike any broadcaster in the totality of baseball, Waite Hoyt aired play-by-play in the past, not present tense. He was a chronicler, not sportscaster; he narrated action after the fact; on radio, his accents, like his life, bridged, not disengaged the years."[7] Furthermore, Donn Burrows stated, "He [Hoyt] had the style, the stories, the knowledge and big league experience. A package that no other broadcaster brought. He loved the game and could talk about it and the participants nonstop and intimately for hours on end."[8]

However, the broadcast of a game in the new millennium is vastly different than the environment that Waite Hoyt broadcast in during the middle part of the 20th century. When Hoyt was broadcasting games on the radio they were for the most part regional events and even in the middle 1950s some teams such as Pirates, Braves and Athletics didn't even televise their games. Today, if someone is listening to the radio broadcast of a major league game they more often than not tuned in on their car radio while they are in transit, rather than sipping beer on the front porch during hot summer evenings. Today cable TV networks such as YES, TBS, WGN, FOX, ESPN and MSG bring baseball games into American homes every day of the season. Also, since 1987 major league baseball has been broadcasting games via satellite to Japan. The 2001 All-Star game, played at Safeco Field in Seattle, was a huge success in Japan. Furthermore, in today's market many ball clubs own or have substantial financial interests in the cable networks that broadcast their games, such as Yankees owner George Steinbrenner with the YES network and Braves owner Ted Turner with TBS. The broadcast of a game today is a vastly more complicated affair. In Waite Hoyt's time in the booth it was just himself with a few assistants and engineers that handled every aspect of the broadcast both on radio and television. Today it requires a cable television network such as MSG to use more than 100 people and 14 cameras to broadcast a major league game.

Donn Burrows agreed with the premise that Waite Hoyt was a pathfinder in leading ex-major league ballplayers into broadcasting. However, Burrows also said he believes that the balance of influence has now tilted in the favor of the players: "I think that Waite's eloquent vocabulary and richly worded stories helped open the doors for the massive entrance of former players to the broadcast booth. I think that is has over evolved now. Today players are automatic because they have access to other players and they have already been so heavily promoted in many cases throughout their careers."[9]

In reality, it does seem that in today's market baseball broadcasting is on the brink of over-saturation with the number former players now behind the microphone. Over the last 40 years since Hoyt broadcast the Cincinnati Reds games the list of his successors has become endless: Richie Ashburn, Bob Uecker, Ralph Kiner, Tony Kubek, Sandy Koufax, Ernie Johnson, Joe Garagiola, Jerry Coleman, Don Drysdale, Pee Wee Reese, Bill White, Ken Harrelson, Phil Rizzuto, Joe Nuxhall, Joe Morgan, Tim McCarver, Steve Blass, Tom Seaver, Keith Hernandez, Bob Tewksbury,

Don Sutton, Jim Kaat, Ken Singleton, Jim Palmer, Steve Stone, Ron Santo, Larry Dierker, Del Shannon, Duke Snider, Frank McCormick, Harmon Killebrew, Lou Boudreau, Charlie Grimm, etc.

It's doubtful if any of these former major league ballplayers-turned-broadcasters has ever felt grateful in any way to Hoyt for the pathways into the booth that he helped clear for them. Hal McCoy stated, "I have never asked, but I've never heard any ex-players now in the booth give any credit whatsoever for what those legends [Hoyt, Dean, Street, Garagiola] did for them, both in paving the way and in helping them become broadcasters. And that's a shame."[10] But still the question remains: If Waite Hoyt as a former major league player had failed in his pioneering broadcasting venture in the early 1940s, how long would it have set back the good fortunes of these legions of former major league players who are now laboriously domiciled in the radio and television broadcasting booths?

Perhaps the real contribution made to the art of baseball broadcasting by Waite Hoyt and his legendary contemporaries such as Dizzy Dean and Joe Garagiola is the enthusiasm for the game that each brought to the broadcasting booth every single day of the season and then took with them outside the stadium gates into communities in which they served. It would be so great for the game today if somehow in the new era of major league baseball — that features empty suit owners and broadcasters, arrogant multi-millionaire players, several franchises struggling to stave off contraction and a commissioner that cares more about marketing the product of baseball than protecting the integrity the game's history — another broadcaster would rise from the ranks, be it a former player or otherwise, who could make the fans throughout American feel connected to the game. In short, become a broadcaster synonymous with the game rather than the business. That's what Waite Hoyt and his contemporaries did; they strived to become part of a community of baseball rather than the business of baseball. When the broadcast ended, their jobs real jobs began as they nurtured their fans and united their communities with the game.

Notes

Chapter 1

1. "The City has no promenade for..." from an article entitled "The City of Brooklyn," New York: *A Collection from Harper's Magazine*, Gallery Books, New York, 1991.

2. "...conduct unbecoming an American boy..." from an article by Rud Rennie, source unknown, from the archives of the National Baseball Hall of Fame and Museum.

3. *Ibid.*

4. *Ibid.*

5. *Ibid.*

6. "During a Brooklyn-New York series..." from a personal letter written by Addison Hoyt to an unknown source, February 9, 1917, from the archives of the National Baseball Hall of Fame and Museum.

7. "Do you belong to the Brooklyn..." from an article by Frank Graham, source unknown, February 8, 1961, from the archives of the National Baseball Hall of Fame and Museum.

8. *Ibid.*

9. *Ibid.*

10. "I'm tired of working this way..." from "Waite Hoyt: Yankees' Schoolboy," Leo Trachtenberg, *Yankees Magazine*, February 21, 1985.

11. "Hoyt put on a uniform..." from a newspaper article, source unknown August 1915, from the archives of the National Baseball Hall of Fame and Museum.

12. "The Giants gave me $5 for signing..." from an article by James Enright, *Sporting News*, July 31, 1965.

13. "It was one of those formal spring dances..." from an article by Rud Rennie, source unknown, from the archives of the National Baseball Hall of Fame and Museum.

14. "Waite Hoyt is about ripe..." from an article by O.B. Keeler published in The New York American, May 20, 1917, from the archives of The National Baseball Hall of Fame and Museum.

15. *Ibid.*

16. *Ibid.*

17. "Howley taught me more about..." from an article by Frederick G. Lieb, March 3, 1927, source unknown, from the archives of The National Baseball Hall of Fame and Museum.

18. "One night as the clock struck 12..." from an article J.G. Taylor Spink, published in The Sporting News, April 2, 1942.

19. *Ibid.*

20. *Ibid.*

21. "We are asking them to join the navy..." from an article in The Daily Home News, July 24, 1918.

22. "The game was a cavalcade of..." from an article published in The New York Times, July 25, 1918.

23. "Frisch couldn't play for McGraw..." from a radio script entitled McGraw's Technique by Waite Hoyt, from the archives of The Cincinnati Historical Society.

24. "We have to have your Regent's Card…" from an article by James D. Bunting and Alan C. Johnson, published in the Purple And Gold, date unknown. From the archives of The National Baseball Hall of Fame and Museum.

25. *Ibid.*

26. *Ibid.*

27. *Ibid.*

28. "Barrow got sore at this…" from an article by Leo Trachtenberg published in Yankees Magazine, February 21, 1985. From the archives of The National Baseball Hall of Fame and Museum.

Chapter 2

1. "His huge head bent toward the floor…" from *Babe Ruth As I Knew Him*, Waite Hoyt, Dell Publishing Co., Inc., 1948.

2. *Ibid.*

3. *Ibid.*

4. *Ibid.*

5. *Ibid.*

6. "In 1919, Babe was kind of…" from a radio script by Waite Hoyt entitled "Miscellaneous Remembrances," the Waite Charles Hoyt Papers and Memorabilia, the Cincinnati Historical Society.

7. "The feature of that game…" from a personal letter written by Waite Hoyt to Frank E. Hanson, date unknown, from the archives of the National Baseball Hall of Fame and Museum.

8. "Accept your offer of…" from a press release by the American League Service Bureau to the Sunday papers, December 9, 1928, from the archives of the National Baseball Hall of Fame and Museum.

9. *Ibid.*

10. "…sing the blues about how…" from *The Best of Waite Hoyt in the Rain*, 1993 Major League Baseball, The Miley Collection, Inc.

11. "I'll pitch high inside…" from *Babe Ruth As I Knew Him*, by Waite Hoyt, Dell Publishing Co., Inc., 1948.

12. *Ibid.*

13. "Between games, Joe Jackson…" from a radio script by Waite Hoyt entitled "Miscellaneous Remembrances," the Waite Charles Hoyt Papers and Memorablia, in the archives of the Cincinnati Historical Society.

14. "Ruth stood firmly on his legs…" from an article in *New York Times,* September 25, 1919.

15. "…Hoyt pitched for Boston," from *Babe Ruth As I Knew Him*, Waite Hoyt, Dell Publishing Co., Inc., 1948.

16. "Waite Hoyt, the Brooklyn schoolboy…" from an article published in *Boston Herald*, September 25, 1919.

17. "He felt secure in Boston…" from *Babe Ruth As I Knew Him* Waite Hoyt, Dell Publishing Co., Inc., 1948.

18. *Ibid.*

19. "Hell, I threw him a curve ball…" from *Babe: The Legend Comes to Life,* Robert W. Creamer, Fireside, New York, New York, 1974.

20. "I cannot recall whether I won…" from *Waite Hoyt's Scrapbook*, "My Most Memorable Christmas," *Greater Cincinnati Sports*, December 1977.

21. *Ibid.*

22. *Ibid.*

23. *Ibid.*

24. *Ibid.*

Chapter 3

1. "In Boston he had been a surprised…" from *Babe Ruth As I Knew Him*, Waite Hoyt, Dell Publishing Co., Inc., 1948.

2. "…had no business sense whatever…" from a radio script by Waite Hoyt entitled "Miscellaneous Remembrances," the Waite Charles Hoyt Papers and Memorabilia, from the archives if the Cincinnati Historical Society.

3. "Don't throw that big baboon…" from *The Giants: Memories and Memorabilia from a Century of Baseball,* by Bruce Chadwick and David M. Spindel, Abbevile Press-Publishers, New York, London, Paris, 1993.

4. "We can't win 'em all…" from an article in *The Daily Home News*, October 8, 1921.

5. "When in that electrical eighth inning…" from an article in *The Daily Home News*, October 11, 1921.

6. "His attitude towards his foes…" from an article in *Philadelphia Inquirer*, October 11, 1921.

7. "Waite Hoyt, star pitcher of the Yankees…" from an article in *Brooklyn Daily Eagle*, November 29, 1921.

8. "The Yankees of 1922 were…" from *Babe Ruth As I Knew Him*, Waite Hoyt, Dell Publishing Co., Inc., 1948.

9. *Ibid.*

10. *Ibid.*

11. *Ibid.*

12. "Hoffman and Devormer had a melee…" from an article by J. G. Taylor Spink, *Sporting News*, October 15, 1952.

13. "If that big monkey…" from *Babe Ruth As I Knew Him*, Waite Hoyt, Dell Publishing Co., Inc. 1948.

14. *Ibid.*

15. "Judged purely by surface appearances…" from an article by Davis J. Walsh *St. Louis Post-Dispatch*, August 26, 1922.

16. "The fact that the Giants have…" from an article by Branch Rickey, *The Daily Home News*, October 2, 1922.

17. "Well, we were licked…" from an article in *The Daily Home News*, October 9, 1922.

18. *Ibid.*

19. "The '22 series was no contest…" from "Why the American League Wins," Waite Hoyt as told to Stanley Frank, *The Saturday Evening Post*, April 2, 1938.

20. "The entire conception as …" from *Waite Hoyt's Scrapbook*, "Thanksgiving in Kobe, Japan," *Greater Cincinnati Sports*, November 1977.

21. *Ibid.*

Chapter 4

1. "Down on the Potomac…" from an article in *New York Times*, April 18, 1923.

2. "He was known as either the Big Bam…" from *Babe Ruth As I Knew Him*, Waite Hoyt, Dell Publishing Co., Inc., 1948.

3. *Ibid.*

4. *Ibid.*

5. *Ibid.*

6. "Years later, Hoyt confessed…" from an article in *Sporting News*, September 3, 1984.

7. "Skip it, you and I…" from *Babe Ruth As I Knew Him*, Waite Hoyt, Dell Publishing Co., Inc., 1948

8. *Ibid.*

9. *Ibid.*

10. *Ibid.*

11. *Ibid.*

12. *Ibid.*

13. *Ibid.*

14. *Ibid.*

15. "If you have a young son…" from "Chronicle of 20th-Century Sport" Ron Smith, *Sporting News*, 1992.

16. "I want to thank you for…" from Babe: The Legend Comes to Life, Robert W. Creamer, Fireside, New York, NY, 1992.

17. *Ibid.*

18. "The Yankees were a great team…" from "Why the American League Wins," Waite Hoyt as told to Stanley Frank, *The Saturday Evening Post*, April 2, 1938.

19. *Ibid.*

20. "Colonel Ruppert owned half of…" from an article by Tom Reilly, *The Walpole Times*, July 28, 1977, from the archives of the Cincinnati Historical Society.

21. "That's my office building…" from an article by Pat Harmon, *The Cincinnati Post*, August 27, 1984.

22. *Ibid.*

23. "Suddenly the Babe burst…" from *Babe Ruth As I Knew Him* Waite Hoyt, Dell Publishing Co., Inc., 1948.

24. *Ibid.*

25. *Ibid.*

26. *Ibid.*

27. *Ibid.*

28. *Ibid.*

29. *Ibid.*

30. "I want you to pitch for me…" from a document in the Waite Charles Hoyt Papers and Memorabilia from archives of the Cincinnati Historical Society.

31. *Ibid.*

Chapter 5

1. "If we keep on beating these guys…" from *Babe: The Legend Comes to Life*, Robert W. Creamer, Fireside, New York, NY, 1992.

2. "So far as any deep strategic…" from an article by Miller Huggins, *St. Louis Post-Dispatch*, October 3, 1926.

3. "We don't have to come back…" from an article by Rogers Hornsby, *St. Louis Post-Dispatch*, October 3, 1926.

4. "There's only one thing to be said…" from an article by Rogers Hornsby, *St. Louis Post-Dispatch*, October 7, 1926.

5. "Experience helped Hoyt a lot…" from an article by John McGraw, *St. Louis Post-Dispatch*, October 7, 1926.

6. "I did not think that Shocker…" from an article by John McGraw, *St. Louis Post-Dispatch*, October 10, 1926.

7. "A tall lank figure, with a gaudy…" from an article by J. Roy Stockton, *St. Louis Post-Dispatch*, October 11, 1926.

8. *Ibid.*

9. *Ibid.*

10. "Hoyt pitched fine ball…" from an article by James B. Harrison, *New York Times*, October 11, 1926.

11. "He won't get it," from an article by Richards Vidmer, *St. Louis Globe-Democrat*, October 12, 1926.

12. "Waite never was better than…" from an article by Frederick G. Lieb, *Sporting News*, March 3, 1927.

13. "We concocted two slogans…" from an article by J. G. Taylor Spink, *Sporting News*, October 15, 1952.

14. *Ibid.*

15. "Three great guys…" from an article by David Wecker, *The Cincinnati Post* online at cincypost.com, 1999.

16. "Don't forget this…" from an article by James Enright, *Sporting News*, August 7, 1965.

17. "Jeez, I'm tied with myself…" from an undated essay in the Waite Charles Hoyt Papers and Memorabilia from the Cincinnati Historical Society.

18. *Ibid.*

19. "Sixty, count 'em…" from *Babe: The Legend Comes to Life*, Robert W. Creamer, Fireside, New York, NY, 1992.

20. "That's easy…" from an article in *Pittsburgh Post-Gazette*, October 4, 1927.

21. "The Yankees like the Pirates…" from an article in *Pittsburgh Post-Gazette*, October 5, 1927.

22. "We're not afraid of any batter…" from an article by Owen J. Bush, Manager Pirates published in *Pittsburgh Post-Gazette*, October 5, 1927.

23. "It won't be long now…" from an article in The *Pittsburgh Post-Gazette*, October 6, 1927.

24. *Ibid.*

25. "Nice hitting Babe…" from an article by Waite Hoyt entitled "In The Dugout with Waite Hoyt," from the archives of the National Baseball Hall of Fame and Museum.

26. *Ibid.*

27. *Ibid.*

28. "Early in the morning…" from an article by Ring Lardner, the *Pittsburgh Post-Gazette*, October 6, 1927.

29. "If I had been pitching against…" from an article by Waite Hoyt entitled "In The Dugout with Waite Hoyt," from the archives of the National Baseball Hall of Fame and Museum.

30. "Some one told me to feed…" from an article in *Pittsburgh Post-Gazette*, October 6, 1927.

31. *Ibid.*

32. *Ibid.*

33. "Great work kid…" from an article in *Pittsburgh Post-Gazette*, October 7, 1927.

34. *Ibid.*

35. "Our traveling for 1927 ended…" from an article by Tony Lazzeri published in *Pittsburgh Post-Gazette*, October 7, 1927.

36. "I rated first in winning…" from an article by Daniel source unknown, January 20, 1928, from the archives of the Baseball Hall of Fame and Museum.

37. "Nobody was overly interested…" from an article by James Enright published in *Sporting News*, August 7, 1965.

38. "This is costing me $2,500…" from a radio script by Waite Hoyt entitled "According to Hoyt," from the archives of the Cincinnati Historical Society.

39. *Ibid.*

40. "That taught me a lesson…" from an article by James Enright, *Sporting News*, August 7, 1965.

41. "In 1926 it was just a breeze…" from an article by J. Roy Stockton, *St. Louis Post-Dispatch*, October 6, 1928.

42. "Waite Hoyt and George Pipgras…" from an article by Herman Wecke, *St. Louis Post-Dispatch,* October 7, 1928.

43. "Huggins pitchers knew what…" from an article by J. Roy Stockton published in The St. Louis Post-Dispatch, October 7, 1928.

44. "In 1921, the Giants lost…" from an article by John J. McGraw, *St. Louis Post-Dispatch*, October 7, 1928.

45. "We've got two victories..." from an article by Babe Ruth, *St. Louis Post-Dispatch*, October 7, 1928.
46. "They didn't beat us..." from an article by Charles W. Dunkley, *St. Louis Post-Dispatch*, October 8, 1928.
47. *Ibid.*
48. "I'm not sure what I will do..." from an article by Miller Huggins, *St. Louis Post-Dispatch*, October 8, 1928.
49. *Ibid.*

Chapter 6

1. [Here I am] "knocking 'em dead..." an article entitled "The Merry Mortician of the Mound," excerpted from *Baseball's Greatest Pitchers*, Tom Meany in *Baseball Digest*, 1952.
2. "Wives of ballplayers, when they..." from *Voices of The Game*, Curt Smith, Diamond Communications, Inc., South Bend, Indiana, 1987.
3. "What happened?" from an article by J. G. Taylor Spink, *Sporting News*, April 2, 1942.
4. *Ibid.*
5. *Ibid.*
6. *Ibid.*
7. *Ibid.*
8. *Ibid.*
9. "Nice pitching..." from an article by James Enright, *Sporting News*, July 31, 1965.
10. "A fast ball..." from an article in *The Cincinnati Enquirer*, August 26, 1984.
11. *Ibid.*
12. *Ibid.*
13. *Ibid.*
14. *Ibid.*
15. "The trouble with this club..." from an article, the National Baseball Hall of Fame and Museum.
16. "It was tough leaving..." from *Babe Ruth As I Knew Him*, Waite Hoyt, Dell Publishing Co., Inc., New York, NY, 1948.
17. "Good-bye, Walter..." from a composition by Waite Hoyt, the Waite Charles Hoyt Papers and Memorabilia, Cincinnati Historical Society.
18. "Hi, Keed..." from *Baseball Anecdotes*, Daniel Okrent and Steve Wulf, Harper & Row Publishers, New York, 1990.
19. *Ibid.*

20. "I played for him in 1931..." from an essay by Waite Hoyt entitled Today is Connie Mack Day in Philadelphia," the Waite Charles Hoyt Papers and Memorabilia, from the archives of the Cincinnati Historical Society.
21. *Ibid.*
22. *Ibid.*
23. "Behind the right-field wall..." from *Babe Ruth As I Knew Him*, Waite Hoyt, Dell Publishing Co., Inc., New York, NY, 1948.
24. "Waite Hoyt, who boasts a record..." from an article by S. O. Grauley, published in *Philadelphia Inquirer*, October 8, 1931.
25. "Just let me find that guy..." from an article in *New York World-Telegram*, April 28, 1932, from the archives of the National Baseball Hall of Fame and Museum.
26. *Ibid.*
27. *Ibid.*
28. "We have a young pitching staff..." from an article by Volney Walsh published in *Pittsburgh Press*, January 21, 1933.
29. "It's the biggest since the Panama Canal..." from an article in *Pittsburgh Press*, January 22, 1933.
30. *Ibid.*
31. *Ibid.*
32. "If you guys don't shut up..." from an article by Leo Trachtenberg, *Yankees Magazine*, February 2, 1985.
33. "I see a different Hoyt..." from an article by C. William Duncan, source unknown, September 20, 1934, from the archives of the National Baseball Hall of Fame and Museum.
34. "If he can't manage himself..." from *Microsoft Complete Baseball*, Microsoft Corporation, 1994.
35. "Babe was a sorry spectacle..." from an essay by Waite Hoyt entitled "According to Hoyt" August 20, the Waite Charles Hoyt Papers and Memorabilia, from the archives of the Cincinnati Historical Society.
36. "My logs are OK..." from an article in *The Boston Globe*, May 24, 1935.
37. *Ibid.*
38. "The best way to pitch to Ruth..." from *Babe Ruth as I Knew Him*, Waite Hoyt, Dell Publishing Co., Inc., New York, NY, 1948.
39. *Ibid.*

40. *Ibid.*

41. *Ibid.*

42 "That's the day I should…" from an essay by Waite Hoyt entitled "According to Hoyt" August 20, the Waite Charles Hoyt Papers and Memorabilia, from the archives of the Cincinnati Historical Society.

43. "George Herman Ruth — the Great Man…" from an article by Volney Walsh, published in *Pittsburgh Press*, May 26, 1935.

44. "I'm going to be president…" from *Bums: An Oral History of the Brooklyn Dodgers*, Peter Golenbock, G. P. Putnam's Sons, New York, 1984.

45. "In sharp contrast, American Leaguers…" from "Why the American League Wins," Waite Hoyt as told to Stanley Frank, *The Saturday Evening Post*, April 2, 1938.

46. *Ibid.*

47. "To say the least, the article…" from an editorial, source unknown, April 14, 1938, from the archives of the National Baseball Hall of Fame and Museum.

48. "Burleigh asked me to advise…" from a Western Union Telegram sent to Waite Hoyt, May 16, 1938, from the archives of the National Baseball Hall of Fame and Museum.

49. "I just joined you…" from an article by James Enright, *Sporting News*, August 7, 1965.

50. "Just as soon as Hoyt's…" from an article entitled "Daniel's Dope," *New York–World Telegram*, May 18, 1938, in the archives of the National Baseball Hall of Fame and Museum.

51. "Then is when I realized…" from an article by James Enright, *Sporting News*, August 7, 1965.

Chapter 7

1. "I knew my real goal was…" from *Voices of the Game*, Curt Smith, Diamond Communications, Inc., South Bend, Indiana, 1987.

2. "It was Cobb's turn to bat…" from a radio script written by Waite Hoyt, the Waite Charles Hoyt Papers and Memorabilia, from the archives of the Cincinnati Historical Society.

3. "In his early days on WNEW…" from an article by Alton Cook published in The New York World-Telegram, April 27, 1939, from the archives of the National Baseball Hall of Fame and Museum.

4. "He had been hired only as a freak…" from *Bums: An Oral History of the Brooklyn Dodgers*, Peter Golenbock, G. P. Putnam's Sons, New York, 1984.

5. "See that picture over there…" from *Babe Ruth As I Knew Him* Waite Hoyt, Dell Publishing Co. Inc., New York, 1948.

6. *Ibid.*

7. *Ibid.*

8. *Ibid.*

9. *Ibid.*

10. *Ibid.*

11. *Ibid.*

12. *Ibid.*

13. *Ibid.*

14. "I enjoyed those programs with…" from *Voices of the Game,* Curt Smith, Diamond Communications, Inc., South Bend, Indiana, 1987.

15. "An agency man came to me…" from an article by Furman Bisher, *Sporting News*, June 21, 1980.

16. "He went into the studio…" from "Waite Hoyt: The Broadcast Years in Cincinnati" Ellen Frell, in *Baseball in Cincinnati: From Wooden Fences to Astroturf,* Cincinnati Historical Society, 1988.

17. "When they offered me the job…" from *Voices of the Game,* Curt Smith, Diamond Communications, Inc., South Bend, Indiana, 1987.

18. "…he was a drinker and a…" from an article by Lonnie Wheeler, *The Cincinnati Enquirer*, August 26, 1984.

19. *Ibid.*

20. *Ibid.*

21. "I found a level of happiness…" from *Voices of the Game,* Curt Smith, Diamond Communications, Inc., South Bend, Indiana, 1987.

22. "Baseball is about to adopt schedules…" from *Baseball: An Illustrated History* Geoffrey C. Ward and Ken Burns, Alfred A. Knopf, New York, 1994.

23. "Folks who watched Waite Hoyt…" from an article by J. G. Taylor Spink, *Sporting News*, April 2, 1942.

24. "Jesus, we could have been killed…" from *Voices of the Game* Curt Smith, Diamond Communications, Inc., South Bend, Indiana, 1987.

25. "It was, indeed dangerous..." from the author's correspondence with Hal McCoy, January 13, 2004.

26. "Read about your case of Amnesia..." from an article by Lonnie Wheeler, *The Cincinnati Enquirer*, August 26, 1984.

27. "Better than all else..." from "Waite Hoyt: The Broadcast Years in Cincinnati," Ellen Frell, in *Baseball in Cincinnati: From Wooden Fences to Astroturf*, Cincinnati Historical Society, 1988.

28. "When it came to alcohol..." from an address by Waite Hoyt presented to a meeting of Alcoholic's Anonymous 1976, from the personal archives of Donn Burrows.

29. "He's No. 1 in my book..." from an article in *The Cincinnati Enquirer*, August 26, 1984.

Chapter 8

1. "Allen and Barber always had great..." from *Voice of the Game* Curt Smith, Diamond Communications, Inc., South Bend, Indiana, 1987.

2. *Ibid.*

3. *Ibid.*

4. *Ibid.*

5. "Ewell Blackwell, had he not hurt..." from a personal letter written by Waite Hoyt to Arthur Daly, May 28, 1967, from archives of the National Baseball Hall of Fame and Museum.

6. "Waite Hoyt is authoritative..." from *Microsoft Complete Baseball*, Microsoft Corporation, 1994.

7. "Radio is a medium..." from *Bunts*, George F. Will, Touchstone, New York, NY, 1999.

8. "Unlike any broadcaster in the..." from *Voices of the Game*, Curt Smith, Diamond Communications, Inc. South Bend, Indiana, 1987.

9. "It was just as much of a sickening..." from *Babe Ruth As I Knew Him*, Waite Hoyt, Dell Publishing Co., Inc., New York, 1948.

10. "This one time I'm not going..." from an article in *The Cincinnati Post*, August 17, 1948.

11. "The world was a big night club..." from a radio script by Waite Hoyt entitled "Miscellaneous Remembrances," the Waite Charles Hoyt Papers and Memorabilia, from the archives of the Cincinnati Historical Society.

12. "Hey Gen...." from an article in *The Cincinnati Post*, August 17, 1948.

13. *Ibid.*

14. *Ibid.*

15. "Lord, I'd give my right arm..." from an article by Bob Broeg, *Sporting News*, November 27, 1973.

16. *Ibid.*

17. "Branch Rickey said my book..." from a personal letter written by Waite Hoyt to Robert W. Creamer, November 8, 1969, from the archives of the National Baseball Hall of Fame and Museum.

18. "When you're broadcasting..." from an article by Pat Harmon, *Sporting News*, April 1964.

19. "'the worst fan clientele..." from *Rogers Hornsby: A Biography*, Charles C. Alexander, Henry Holt and Company, Inc., New York, New York, 1995.

20. *Ibid.*

21. "As a person..." from *Cincinnati Seasons—My 34 years with the Reds*, by Earl Lawson, Diamond Communications, South Bend, Indiana, 1987.

22. "I had studied him..." from an essay Hornsby 6 for 6 against Hoyt, by Waite Hoyt in the Waite Charles Hoyt, Papers and Memorabilia, ca.1907—1978, MSS 866, Cincinnati Historical Society.

23. *Ibid.*

24. "I'd rather have old Grover Cleveland Alexander..." from *Rogers Hornsby: A Biography*, Charles C. Alexander, Henry Holt and Company, Inc., New York, New York, 1995.

25. "The funny thing is..." from *Voices of the Game*, by Curt Smith, Diamond Communications, Inc., South Bend, Indiana, 1987.

26. "My visits to Yankee Stadium..." from an article by J. G. Taylor Spink, *Sporting News*, October 15, 1952.

27. "Tom Zachary was peeved..." from a personal letter written by Waite Hoyt to Lee Allen, December 9, 1959, for the archives of the Baseball Hall of Fame and Museum.

28. *Ibid.*

29. "I think that growing up with a

father…" from the author's correspondence with Donn Burrows, December 2, 2003.

30. *Ibid.*

31. "A conglomeration of castoffs…" from *Voices of the Game*, Curt Smith, Diamond Communications, Inc., South Bend, Indiana, 1987.

32. *Ibid.*

33. "When the show was over…" from an article by Red Barber, *The Miami Herald*, August 17, 1969, the Waite Charles Hoyt Papers and Memorabilia, for the archives of the Cincinnati Historical Society.

34. "…was like V-J day and V-E day…" from an article by Jack McDonald, *The Cincinnati Enquirer*, September 27, 1961.

35. "This is the Burger Beer…" from an article by John Fay, *The Cincinnati Enquirer*, August 26, 1984.

36. *Ibid.*

37. "He sat with his chin…" from a personal letter written by Waite Hoyt to Lee Allen, January 22, 1962, for the archives of the National Baseball Hall of Fame and Museum.

38. "Jack really thought a lot…" from the author's correspondence with Barbara Moran, August 2003.

39. "I hated to see Ken Johnson…" from an article by Pat Harmon, *Sporting News*, April 1962.

40. "If Hutchinson had a little pitching…" from *Cincinnati's Crosley Field: The Illustrated History of a Classic Ballpark*, Greg Rhodes and John Erardi, Road West Publishing Company, Cincinnati, Ohio, 1995.

41. *Ibid.*

42. "I felt the pain when I…" from an article in *Pittsburgh Press*, August 17, 1967.

43. "I believe in telling the people…" from *Microsoft Complete Baseball*, Microsoft Corporation, 1994.

44. *Ibid.*

45. *Ibid.*

46. "…made the rainy day famous…" from an article by Marty Hogan, The Cincinnati Enquirer, September 6, 1965.

47. *Ibid.*

Chapter 9

1. "I suppose that most of you…" from an address by Waite Hoyt to a meeting of Alcoholics Anonymous, November 1965, source anonymous.

2. "I am reading constantly about the…" from a personal letter written by Waite Hoyt to Lee Allen, July 27, 1968, from in the archives of the National Baseball Hall of Fame.

3. "Meusel should be in the Hall of Fame…" from a letter by Waite Hoyt to Bill, date unknown, in the archives of The National Baseball Hall of Fame.

4. *Ibid.*

5. "Bob Meusel put up numbers…" from *The Greatest Baseball Players from McGraw to Mantle*, Bert Randolph Sugar Dover Publications Inc., 1997.

6. "What do you think…" from an address by Waite Hoyt at the induction ceremonies of the National Baseball Hall of Fame, July 28, 1969, National Baseball Hall of Fame.

7. "I went to Maz's induction…" from the author's interview with Steve Blass, November 2001.

8. "When you love a game like this…" from an address by Roy Campanella at the induction ceremonies of the National Baseball Hall of Fame, July 28, 1969, National Baseball Hall of Fame.

9. "Standing here before you this morning…" from an address by Waite Hoyt at the induction ceremonies of the National Baseball Hall of Fame, July 28, 1969, National Baseball Hall of Fame.

10. "Waite Hoyt classed up baseball's…" from an article by Bob Considine, King Features Syndicate, New York, NY, November 11, 1970, from the archives of the Cincinnati Historical Society.

11. Campanella was a joy on…" from an address by Stan Musial at the induction ceremonies of the National Baseball Hall of Fame, July 28, 1969, National Baseball Hall of Fame.

12. *Ibid.*

13. *Ibid.*

Chapter 10

1. "Waite liked to sit in the dugout…" from *Pete Rose: My Story*, Pete Rose and Roger Kahn, Macmillan Publishing Company, New York, NY, 1989.

2. "In broadcasting Hoyt had found…" from "Waite Hoyt: The Broadcast Years in Cincinnati" Ellen Frell, in Baseball in Cincinnati: From Wooden Fences to Astro Turfs, the Cincinnati Historical Society, 1988.

3. "You were close to the fans…" from *Voices of the Game*: Curt Smith Diamond Communications, Inc., South Bend, Indiana, 1987.

4. "She's my darling…" from the poem "The Immortal" Waite Hoyt, Waite Charles Hoyt Papers and Memorabilia, from the archives of the Cincinnati Historical Society.

5. "To me, no question…" from an article in *The Miami Herald* by Red Barber, August 17, 1969.

6. "I have read pieces…" from a personal letter written by Waite Hoyt to Robert W. Creamer, dated November 8, 1969, from the archives of the National Baseball Hall of Fame and Museum.

7. "Of all the people I talked to…" from an article by Brian White, in *The Cincinnati Enquirer*, August 26, 1984.

8. "I am under contract to do a…" from a personal letter by Waite Hoyt, to Doctor Marshall Smelser, March 5, 1972, from the archives of the National Baseball Hall of Fame and Museum.

9. "It was also amusing to me…" from a personal letter written by Waite Hoyt to Arthur Daly, May 28, 1967 from the archives of the National Baseball Hall of Fame and Museum.

10. "Unlike Maris and McGwire…" from an article entitled "The Burden of History," Robert W. Creamer, sportsillustrated.cnn.com, CNN/SI, 1998.

11. "Now comes the great ado…" from a personal letter written by Waite Hoyt to Arthur Daly, May 28, 1967, from the archives of the National Baseball Hall of Fame and Museum.

12. "I assume, one man blessed with…" from a document in the Waite Charles Hoyt Papers and Memorabilia, from the archives of the Cincinnati Historical Society.

13. "Willie is the best player I ever…" from an article entitled in *The Cincinnati Enquirer*, August 3, 2003.

14. *Ibid.*

15. "The man [Ruth] was so…" from *I Had a Hammer: The Hank Aaron Story* Hank Aaron and Lonnie Wheeler, Harper Paperbacks, New York, NY, 1991.

16. *Ibid.*

17. "Closest in proximity in times at bat…" from a document in the Waite Charles Hoyt Papers and Memorabilia, from the archives of the Cincinnati Historical Society.

18. "Ruth is vastly superior in most…" from a document in the Waite Charles Hoyt Papers and Memorabilia, from the archives of the Cincinnati Historical Society.

19. "I am almost convinced, you will…" from a personal letter written by Waite Hoyt to Robert W. Creamer, dated November 8, 1969, from the archives of the National Baseball Hall of Fame and Museum.

Chapter 11

1. "Only two…" from an article in *The Washington Star*, November 11, 1976.

2. *Ibid.*

3. *Ibid.*

4. *Ibid.*

5. "I'm very close to Pete…" from an article by Peter Pascarelli, *Philadelphia Inquirer*, June 23, 1982.

6. *Ibid.*

7. *Ibid.*

8. "As this is to be my bow out…" from a document in the Waite Charles Hoyt Papers and Memorabilia, from the archives of the Cincinnati Historical Society.

9. "Bill Dickey…" from an article by Furman Bisher, *Sporting News*, June 21, 1980.

10. *Ibid.*

11. *Ibid.*

12. *Ibid.*

13. *Ibid.*

14. "I sent him a fan letter…" from a column by David Wecker entitled "Mrs. Hoyt recalls love of her life!," www.cincy.post.com., 1999.

15. *Ibid.*

16. "You ain't nothing until…" from a personal letter written by Waite Hoyt, to Lee Allen July 27, 1968, from in the archives of the National Baseball Hall of Fame and Museum.

17. "Waite Hoyt was special..." from the author's correspondence with Hal McCoy, January 14, 2004.

18. "And you always think that..." from an address by Waite Hoyt at the induction ceremonies of the National Baseball Hall of Fame July 28, 1969, National Baseball Hall of Fame.

Chapter 12

1. "I would sit with him at a table..." from the author's correspondence with Donn Burrows, December 2, 2003.

2. "When a critic asked if he knew..." from *Microsoft Complete Baseball*. Microsoft Corporation, 1994.

3. "How do you like that..." from *The Boys of Summer*, Roger Kahn, Harper & Row Publishers, New York, 1987.

4. "I think he loved Cincinnati..." from the author's correspondence with Donn Burrows, December 2, 2003.

5. "I think that Bob Uecker helped make me..." from an article by Robert S. Wieder entitled "Playboy's 20 Q with Joe Morgan," *Playboy*, Vol. 46, no. 10, October 1999.

6. *Ibid.*

7. "Unlike any broadcaster..." from *Voices of the Game*, Curt Smith, Diamond Communications, South Bend, Indiana, 1987.

8. He had the style..." from the author's correspondence with Donn Burrows, December 2, 2003.

9. *Ibid.*

10. "I have never asked..." from the author's correspondence with Hal McCoy, January 14, 2004.

Bibliography

Aaron, Hank, with Lonnie Wheeler. *I Had a Hammer: The Hank Aaron Story*. New York: HarperTorch, 1991.

Alexander, Charles C. *Rogers Hornsby: A Biography*. New York: Holt, 1995.

Astor, Gerald. *The Baseball Hall of Fame 50th Anniversary Book*. Englewood Cliffs NJ: Prentice Hall, 1988.

Baseball on the Air. www.enel.net/beisbol/history.

Burrows, Don. *The Life & Times of Waite Hoyt — Waite's World*. Pro Cam Video, 1997.

Chadwick, Bruce, and David M. Spindel. *The Giants — Memories and Memorabilia from a Century of Baseball*. New York: Abbeville, 1993.

Clayton, Skip, and Jeff Moeller. *50 Phabulous Phillies*. Champaign IL: Sports Publishing, 2000.

Complete Baseball. 1994 Edition. Microsoft Home, Microsoft Corporation, 1994.

Creamer, Robert W. *Babe: The Legend Comes to Life*. New York: Fireside/ Simon & Schuster, 1974.

Frell, Ellen. "Waite Hoyt: The Broadcast Years in Cincinnati." In *Baseball in Cincinnati: From Wooden Fences to Astroturf*. Cincinnati: The Cincinnati Historical Society, 1988.

Golenbock, Peter. *Bums: An Oral History of the Brooklyn Dodgers*. New York: Putnam, 1984.

Hoyt, Waite. *Babe Ruth as I Knew Him*. New York: Dell, 1948.

_____, as told to Stanley Frank. "Why the American League Wins." *Saturday Evening Post*, April 2, 1938.

Neft, David S., Michael L. Neft, Bob Carroll, and Richard M. Cohen. *The Boston Red Sox Fan Book*. New York: St. Martin's Griffin, 2002.

New York: A Collection from Harper's *Magazine*. New York: Gallery, 1991.

Okrent, Daniel, and Steve Woulf. *Baseball Anecdotes*. New York: HarperPerennial, 1990.

Rhodes, Greg, and John Erardi. *Cincinnati's Crosley Field: The Illustrated History of a Classic Ballpark*. Cincinnati: Road West, 1995.

Smith, Curt. *Voices of the Game: The First Full-Scale Overview of Baseball Broad-casting, 1921 to the Present.* South Bend IN: Diamond Communications, 1987.

The Baseball Encyclopedia. 7th ed. Joseph L. Reichler, editor. New York: Macmillan, 1988.

The Baseball Encyclopedia. 8th ed. New York: Macmillian,1990.

The Best of Waite Hoyt in the Rain. Major League Baseball, The Miley Collection, Inc., 1993.

Waite Charles Hoyt Papers and Memorabilia, Ca. 1907–1978. The Cincinnati Historical Society, Cincinnati, Ohio

Waite Hoyt Collection. The National Baseball Hall of Fame and Museum Library, Cooperstown, New York.

Index